# ORIGIN STORIES

## THE PIONEERS WHO TOOK FOOTBALL TO THE WORLD

CHRIS LEE

First published by Pitch Publishing, 2021

Pitch Publishing
A2 Yeoman Gate
Yeoman Way
Worthing
Sussex
BN13 3QZ
www.pitchpublishing.co.uk
info@pitchpublishing.co.uk

ISBN 978 1 78531 769 9

Typesetting and origination by Pitch Publishing
Printed and bound in India by Replika Press Pvt. Ltd.

# Contents

# Introduction

EACH SUMMER, a preseason friendly football match takes place in the outskirts of Sheffield in Northern England. Here, Sheffield FC and nearby Hallam FC contest the 'Rules derby'. It is the world's oldest football rivalry, played by the world's oldest surviving Association rules football clubs. When the players of this fixture first took to the field on Boxing Day 1860, the two clubs were following the 'Sheffield Rules'. The Football Association (FA) rules – the basis for the modern game – were still nearly three years away from agreement. All 'football' in the mid-19th century was played under myriad codes, most famously those devised on the playing fields of Eton, Harrow, Cambridge, Charterhouse and Rugby. In August 2017, I made my way up to the outskirts of Sheffield to take in the 157th year of this fixture armed only with the kernel of an idea for a story on the world's football pioneers. I was joined by around 500 other people who understood fully the significance of this clash between these two historic clubs. Both clubs now reside in the lower echelons of the English non-league tier system.

*Origin Stories: The Pioneers Who Took Football to the World* tells the history of the first Association rules football clubs, organisations and tournaments in the major footballing countries across the world. We follow the story from the very first kick of the round ball in each major country in rough chronological order up until the inaugural World Cup in Uruguay in 1930, by which time football had truly gone global. We uncover the pioneers behind Association football's growth and their influence in forging the game. We learn the challenges they faced and see how they overcame them to lay the foundations for what would become the most popular and lucrative sport in the world. I aim to bust some myths of football's foundation stories along the way.

There is a familiar theme that emerges time and again: British workers carrying a ball and a rule book with them to all corners of the globe to keep them entertained during downtime. This global interconnectivity is often the reason why so many pioneer clubs started life in port cities – as in Genoa, Huelva, Antwerp, Le Havre, São Paulo, Montevideo and Buenos Aires. There are also occasions when enthusiastic sportsmen who spent time in England or Scotland and saw the game first hand caught the bug and set up footballing societies at home. This was the case in Northern Ireland with Cliftonville, Koninklijke HFC of the Netherlands and many other countries. We will also learn of the critical role that royal approval would play in the promotion of the new sport in Scandinavia, Spain, the Netherlands, Romania and elsewhere.

In the second half of the 19th century, conditions were perfect for the rapid global spread of Association football. Domestically in the UK, the rise of urban, industrialised working and middle classes with Saturday afternoon now at their leisure from the 1870s enabled people to gravitate towards their local football club. The growing railway network made getting to and from matches easier for fans, players and officials. Globally, the British Empire was at its peak, joined together by the speed of the steamship and a growing telegraph network. Yet football's popularity would not be imposed by imperial masters, because it attracted local interest of its own accord. Besides, it was via trade connections that the British spread the game, rather than via imperial links. Association rules football is, after all, not as popular in many of the major Commonwealth countries as cricket, or other codes of football, such as rugby or Australian Rules. Here, as in the US and Ireland, the game is known as 'soccer', to distinguish the Association game from other, more prominent, codes of football.

Dr Kevin Moore, former CEO of the National Football Museum in England and an academic scholar on the history of football, tells me that, were it not for crucial decisions made both by the Football Association and the Rugby Football Union (RFU) in the 1870s, things could have been very different worldwide. According to Dr Moore, *rugby* could have been the global football game rather than soccer.

The key differentiator was professionalism. In the 1870s, when both rugby and Association football began attracting paying crowds, clubs of either code began to pay players. While many in the FA were against payment of players, when the clubs of the north threatened to break away and go their own way, the FA accepted professionalism in 1885. A potential chasm over payment of players – one that would ultimately divide rugby later in the 19th century – was averted. This paved the way for the creation of the Football League in 1888, which was the first of its kind in the world and one which Dr Moore believes helped drive the sport's popularity. As Dr Moore has written, 'Soccer chose professionalism and a league. Rugby chose amateurism and no league. This is the moment when it was effectively decided that soccer, rather than rugby, would become the world's leading football game.'[1]

The period we cover in this book is when the football code war was settled. Historian Tony Collins observes that no football code other than the Association game has qualitatively expanded beyond national boundaries since 1914 – and it still gains in popularity worldwide now, 160 years after its codification.[2] Often, where the Brits went there followed a story of exclusivity; locals often had to wait their turn to get a crack at the game. And it was often the British coaches – who would become known in some parts as 'Mister' – who taught the world in time to eclipse football's mother country at its own game. Local influencers took on the mantle from there and never looked back. This British legacy endures in the lexicon of the global game. That's why you find teams in South America called Newell's Old Boys, River Plate, Everton and Albion FC. It's also why a 'crack' is a striker in some countries, or in Brazil a team is a 'time' (pronounced 'chee-may'), and in Italy they're keen on 'pressing' and fond of a good 'cross'.

The clubs we encounter in this journey are often not the biggest names in their country, and few even appear in their country's top leagues, but the contribution the pioneers have made is not forgotten. They even have their own association! Sheffield FC's chairman is Richard Tims. Under Tims's stewardship, Sheffield FC has been at the forefront of keeping the story of the pioneers alive. Sheffield FC is behind the Club of Pioneers, a worldwide network of the oldest continuing football clubs from each country. Every so often the family gets together and competes in Sheffield and has attracted guest appearances from high-profile former players. Retired England stars Chris Waddle and Carlton Palmer have turned out for Sheffield FC, while

Tomáš Skuhravý and Gennaro Ruotolo have pulled on the blue and burgundy Genoa jersey.

'The inspiration for the Club of Pioneers was to unite the heritage and history of football around the world,' Tims tells me. 'As "The World's First Football Club" we believe that football's roots should be valued throughout the world. Through our Club of Pioneers project, we aim to recognise the impact that these clubs have had on the development of football in each country.' The Club of Pioneers now has registered members stretching across Europe, Africa, Asia and as far away as New Zealand. Tims hopes that by recognising the impact of these clubs they will receive greater recognition and support within their own communities.

This book started as a side project, a theme on my football culture blog and podcast, *Outside Write*, where I collected stories about the roots of football in the major footballing countries across the world. On this journey, I've visited Sheffield and Manchester, Glasgow, Italy, Belgium, Berlin and Paris, and spoken to many of the pioneer clubs and prominent local football historians. I've even had the privilege to meet with and talk to descendants of those footballing pioneers. We'll piece together the contribution of clubs, sponsors, administrators and associations in the nascent era of football.

In some countries, the distinction between 'British' and 'English' is not often understood. In this book I make the distinction where possible, and I am very keen that the role that Scots played in the Victorian era is not overlooked, because it is substantial. 'History and heritage can never be valued enough,' Sheffield FC's Richard Tims told me, and I couldn't agree more.

So, join us on the journey, as we meet the characters and clubs who helped put together the earliest rule books, associations and competitions, and generated the first football cultures across the world. Because without them, we would not be discussing the beautiful game at all.

1   Moore, Dr Kevin, *What You Think You Know About Football is Wrong: The Global Game's Greatest Myths and Untruths* (London, Bloomsbury: 2019, p15)

2   Collins, Tony, *How Football Began: A Global History of How the World's Football Codes Were Born* (London: Routledge, 2019, p180)

# 1.

# England

IN THE summer of 2011, an archive went under the hammer at the auctioneer, Sotheby's. It was bought by an anonymous telephone bidder for the sum of £881,250, and its sale achieved global media attention. The archive included what is believed to be the world's first football rule book, dating from October 1858. The vendor was Sheffield Football Club, which is recognised by football's governing body FIFA as the world's first football club. The 'Sheffield Rules' were drafted in Sheffield FC's minute book five years before the foundation of the Football Association in London in 1863, and contain the first recorded mentions of the centre kick, the goal kick, free kicks, corners and throw-ins. The first handwritten document contains crossings out, where the rules were adapted over time and published in print a year later, of which there is just one known surviving copy in the world. The archive also included early match reports, the very earliest examples of football journalism. Sotheby's described the collection as entirely unique.[1] One rule demanded players bring both a red and a dark-blue flannel cap to distinguish between the teams on the pitch. This is the world's first mention of a football kit.

The Sheffield Rules collection takes us right back to a time in the middle of the 19th century when football's code was inconsistent and varied across the country, chiefly from public school to public school. Here, the future leaders of the British Empire were honed for leadership on the playing field. By the time the schoolboys of Eton and Rugby moved on to meet at university in Oxford or Cambridge and wanted to continue playing, they had all become accustomed to different rules. At the Rugby School, they favoured picking up the ball and running with it rather than the rough and tumble kicking game preferred at Charterhouse, Eton and Harrow schools. At Cambridge in 1848, students pinned the rules of their university's football game to the trees around Parker's Piece, the field in which they played. This may have been the first attempt to publish footballing codes.

'Football was what you wanted to make of it, there was no codification or regulation,' football historian Andy Mitchell tells me. 'It was basically the fact that you had people – almost exclusively men – kicking a ball about, sometimes carrying it, with different codes of how to score a goal. All these different games came together, and you ended up with a codification of the game in 1863 to create Association football, which was a way of combining the different rules to create a common match that everyone can understand.' It was the round-ball game that was to evolve into Association football, or 'soccer', as the England and Corinthian FC player Charles Wreford Brown would later call it. This was an abbreviation of the word 'Association', much as 'rugger' familiarises rugby. The word 'soccer' is not, as it is often thought, a recent Americanisation; it's a very English word from a very English source.

Kicking games were not the exclusive reserve of the public schools. Folk football had been a tradition throughout

Britain for centuries. I attended an Easter folk football match in Chiddingstone, Kent, to get a sense of how it might have looked in the past. Here, two teams of more than a hundred keen participants of all ages aimed to transport a ball across farmland and woodland to score a 'goal' at two pubs situated one mile (1.6km) apart. These ancient folk games would provide a diversion for Britain's workers but also often resulted in injuries and even death. They sometimes prompted fines and even royal banning orders.

But the popularity of a kicking game could not be denied. At this time in the mid-19th century, when the primary summer sport in England was cricket, people wanted a pursuit to keep themselves active over the long, cold winter. Football's time had come.

## Sheffield FC: the world's first football club

The Sheffield Football Club was formed on 24 October 1857 by William Prest – a wine merchant and captain of Yorkshire at cricket – and solicitor Nathaniel Creswick. Prest and Creswick were cricketers themselves and would have been involved in ball games already. To create the Sheffield Rules, Prest and Creswick drew on football codes already being deployed by various universities to put together a set of laws, which is why Sheffield FC is regarded as the world's first football club and the universities are not. 'We formed the first specific organisation with the sole intention of playing football,' Sheffield FC's chairman, Richard Tims, explains. 'We're not a school, we're not a village, we're not a university, we are a football club.' Creswick and Prest's Sheffield Rules banned almost all use of hands, setting a clear distinction from the Rugby code. The original Sheffield Rules allowed a bouncing ball to be stopped by hand, but not a rolling ball. The Sheffield FC rule book published in 1859 also defined fouls, introduced the corner kick, throw-in and free kick, and the crossbar. The club continued to use its rule book up until 1877.

In the early days of football, teams often adopted the home side's rules when playing, or split them as a compromise, using one side's rules in the first half and the other's in the second. This inconsistency often led to confusion, such as when Sheffield FC played a London XI in the early years and the height of the bar had to be reduced at half-time as Sheffield's was nine feet high and London's eight. Sheffield FC evolved its rules over the years and appears to have taken a flexible approach to them, such as allowing the weaker team to field additional players. While the Sheffield Rules advocated 11 versus 11, in one game Sheffield FC fielded 12 men against Norton's 18. There was even a 20-a-side game against Sheffield Barracks where Creswick had complained that the opposition fielded 38 players! Football was, in short, pretty anarchic in its early years. Driven by goalless or low-scoring games, later amendments to the Sheffield Rules in 1862 included the addition of scoring a 'rouge'. A rouge was scored if an attacking player touched the ball after it had crossed the 'rouge line', much like a 'try' in the Rugby code, although the concept originated from Eton's rules. Goals outweighed rouges, but if scores were level, the number of rouges could decide the game. The 'rouge' did not last in the Sheffield Rules into the 1870s, however.

As the men of Sheffield FC did not have anyone outside the club to play from its foundation in October 1857 until the creation of the Hallam Football Club three years later, who did they play against? It's a question club chairman Richard Tims is asked all across the world. 'For three years we didn't have any opposition, hence our nickname of "the club",' Tims says. 'We played amongst ourselves – married men versus unmarried men, letters of the alphabet and so on, until we convinced another local cricket club, Hallam, to form a football club.' Nearby Hallam FC sprung out from the town's cricket club in 1860, providing the men of Sheffield FC with a rival. A notice appeared in the *Sheffield Independent* on Saturday, 22 December 1860 announcing a 16-a-side match at Sandygate Cricket Ground on 26 December – Boxing Day – between Sheffield FC and the Hallam and Stumperlowe Club.[2] Subsequent advertisements in local press advertise the time as one o'clock, with an omnibus for spectators leaving the Angel Hotel at noon. Despite the rules, it was still a rough and tumble affair, with Sheffield FC founder and captain Creswick receiving a punch to the nose.

A match report from the *Sheffield Daily Telegraph* published on Friday, 28 December 1860 must surely be the first such post-match report in history. It records a large number of spectators, many of whom were 'extremely liberal with their plaudits' when physical contact occurred, while 'equally unsparing' when players slipped in the snowy conditions.[3] The game was conducted in a good temper and, despite inferior numbers, Sheffield FC, decked in scarlet and white, won 2-0. While Sheffield FC has moved grounds since its foundation, Hallam FC still plays at Sandygate Road. The stadium is recognised in the *Guinness Book of World Records* as the oldest dedicated football ground in the world.[4]

Early photos of Sheffield FC are grainy black and white shots. Stern-faced men – many of whom are bearded – are pictured wearing buttoned shirts and trousers, long socks and sturdy boots. These must be among the first football team photos in history, but little did this set of players know it – or what would follow.

## The foundation of the Football Association

Fans of the art deco architectural style will love the white behemoth of the Freemasons' Hall off London's Kingsway thoroughfare. On a clear day, it gleams brilliant white in the morning sun while its clean, straight lines cast neat shadows. Next door on the Great Queen Street wall hangs a plaque that reads: *The Football Association was formed on the proposal of Ebenezer Cobb Morley at the Freemasons' Tavern, which stood on this site. The modern game of football was born on this day. 26 October 1863.* Through the lens of the modern global game, it's hard to remember there was a time when football was a novelty. In the late 1850s going into the 1860s, the public schools still had their own football codes. Sheffield also had its rules and in London a nascent gaggle of clubs was emerging that would form the year zero of the modern game.

Ebenezer Cobb Morley was a solicitor from Hull. The son of a minister, he had formed the Barnes Football Club in 1862. Although he had not gone through the public-school system himself, many of the Barnes FC players had, and they brought with them their own interpretations of how the game should be played. Morley wanted to standardise the rules, so sent an advert out to the sporting press of the day advertising a meeting at the Freemasons' Tavern in Queen Street, Lincoln's Inn, London. Captains of all football clubs were invited to attend and work to agree a general code for the rules of football.[5] Representatives of 12 clubs from London and its surrounds attended: Morley's own Barnes FC, Blackheath, Blackheath Proprietary School, Charterhouse School, War Office (now Civil Service FC), Crusaders, Crystal Palace*, Kensington School, No Names Club (Kilburn), Perceval House (also from Blackheath), Surbiton FC and the Forest Club of Leytonstone. The Forest

Club was run by the Alcock brothers, Charles (C.W.) and John, who would go on to play influential roles in the game's early development.

The resolution was that a football association should be formed to set an agreed, uniform code for football. Six meetings took place between 26 October and 8 December 1863. The Association was founded at the first meeting, with the journalist Arthur Pember of the No Names Club from Kilburn appointed president. The Association failed to galvanise interest from many of the leading public schools. While Charterhouse School attended the first meeting, it declined to join the Association. Even without the public schools and their potential to quibble over rules, the Football Association committee found consensus hard. The key issues at stake when putting together the Association's laws were the pitch dimensions and outline, starting the game, offside rules, physical contact and handling. Those rules were thrashed out over the second and third meetings. This would be a blend of handling and dribbling.[6] The sticking point was whether or not hacking – kicking an opponent on the leg – would be permitted. It was agreed that hacking would not be permitted, and the laws were approved at the sixth meeting.

By this time, Blackheath FC – which favoured the Rugby School code – Perceval House and Crusaders had left. They were replaced before the end of 1863 by Royal Engineers, Forest School, Uppingham School and, notably, Sheffield FC. Blackheath had insisted on a clause allowing a player who had made a fair catch to run towards his opponents' goal, and also wanted provision for hacking and tripping.[7] The motion was voted down by 13 to four. Blackheath has the distinction of being a founder member of both the Football Association and the Rugby Football

Union (RFU) in 1871, along with Civil Service. Of those dozen clubs that attended the very first meeting to form the Football Association, only Civil Service FC still survives, although the Alcock brothers' Forest Club, later renamed Wanderers, has been revived by enthusiasts in recent years.

* The first Crystal Palace, founded 1861, played its inaugural match against the Alcocks' Forest FC on 15 March 1862. The club reached the semi-finals of the first FA Cup ten years later. The club then appears not to have played football between 1875 and 1895. A new company was set up and the current Crystal Palace FC was established in 1905. In 2020, a historian claimed a link between the two entities exists, which would make the club the world's oldest professional football club,[8] although several football historians dispute the claim.

## The Football Association rule book

What emerged from the meetings was a set of laws that very much echoed the Cambridge Rules of 1848. The 13 rules published by John Lillywhite cost a shilling and sixpence, and the first rule marks out the size of the playing area – a maximum of 200 yards long and 100 yards wide – and goal size (eight yards wide). There was no crossbar or net at this point. The rules outlawed pushing and hacking, covered early throw-ins and teams changed ends after a goal was scored. Players could catch the ball, but not pick up, carry or throw it to a team-mate. And gutta-percha was banned.[9] Gutta-percha is a form of latex used in the Victorian era for insulating telegraph cables. However, the references to nails and iron plates hint at the aggressive nature of football at that time. The first match to be played using the FA's new rules took place at Limes Field in Barnes on 19 December 1863, where Morley's home side drew 0-0 with

Richmond. While the Football Association had influence within London, its activity and wider reach appears to have been limited.[10] There was not a single entry in the FA minute book between 28 October 1864 and 22 February 1866.[11] Meanwhile, further north, Sheffield's rules were in use in its locale, where a growing number of football clubs were founded. In nearby Nottingham, the Notts County Football Club was also formed in 1862, playing its own defined rules. Nottingham Forest followed three years later in its 'Garibaldi red' shirts, a tribute to the hero of the recent unification of Italy.

At the FA's 1866 meeting, the offside rule was relaxed in response to debate. There could now be three opponents between the player and the opposing goal to create a more exciting game. A tape was also introduced across the goalposts to clearly define the scoring height, an early forerunner of today's crossbar. Touch downs – like Sheffield's 'rouges' – were also added. At this point, Sheffield FC took the initiative, suggesting an Association rules match between London and Sheffield at Battersea Park, which took place on Saturday, 31 March 1866. The London team won by two goals and four touch downs, with Sheffield failing to score. Charles W. Alcock had a goal disallowed for offside, testing the new rules for possibly the first time. The London team also featured Morley of Barnes and No Names' Pember as captain. The Sheffield team was led by club secretary W. Chesterman, who had instigated the match. Reports imply that the London team received rough treatment from their Yorkshire opponents in earning the win.[12] The difference in approach may well reflect the more physical game in the north. Regardless, there were no hard feelings, and the teams decamped to The Albion pub on Russell Street in Covent Garden to dine after the match.

By February 1867, when only a handful of member clubs attended the FA meeting, Morley apparently considered winding up the Association, despite the growing number of football clubs in the London area. But the despondent Morley was encouraged by letters from Yorkshire. Here, Sheffield FC had become something of a cheerleader for the FA in the north, as its only member outside London and its surrounds. The Sheffield Football Association now included more than a thousand members and 14 clubs, and Sheffield FC wanted a return match. Without Sheffield's positivity, the FA may have folded there and then, and who knows what direction football would have gone in. New laws were introduced designed to appeal to the public schools, and Charterhouse signed up to the Association in 1868. The founders of Scotland's first football club, Queen's Park FC, had also written to Charles W. Alcock for a set of the Association rules in the previous year. We will explore the first internationals between England and Scotland in the next chapter. The year 1868 also saw the launch of the first *Football Annual*, which was an 84-page directory of active football clubs of any code.[13] Again, Lillywhite was the publisher.

## How the FA Cup boosted the Association game

For the Association code, 1871 was a pivotal year. On 26 January, at the instigation of Blackheath, 21 clubs met at the Pall Mall Restaurant in London. The meeting, chaired by E.C. Holmes of the Richmond Club, led to the creation of the Rugby Football Union. The split of the two leading football codes in England was complete. The following month, the Association adopted a proposal from the Upton Park club that the goalkeeper be able to handle the ball. Members also accepted a Sheffield FC innovation, the corner kick, to restart the game for the attacking team

once the defending side had put the ball out of play behind
its goal line. But it was a short announcement made by
Wanderers' Charles W. Alcock, aged 29 and now secretary
of the FA, at the offices of *The Sportsman* newspaper on
20 July 1871 that truly bolstered the Football Association's
influence: 'That it is desirable that a Challenge Cup should
be established in connection with the Association for which
all clubs belonging to the Association should be invited to
compete.'[14] An Old Harrovian like many of his Wanderers
team, Alcock's Football Association Challenge Cup was
based on the Harrow School knockout competition, except
this one would be open to clubs nationwide.

The first 15 clubs to enter what is the world's oldest
surviving football tournament were Barnes, Civil Service,
(the original) Crystal Palace, Clapham Rovers, Hitchin,
Maidenhead, Marlow, Queen's Park from Glasgow – the
Scottish Football Association was still two years away from
being founded – Donington Grammar School, Hampstead
Heathens, Harrow Chequers, Reigate Priory, Royal
Engineers, Upton Park and Alcock's own club, Wanderers. It
was a sketchy start for the FA Cup. All 50 members had been
invited, with some declining on the basis that a competition
could lead to unhealthy rivalry.[15] Due to distances between
fixtures, only 12 teams actually ended up playing, with
Queen's Park unable to afford to stay in London for a
replay once it had drawn with Alcock's Wanderers. The
first FA Cup became something of a London gentlemen's
tournament, but its importance must not be underestimated
as a genus of what could follow.

The first final was held at the Kennington Oval in
London – home of Surrey County Cricket Club, where
Alcock was also secretary – on Saturday, 16 March 1872.
The competition was immediately described by the press

as the 'Blue Riband of Foot-ball'.[16] The strongest team in that first FA Cup Final was Wanderers, with Charles W. Alcock as its captain. Wanderers defeated Royal Engineers with a single goal from Morton Betts after 15 minutes. Once more in a high-profile match, Charles W. Alcock had a goal disallowed after his team-mate Charles Wollaston handled the ball. Two thousand people had come to see the game. When Wanderers took on Oxford University in the final of the following year at London's Lillie Bridge ground in Fulham, the crowd had grown to 3,000. By the tenth anniversary of the competition in 1882, the cup final attendance had doubled to 6,000 as Old Etonians became the last of the gentleman amateur sides to win the FA Cup. Alcock's FA Cup had given the advantage to the Association game over rugby as the predominant winter game. In 1886, the football associations of England, Ireland, Scotland and Wales came together to create the International Football Association Board (IFAB) to oversee the evolution of the game's laws. To this day, IFAB is the guardian of the laws of football and they can only be changed by the board, with world football's governing body FIFA sitting alongside the four Home Nations associations with 50 per cent voting influence.

## The game of the people

By now, football was really catching on in the public consciousness. Workers had started getting Saturday afternoon off work since the 1850s in England and, coupled with the growth in the railway network, football was able to spread around the country. In keeping with the Victorian ethos of personal improvement through physical activity, Britain's factories, mills and foundries were establishing football clubs to keep their workers active. The Dial

Square club – now known as Arsenal – was formed at an armament factory in Woolwich, Kent. Newton Heath – now Manchester United – was founded at a railway depot. Manchester City, Wolverhampton Wanderers and Everton came out of churches, while Sheffield Wednesday was formed out of the Wednesday Cricket Club, the day of the week that the team played. 'We've perhaps forgotten over the course of history the original purpose for football clubs, which was that they were formed for the benefit of their members so that their members could play football,' Paul Brown, author of *Savage Enthusiasm*, a history of football fandom, informs me. 'Football wasn't invented as a spectator sport; it was invented to be played, not necessarily watched.' But people were coming to watch footballers play. Originally, these spectators would be non-playing members of the club who would stand around the touchline. However, when clubs started playing other clubs, non-players began cheering for either side. This was particularly the case for institutions – such as the factories, churches or railways – where there was a ready-made pocket of support. This interest spread into the wider community. *The Goal* newspaper was launched in 1873, and the football fan was born.

Existing narratives, such as rivalries between towns and institutions, would now be channelled on the football pitch. Brown cites the example of Blackburn versus Burnley, two Lancashire mill towns who had a pre-existing rivalry in the cotton industry. 'Football came along at the right time. People, particularly working people, were looking for something to do with their time,' Brown adds. 'For the first time, workers in factories had Saturday afternoons free and they had a little bit of money in their pocket. Football was ideal because it was accessible, it was exciting, and that was the basis for the first real growth in popularity.' Football was being played on parkland and rudimentary grounds, except the FA Cup Final and internationals, hosted at Kennington Oval, which had been built for cricket in 1845. The Oval had hosted the Surrey Football Club, founded by members of the county's cricket club in 1849 and the first club in England not from a school background to publish its own football rules. The club would later fold. It was not until 1892 that England's first purpose-built football stadium was built at Goodison Park, Liverpool, for the Everton Football Club. The ground originally had stands on three sides – two uncovered stands that could each hold 4,000 spectators, while a main stand contained 3,000 seats. The FA's Lord Kinnaird and Frederick Wall opened the ground in August 1892, although Everton did not play its first game there until 2 September, with a 4-2 win against Bolton Wanderers.[17]

## Football undergoes social change

During the 1870s and 1880s, the game started to migrate away from the gentlemen footballers and public-school old boys. In 1872, Charles Clegg from Sheffield was the only player selected by the FA to represent England in the first 'official' international against Scotland that had not attended a public school. He found himself ignored by the rest of the team, both on and off the pitch. The Scots teams, led by Queen's Park, pioneered the passing or 'combination' game – a style also favoured by English working institution teams, like Royal Engineers of the Chatham Dockyard. However, the English gentlemen were playing for themselves. On one famous occasion, when Sheffield's Billy Mosforth confronted the gentleman player Alfred Lyttelton for not passing during an international against Scotland in 1877, Lyttelton replied that he was playing for his *own* pleasure.[18]

The gradual changing of the guard was reflected in the performances of working-class teams in the first decade of the FA Cup, where they were pitted directly against the gentleman teams. Nottingham Forest and Blackburn Rovers had particularly good cup runs, but it was Rovers' cross-town rival, Blackburn Olympic, that finally overturned the apple cart in the 1882/83 season. Blackburn Olympic was founded in 1877 and was backed by a Lancastrian iron magnate, Sid Yates. Olympic's players were factory and mill men while the team's player-coach was a publican from Sheffield, Jack Hunter. Hunter had skippered England and marshalled from the back, bringing an extra man into midfield in order to play a more expansive passing game. In the quarter-finals of the 1882/83 tournament, Olympic thrashed much-fancied Welsh side Ruabon Druids 4-1 at home in front of 8,000 people. Ahead of the semi-final against Old Carthusians, the Charterhouse alumni team, Hunter took the team for a week's training break in Blackpool. Olympic won the match 4-0. Ahead of the final, Hunter again took the team to the coast. These working-class lads would need to be fitter and faster than their larger, healthier, upper-class opponents – the Old Etonians – if they would have a chance of winning. The Old Etonians featured early football superstar Arthur Kinnaird – later Lord Kinnaird of the FA – in a story retold with some dramatic licence in the Netflix series *The English Game* in 2020.

Cup final day arrived on 31 March 1883. A crowd of 8,000 gathered at the Kennington Oval, where the pitch was marked out with flags. Around 300 Lancastrians made the long journey south to watch Olympic, their cloth caps distinguishing them from the top-hatted Eton support. Kinnaird won the toss, and the Old Etonians started well, taking a first-half lead through Harry Goodhart. Olympic's dexterous keeper Thomas Hacking was busy throughout, according to reports. Olympic clawed their way back into the game and their cross-field passing confounded the Old Etonians, who lost a man to injury before the Lancastrians levelled to take the game into extra time. Early in the extra period, Costley netted early for Olympic, whose fitness and one-man advantage helped them control play until full time was called. Blackburn Olympic had made history and, unlike many of their Lancastrian neighbours, counted not a single Scot among their XI and included just two Yorkshiremen. For the first time, the trophy was presented on the field of play at the end of the match, by Major Francis Mandarin, president of the Football Association.

The *Bolton Evening News* heralded Olympic for being the first to break through the 'magic circle' of London-based cup winners. 'Bravo, Olympic, may you long enjoy the great name you have so bravely earned,' the paper adds.[19] Alas, Olympic had folded by the end of the decade. The club failed to attract the support to sustain itself in the Blackburn area, where several clubs were active, most notably the increasingly powerful Blackburn Rovers, who won the next three editions of the FA Cup. Blackburn Olympic's plight highlights another aspect of the game that rose to prominence during the 1880s. It caused divisions and, ultimately, drove some clubs out of business altogether – professionalism.

## The onset of professionalism

By the 1870s, football was a big money spinner. With their Saturday afternoons free to do as they pleased, the working man and woman chose football increasingly as their weekend diversion. Payment of players was outlawed by FA Rule 15, the spirit of which was built very much on the public-school Victorian ethos of muscular Christianity.

It was easy enough for the gentlemen footballers with their highly paid careers or private incomes to draw on, but the working-class players from the mills and factories did not enjoy such luxuries. While professionalism was not allowed, clubs had got around the rules with 'expenses' for players, or even job offers to players for them to turn out for a particular team. This was the case for Glaswegian docker James Lang of Third Lanark, who took a knife-making job in Sheffield in order to turn out for The Wednesday club in 1876. In Lancashire, Blackburn Rovers, Bolton Wanderers, Preston North End and Darwen were enjoying rising gate receipts to the point that they were able to attract more of what became known as the 'Scotch Professors' south, in order to bring the attractive Scots passing game. One of these early professionals, Fergus Suter, moved from Partick FC to Darwen in 1878. His story is also dramatised in the Netflix series, *The English Game*. He moved south along with compatriot Jimmy Love to turn out for Darwen before an acrimonious move to Blackburn Rovers in 1880, where he spent the final nine years of his playing life. In contrast to the narrative of *The English Game*, Suter lost the 1882 FA Cup Final with Rovers to Old Etonians before winning three consecutive FA Cups with the club between 1884 and 1886.

It was Preston North End's chairman, William Sudell, who was the driving force behind open professionalism. Sudell became a member of what would become the Preston North End Football Club in 1867, aged 16, when the establishment was a cricket club. Sudell was something of an all-round sportsman, accomplished at swimming, cycling, cricket and rugby, and by 1874 he was chairman of the club. It was the Rugby code that the club opted to play first – albeit briefly – in 1877 but found themselves edged out by more established clubs. So, inspired by the other growing Lancashire clubs from neighbouring mill towns, Preston North End switched codes. On 5 October 1878 the club played its first match under FA rules at its Deepdale ground. Sudell played in the 1-0 defeat to fellow Lancastrians, Eagley. It was not until May 1880 that Preston North End officially adopted the Association code in a motion that was carried unanimously by members. Despite early setbacks – including a 10-0 defeat to Blackburn Rovers – enthusiasm for the game was fierce and, with Sudell at the helm, Preston North End was ambitious. By 1883, Sudell was perfectly comfortable with tempting Scottish players south in exchange for jobs. He brought down full-back Nick Ross from Heart of Midlothian, Ross's brother James, as well as midfielders George Drummond, David Russell and Jack Gordon. Events came to a head during an FA Cup tie with Upton Park from East London at Deepdale in 1884. The Preston players had even been relaxing at the seaside resort of Lytham for the week running up to the match. A protest was lodged to the Football Association over the eligibility of Preston North End's players. The FA was finally forced to confront professionalism head-on to avoid a split in the game. The Lancashire clubs had strong opponents inside the FA and their key challenge did not come from the southern gentleman amateurs, but from the Midlands and the North.

In January 1885, the Notts Football Association had asked delegates from the Birmingham, Derbyshire, Staffordshire, Lincolnshire and Hallamshire Associations to meet its representative to 'propose alterations'. [20] Influential men like Charles Clegg of Sheffield – who we met earlier in his England playing days – and Charles Crump of the Birmingham FA were opposed to the payment of players. Some Midlands clubs along with prominent Lancashire club Darwen were in favour of payment to players to cover wages lost rather than payment for playing. The opponents of professionalism pushed the FA to issue a questionnaire to members in 1884 asking for details on their players, including any wages, under threat of expulsion on refusal. Recognising this existential threat, the Lancashire clubs got together and were ready to face the Football Association in London head-on. They promised not to dignify the questionnaire with a response, as well as to pull out of the FA Cup, and even form their own professional league. As he had with the creation of international football and the FA Challenge Cup, it was Charles W. Alcock again who made the breakthrough at the Football Association. By 1885, Alcock had sensed the way the wind was blowing and proposed the legalisation of professionalism based on cricket's example. Cricket, for some time the national sport in that era, had experienced its own professionalism debate since the 1770s.

In July 1885, after months of debate, the Football Association finally allowed the payment of players. Footballers would now have the same recognised professional status as cricketers, and a potentially seismic divide in the game – one that would later split the rugby code – was avoided. A year later, the Glaswegian George Ramsay became the first professional football manager when he took the helm at Aston Villa.[21] The argument over professionalism in football would appear time and again over the coming decades, not least around the participation of teams in the amateur Olympic tournaments.

## The foundation of the Football League
Popular though the FA Challenge Cup was, one tournament and a series of friendlies was not enough to sustain public interest in football. Aston Villa director William McGregor, another Scot shaping the future of the sport, suggested a

league format to provide a regular revenue stream for clubs and something to play for. The formation of a Football League was discussed initially ahead of the 1888 FA Cup Final and agreed over subsequent meetings in Manchester and Birmingham. The founding clubs of the Football League were McGregor's Aston Villa, Sudell's Preston North End, Wolverhampton Wanderers, Blackburn Rovers, Bolton Wanderers, West Bromwich Albion, Everton, Burnley, Derby County, Notts County and Stoke (City). All these clubs still exist but the 12th team – Accrington FC of Lancashire, not to be confused with Accrington Stanley – folded in 1896. Nottingham Forest, The Wednesday and Lancashire's Halliwell Rovers were not admitted as the organisers feared there would not be time for additional fixtures in the calendar.[22] It was Sudell's Preston North End team that dominated the first season of the Football League, winning the league and cup double undefeated. The 'Invincibles' did not even concede a goal in their five-match FA Cup run and striker John Goodall netted 21 goals to become the Football League's first-ever top scorer. The Football League inspired the formation of other leagues, such as the short-lived Combination, which featured Blackburn Olympic, Port Vale, Northwich Victoria and Newton Heath. The Combination failed to complete its first season. In 1889, the Northern League was founded, making it the second-oldest league in the world, featuring clubs in the north-east of England, while the Football Alliance was also formed, featuring Newton Heath again, Crewe Alexandra, The Wednesday and Nottingham Forest. After three seasons, the Alliance was absorbed into the Football League as Division Two.

So far, the various attempts at league football had been centred in the Midlands and the North of England, enabled by the growing railway network and more flexible working practices. The South took a few more years to respond, but in 1895 the Southern League was formed, featuring some familiar names. The first champions were Millwall Athletic (now simply Millwall). The league also featured Tottenham Hotspur, Southampton St. Mary's (now Southampton), Luton Town and Queens Park Rangers.

## Bramall Lane: the pioneer stadium

The Bramall Lane stadium in Sheffield rises above the rows of tight-knit terraced houses in the heart of England's steel city. Home fans and visitors alike may not be aware of the significance of the ground despite the profile of its home side, Sheffield United. Bramall Lane, along with the Kennington Oval in London, are the only arenas in England to have hosted both Test match cricket and the FA Cup Final. The ground, easily accessible on foot from the city centre, was where Messrs Creswick and Prest had met to discuss forming Sheffield FC back in the 1850s. The cricket ground had opened in 1855, with the first football match being played at the ground on 29 December 1862 between Creswick and Prest's Sheffield and cross-town rivals Hallam. The game ended goalless. In early 1867, Bramall Lane was host to the final stages of England's – and the world's – first-ever football tournament. The Youdan Cup, a small silver jug, was provided by the sponsor, theatre owner Thomas Youdan. The tournament was played over three weeks under Sheffield Rules, which still involved 'rouges' as a method of scoring. These were only used in case of a tie. Hallam beat Norfolk from Norfolk Park, Sheffield, in the final. The world's oldest football trophy remains the property of Hallam FC, despite going missing for several years before it resurfaced at an antique dealers in Scotland in 1997.[23] A year later, local theatre owner Oliver Cromwell sponsored a tournament played under Sheffield Rules, which The Wednesday club won in a final held at Bramall Lane. The trophy now resides in the trophy cabinet of what is now Sheffield Wednesday FC.

On 14 October 1878, Bramall Lane was the scene of the 'decided novelty in football – a match with the assistance of the electric light', as the *Sheffield Independent* enthused.[24] Floodlit football had arrived! The Monday night match was arranged between two sides picked by the Sheffield Football Association with one side captained by Sheffield mayor William Clegg and the other by his brother, Charles, both of whom had been capped by England. The referee was W. Peirce Dix of the Sheffield FA, who would oppose professionalism in the coming decade. Electric light was a relatively new technology, and John Tasker, a local businessman, derived the idea to promote the commercial use of electricity. Tasker built a wooden stage, around ten metres high, on each corner of the ground, each of which hosted a lamp and reflector. They were powered by engines behind each goal that drove two Siemens dynamo machines, one for each lamp. Newspaper reports state that the total power equalled 8,000 candles at the cost of 3½d per light per hour. The result was 'brilliant and effective'.[25] While 12,000 tickets were sold, many thousands scrambled for vantage points to view this historic match, with an estimated 20,000 people watching the game. Floodlights would not become a regular fixture in English football until the 1950s, when Portsmouth FC became the first club to host a Football League match under lights.[26]

The Wednesday club had been using Bramall Lane before moving to its own ground. By the late 1880s, Bramall Lane's owners decided it needed a club to keep the money coming in during the winter months. The committee of the Sheffield United Cricket Club met at the offices of club secretary Joseph Wostinholm at 10 Norfolk Row, Sheffield, on 22 March 1889 and agreed to form a new football club for the 1889/90 season. Newspaper advertisements appeared around Sheffield that week inviting professional players to submit their testimonials. Sheffield United Football Club is the oldest 'United' in world football, and Bramall Lane is the oldest ground in the world to still host professional football.

Sheffield United also fielded the world's first black professional footballer. Arthur Wharton was born in the Gold Coast – modern-day Ghana – and as a 19-year-old moved to England to train as a missionary in 1882. Despite his extraordinary pace – Wharton ran 100 metres in ten seconds at Stamford Bridge in 1886 – the all-rounder excelled in goal. He signed for Preston North End, then moved to Yorkshire with Rotherham Town, before becoming legendary goalkeeper William 'Fatty' Foulkes's understudy at Sheffield United. Wharton never settled at any club and, following retirement from football in 1902, worked in a colliery. He died penniless in 1930 and was laid to rest in an unmarked grave. Wharton remained largely forgotten until 1997, but he has since received a headstone and his story appears in the National Football Museum in Manchester. Sheffield United would also make history on 22 January 1927 away to Arsenal at Highbury. This is when the BBC's Henry Blythe Thornhill Wakelam, himself a former Harlequins rugby player, delivered the world's first radio football commentary operating out of a wooden hut. A numbered grid system was devised to help listeners follow play around the pitch, giving rise – some argue – to the phrase 'back to square one'.[27]

## The pioneers of women's football

Things started to really accelerate for the women's game in Britain after the London 2012 Olympics. In that tournament, Team GB's women's team played to a full house at Wembley and beat Brazil 1-0. I was there and the atmosphere was fantastic. Three years later, England's performance finishing third in the 2015 Women's World Cup marked another milestone and, by 2019, the women's game received record TV viewing numbers during the World Cup in France. In 2017, Lewes FC in Sussex became the first professional or semi-professional team in the UK to pay its women's team players the same as their male counterparts. It marked the latest inroads for the women's game in England, whose early success was stifled by a Football Association ban in 1921. However, it was not in England but Scotland that Britain's first female football team was founded. The suffragette Helen Matthews, who played under the pseudonym 'Mrs Graham', founded Mrs Graham's XI in Stirling in 1881. The first recorded women's football match was between a team from Scotland and a team from England at Easter Road, Edinburgh, which resulted in a 3-0 win for the Scots. An editorial in Scotland from May 1881 sums up the attitude of many men in the country at the time, describing the women's match in Edinburgh as 'women's rights with a vengeance ... we want no such importations here'.[28] The team had created enough interest to attract at least 400 paying customers. A good few hundred more than that jumped the fence for its next match at the Shawfield Grounds in Rutherglen Bridge, near Glasgow, the following week. With the game goalless after 55 minutes the 'rougher element' of the crowd broke the rope and invaded the pitch, forcing the police to charge with batons and rescue the players. Players were 'hissed' at by the crowd when the police escorted them from the ground.[29]

Women persevered nevertheless and in 1895 the British Ladies Football Club was founded with Mary Hutson – who also played under the wonderful pseudonym, Nettie Honeyball – as its captain. Honeyball made the teams' kits herself. One was dark and light blue, the other red and white. The teams were made up mostly from London and surrounds and included a mixture of married and single young women of independent means. Honeyball received a mixed response by mail, some in favour, some opposed and one so very offensive that Honeyball handed it over to the police. The first match at Crouch End between Honeyball's 'North' and the 'South' attracted a huge crowd, was 60 minutes in length and ended 7-1 to the North. The event drew criticism from *The Sketch*, which described the spectacle as a 'huge farce' and women as unsuited to the rough and tumble of the football field, concluding that 'as a public entertainment it is to be deplored'.[30] Yet the British Ladies Football Club drew support from a wide cross-section of society. Its patron was the aristocrat Lady Florence Dixie, many of its members were middle class and it included Britain's first black female footballer, Emma Clarke. In December 2019, Clarke was honoured with a blue plaque in Crouch End where she and her sister Florence also played football.[31]

Women's sport was growing by the 1890s. The All England Lawn Tennis and Croquet Club had opened its annual championships to women in 1884, seven years after the first men's singles tournament. Cycling was also a popular pursuit for women in the 1890s and was a key mode of transport for the suffragettes. The First World War provided a brief moment in the limelight for the women's game. With so many men – including many professional footballers – away in the trenches, women had picked up the mantle on the land and on the factory floor. Alfred

Frankland of the Dick, Kerr munitions factory in Preston observed women working at the plant hosting kickabouts during breaks. These impromptu games were arranged by a worker named Grace Sibbert, and in 1917 Frankland suggested to Sibbert that the women form a football team. He even arranged for the 'Dick, Kerr Ladies FC' to play a Christmas Day charity match at Preston North End's Deepdale ground to raise money for wounded soldiers.

A crowd of more than 10,000 turned up to watch the Dick, Kerr Ladies take on a women's team from Coulthard's Foundry. Unlike the British Ladies' team of the previous century, Dick, Kerr and Coulthard's were dressed as men would have been, with shorts, long shirts and socks, but with matching hats. Corsets were barred.[32] There was no derision from the watching local newspapermen this time, with the *Lancashire Evening Post* praising the ladies' combination play.[33] Dick, Kerr Ladies beat Coulthard's 4-0 and raised more than £600 for the wounded – £50,000 in modern money. The team received training from former Preston North End players, including 'Invincibles' member Bob Holmes, and were playing sometimes twice a week at exhibition games across the country. Despite the end of the war and many of the women losing their jobs as men returned from the front, the Dick, Kerr Ladies continued to play. In 1920, a then record crowd for a women's game saw Dick, Kerr Ladies beat a French team 2-0. And on Boxing Day 1920 they drew a crowd of more than 50,000 to Goodison Park for a match against St. Helens Ladies, raising £3,000 for disabled soldiers. Again, the Preston team triumphed 4-0.

One year later, however, the FA dealt a blow to women's football that would set it back for decades, saying that the game was 'quite unsuitable' for women and requesting its members refuse access to their grounds for women's matches.[34] That blanket ban, based apparently on doctors' concerns over the future fertility of female players, meant that grounds like Preston North End's Deepdale and Everton's Goodison Park could no longer host women's matches. The ban would last half a century until lifted in 1971.

Belinda Scarlett is a curator at the National Football Museum in Manchester. She tells me that the Dick, Kerr Ladies were among the most well known and successful of the women's munitions teams that started playing during the First World War. 'Then in 1921, the FA brings in its restrictions arguing that football is unsuitable for women, and that really changes the course of women's football going forward,' she explains. 'It's very difficult to look at the FA ban in isolation. It was a result of many factors, including society's attitude towards what women could or should do in the 1920s. This was obviously just post-war and there were concerns that men that had returned from the war weren't able to fulfil their previous role in society and that women should make way and go back to what they were doing before the war.' Scarlett adds that the FA did not have control over the women's game, so this was also a potential contributing factor to the ban. Both on and off the pitch, the Dick, Kerr Ladies dressed and acted like modern, independent women, Scarlett explains.

Dick, Kerr Ladies – once the unofficial England team and regarded as the greatest women's team ever – played on until 1965, but we will never know what might have been for the women's game in England had it never been banned. In 2017, to mark the centenary of the Dick, Kerr Ladies' first charity match, a wall mural was unveiled at Deepdale based on an iconic photograph of the team. The ladies stand in a line in the goalmouth, each with their hands on the shoulders of the woman in front. In the same year, a blue plaque was unveiled by Valerie Conn, a founding player's granddaughter, at the Dick, Kerr factory building. In 2019, to coincide with the FIFA Women's World Cup in France, the National Football Museum unveiled a statue of the Dick, Kerr Ladies' prolific goalscorer, Lily Parr, who netted more than 980 goals over a 32-year career. It is the first statue ever created of a woman footballer.[35] The female pioneers' legacy is finally being recognised and built on.

## The evangelists: football clubs on tour

With the game firmly established in the motherland, English clubs started touring Europe in the last decade of the 19th century to spread the game and help the fledgling clubs abroad to develop. Clapton FC of East London was the first to play on the continent, thrashing Belgium's pioneer club Antwerp 8-1 in 1890. Three years later, they returned, to win by seven goals again. Cambridge University also travelled to Belgium in 1893, beating a Brussels FA team 3-0. Tunbridge Wells FC played three games in Brussels and one in Bruges in 1896, winning all four handsomely. The most famous touring side of all, however, can also now be found playing in the lower tiers of the English football league system.

It's a clear September night in the suburbs of South London. The mellow golden sun makes silhouettes of the skeletal floodlights of the War Memorial Sports Ground, home of Carshalton Athletic. In the small crowd of 225 is a dedicated group of visiting supporters with apparently more banners than actual fans. Among them is a Brazilian flag and messages in Portuguese, including *Camisa 12* (Twelfth man) and *Obrigado por fazer parte da nossa história* (Thank you for being part of our history). These are the fans of Corinthian-

Casuals, a club formed by merger in 1939 but with roots that go far deeper. The Corinthians' legacy is probably better known for inspiring the eponymous São Paulo club, who became champions of South America by winning the Copa Libertadores in 2012. Corinthian Football Club was formed in 1882 by Football Association representatives, including Nicholas Lane 'Pa' Jackson. He had been assistant honorary secretary of the Football Association. The FA was keen to develop an amateur team that could take on and beat Scotland in the model of Queen's Park, whose passing combination and knowledge of each other's game had enabled them to play England off the park. England only beat Scotland *once* in the entire 1880s. Corinthians' tours became legendary. On an early tour of the north of England in December 1884, Corinthians thrashed FA Cup holders Blackburn Rovers 8-1 in front of 10,000 spectators. Corinthians played seven games in eight days on its northern tour as the age of professionalism closed in.

The amateurs were living through a sea change in the sport. When Blackburn Olympic beat the Old Etonians in the 1883 FA Cup Final, the power shifted away finally from the gentleman amateurs. In 1885, football had turned professional, and in 1888 the Football League kicked off without any of the original amateur pioneer clubs. Yet the FA, which accepted professionalism after much heated debate, was still run by public-school men, and in 1886 nine Corinthians represented England against Scotland in a 3-0 defeat at Hamilton Crescent, Glasgow. In both 1894 and 1895, all 11 men representing England against Wales were Corinthian FC players. In July 1897, Corinthians toured South Africa, its first overseas tour. Playing 23 matches over almost two months, the tourists won 21, drew twice and scored 113 goals to just 15 against. The team returned in

1903, winning 22 of 25 matches, drawing two and facing its first overseas defeat to Durban – 1-0.

The public schools that adopted Association rules still played a leading role in football in the 1880s. Just one year after Corinthian FC was founded, Casuals FC was formed as a feeder club for the Corinthians. The Casuals fielded five teams, meaning they could source more players and, unlike Corinthians, entered competitions and in 1905 became founding members of the Isthmian League. During the 1890s, Corinthians were graced by sporting legends. One was the 17-year-old Charles Miller in 1892, who would later be credited with introducing football to Brazil. Miller was a last-minute stand-in for Corinthians against Hampshire in a side that included the sporting all-rounder, Charles Burgess (C.B.) Fry, who was the same age. Fry is best known for his illustrious cricketing career, where he captained England for six unbeaten Tests, winning four and drawing two. He scored two centuries in his 26-Test international career and notched up more than 30,000 first-class runs in total. In athletics, he equalled the world record for the long jump (7.176m). Fry had played football at Repton School, which had a strong reputation in the Association game, and established himself as a formidable and pacy defender. By 16, he was playing in the FA Cup for Casuals, before captaining Oxford University and joining Corinthian FC in 1891. Like Miller, he would later turn out for Southampton FC – albeit as an amateur – for two years, helping the club win the Southern League and make the FA Cup Final. In 1901 he played his one and only England match as full-back against Ireland, which was held at Southampton. In the 1880s, Corinthians fielded brothers A.M. and P.M. Walters, who were nicknamed 'Morning' and 'Afternoon' according to their initials.

In 1904, Corinthians smashed Manchester United 11-3, still the Red Devils' biggest-ever defeat. During the course of this book, we will see Corinthians' impact on the nascent game in several countries, nowhere more so than Brazil, which the club toured at Miller's behest in 1910. The club provided 86 members of the England team – which no other club surpassed until Tottenham Hotspur in the 21st century – and 16 captains, more than any club. Nearly a century and a half after its foundation, Corinthian-Casuals remains true to its roots. Corinthian-Casuals' community manager is John Forrest. 'At their inception in 1882, the Corinthians' aim was to attract the best amateur footballers in England in an effort to improve the fortunes of the national team who, at the time, were regularly being beaten by Scotland,' he explains. 'That's a pretty ambitious mission statement to say the least! It's also fair to say that the plan worked and for the first 30 years or so of the club's existence, they were justifiably considered to be the best football club in the world.' Forrest continues: 'Today, our continued adherence to the ethos of amateurism obviously means that our ambitions are rather more modest! However, we are still the highest ranked amateur club in the country competing as we do in an otherwise entirely semi-professional league. Although the club's heyday is a distant memory, we believe that the "Corinthian Spirit" of fair play and sportsmanship still has a vital role to play in the development of young people and we try to instil those virtues through our youth system both on and off the field of play.'

## The Association rules game goes global
By the turn of the 20th century, the Association game had put down roots in most corners of the world. There was a professional season in the United States and cross-national

tournaments in South America in the 1890s. The foundation of the *Fédération Internationale de Football Association* (FIFA) in Paris in May 1904 signalled a sea change in the way the game would be run outside Britain. Initially resistant, the Football Association declined to participate in FIFA, only to recognise it officially in April 1905. This was thanks mainly to the diplomatic efforts of Baron Édouard de Laveleye from Belgium's governing body, the *Union Belge des Sociétés de Sports Athlétiques* (UBSSA).

From then on until the 1920s, when debates around professionalism and a reticence to cooperate with the Germans in the bitter aftermath of the First World War soured the waters, the FA was a constructive FIFA partner. Blackburn-born administrator Daniel Burley Woolfall succeeded French founder Robert Guérin as FIFA's president in 1906 until his death in October 1918. Woolfall was instrumental in arranging the 1908 Olympic football tournament at White City, London, where Great Britain – essentially an English amateur side – won the gold medal. Great Britain retained gold at the 1912 Olympics in Stockholm. The country had won the first football gold on offer at the Olympics in 1900 in Paris, where Great Britain was represented by the amateur side Upton Park. The FA was still influential, but its game had gone global. The pioneers were taking the game to the world, forming new football cultures and moulding new identities.

## The pioneer clubs today

Sheffield FC may not have achieved the heights enjoyed by its more illustrious professional neighbours, United and Wednesday, but its legacy as the world's first club remains. The club's badge has always retained a nod to its Victorian roots. In its current guise, the central shield is split into two black and two dark red checks, its current colours, with 'Sheffield FC' emblazoned across it. In the top-left black quadrant is the year of foundation, 1857, while an old sewn football sits in the bottom-right black quadrant. Either side of the shield stand two players. On the left stands a moustached man from the founder era holding his Victorian ball and dressed in a blue cap, blue jersey, white long johns and knee-high blue socks. To the right, the modern player is dressed in red, sporting a contemporary ball and haircut. Under the shield and players reads the proud statement: *The World's First Football Club.*

In 2004, FIFA awarded the club with its Centennial Order of Merit for its contributions to football. The only other club to share this distinction is the world's most successful club, Real Madrid. Three years later, Pelé was guest of honour at Bramall Lane in a match between Sheffield FC and Inter Milan to mark the club's 150th anniversary. Chairman Richard Tims has been invited all over the world as an ambassador of the world's oldest club and even addressed the famous Yellow Wall at Borussia Dortmund's Westfalenstadion. Mementoes of Sheffield FC's early trophies and subsequent fame adorn a modest members' room at the Coach & Horses ground. I poked my head in prematch and the weight of history feels almost too much for that small space. Sheffield FC stayed amateur while across town The Wednesday went professional and Sheffield United was formed as a professional club, even borrowing players from Sheffield FC to get them started.

'Creswick and Prest wrote the Sheffield Rules of football to keep themselves fit for cricket. These were gentlemen who didn't need to derive an income from sports; they did it for the love of the game,' Tims told me. 'Professionalism rose to prominence with the formation of the football league [1888], and Sheffield FC got left behind. Although in the 1870s and 1880s the amateur game was still considered as good as the professional game, by the turn of the century, you've seen what's happened now,' he adds. Instead, the club proposed the creation of a cup competition specifically for amateur sides and in the 1903/04 season won the FA Amateur Cup. The club finished runners-up in the FA Vase Final in 1977 to Billericay Town and has reached the FA Cup fourth round on two occasions. In 2009, Charles W. Alcock's Wanderers was reformed by enthusiasts in London 122 years after the original club folded. After football's earliest years in London, the Midlands and the North, it's to Glasgow that football moved next.

1  http://www.bbc.co.uk/news/uk-england-south-yorkshire-14153913

2  *Sheffield Independent*, 22 December 1860

3  *Sheffield Daily Telegraph*, 28 December 1860

4  https://www.guinnessworldrecords.com/world-records/75073-oldest-football-ground

5  Brown, Paul, *The Victorian Football Miscellany* (County Durham: Goal-Post, 2013)

6  http://www.thefa.com/about-football-association/what-we-do/history

7  *The Rules of Association Football 1863* (Oxford: Bodleian Library, 2006, p18)

8  https://www.cpfc.co.uk/news/2020/april/crystal-palace-the-oldest-professional-football-club-in-the-world-formed-1861/

9  *The Rules of Association Football 1863* (Oxford: Bodleian Library, 2006, p35)

10 https://www.thefa.com/about-football-association/what-we-do/history

11 Morris, Terry, *Vain Games of No Value? A Social History of Association Football in Britain During its First Long Century* (Bloomington: AuthorHouse, 2016, p187)

12 *Bell's Life*, 7 April 1866 (p10)

13 Westby, Martin, *England's Oldest Football Clubs 1815–1889* (Self-published, 2019, p61)

14 http://www.thefa.com/about-football-association/what-we-do/history

15 Ibid.

16 *Morning Post*, 16 March 1872 (p5)

17 http://www.evertonfc.com/content/history/history-of-goodison-park

18 Sanders, Richard, *Beastly Fury: The Strange Birth of British Football*

(London: Bantam, 2010)

19 *Bolton Evening News*, 2 April 1883 (p4)

20 *Preston Herald*, 10 January 1885 (p2)

21 https://scottishfootballmuseum.org.uk/george-ramsay-the-worlds-first-football-manager/

22 Brown, Paul, *The Victorian Football Miscellany* (County Durham: Goal-Post, 2013)

23 https://www.hallamfc.co.uk/index.php/our-club/our-history

24 *Sheffield Independent*, 19 October 1878 (p10)

25 Ibid.

26 https://www.portsmouth.co.uk/sport/football/portsmouth-fc/portsmouth-s-fratton-park-presence-in-football-history-as-floodlight-pioneers-1-8884719

27 http://news.bbc.co.uk/sport1/hi/football/1760579.stm

28 *Jedburgh Gazette*, 14 May 1881 (p2)

29 *Manchester Evening News*, 18 May 1881 (p2)

30 *The Sketch*, 27 March 1895

31 https://www.womeninfootball.co.uk/news/2019/11/30/emma-clarke-honoured-last-lat/

32 *Lancashire Evening Post*, 26 December 1917 (p4)

33 Ibid.

34 *Hull Daily Mail*, 6 December 1921 (p4)

35 https://www.nationalfootballmuseum.com/halloffame/lily-parr/

# 2.

# Scotland

IF YOU pop into the tourist shops that flank Edinburgh's Royal Mile, the chances are you'll spot a tea towel titled 'Wha's Like Us?' In Scots dialect it means 'Who's as good as us?' and contains the words of a poem that lists Scottish inventions that an Englishman will come across in the course of his day-to-day life. Could this long line of Scottish inventions also stretch to football? There is an argument that the world's first football club was founded in Edinburgh in 1824, a full 33 years before Messrs Creswick and Prest founded Sheffield FC.

When it comes to Association football, Scotland's role is indeed pivotal. The 'founding fathers' of football in three of the major footballing powers – Spain, Brazil and Argentina – were all Scots or from Scots families, as were those pivotal to launching the game in Scandinavia, Japan, Czech Republic, Ukraine and elsewhere. The world's oldest known football, found during renovations at Stirling Castle, dates from around 1540. Scottish football historian Andy Mitchell tells me that – as in England – football had been played in Scotland, even as far north as the Orkney Islands, since mediaeval times. '[Football] was also played in the schools, and whilst we tend to focus on the development of football at Eton, Harrow, Charterhouse, Westminster and Rugby, what's not so well known is that a lot of other schools also had their own football games,' Mitchell told me. 'My particular focus is on Edinburgh, where a kicking game of football was played at the High School of Edinburgh from the late 18th century. It was a very popular game, it was in an enclosed space, so you didn't run and carry with the ball, you kicked it around.' Mitchell recounts that in 1824, John Hope, one of the former pupils of the High School of Edinburgh, went up to Edinburgh University, where he was training to be a lawyer. He wanted to keep on playing the game, so he set up 'The Foot-ball Club'. Rather like the Football Association four decades later, there was no prefix. The club was not called 'The Edinburgh Foot-ball Club' because it was the very first of its kind.

'It was an open club, it wasn't exclusive to students or former pupils at the High School, and it was a great success,' Mitchell continues. 'It attracted 70 or 80 members per year for the first ten years of its life and had a very vibrant football culture, and the reason we know all this is because John Hope – the founder – kept incredibly detailed records.' Hope – who was just 17 when he set up The Foot-ball Club in Dalry, south-west Edinburgh – kept membership lists, accounts and descriptions of the events that they had played. He even kept the letters from his club members and a description of how to make a football. 'So, here we have quite a long-lived football club which kept on going until about 1841, so that's 17 years of activity in Edinburgh. Very clearly, this was the first football club of any kind in the world, which predates Sheffield by quite a considerable time and shows that there was a football culture in Scotland long before Sheffield or London, or anywhere else,' Mitchell argues.

John Hope's team were a mix of middle-class professionals, and, while there are similarities, his rough and tumble kicking game did not use the same rules as those that became the Association rules.[1] All the John Hope papers are kept in the Scottish National Archives now, so his basic rules survive. 'The rules quite clearly specify a code of behaviour, no tripping, goalposts, free kicks, lineation of a field of play,' Mitchell adds. Hope's summer matches raised money for poor children in Edinburgh. Although The Foot-Ball Club is not mentioned in any contemporary media reports, Hope left a wealth of documents, which Mitchell has analysed. Mitchell and fellow sports historian John Hutchison have identified 324 members of the club during its 17-year existence. Although the club folded in 1841, it left a legacy. Club member Charles Kirkpatrick's son James went on to win the FA Cup with Wanderers FC in 1877. James Kirkpatrick also captained Scotland in the first recorded international against England in 1870.[2]

## For the sake of playing

Between the disappearance of The Foot-Ball Club of Edinburgh in 1841 and the foundation of Scotland's first Association side – Queen's Park Football Club in Glasgow on 9 July 1867 – rugby football was played quite widely in both Edinburgh and Glasgow. Queen's Park FC was founded by a group of men from the north of Scotland who had come down to Glasgow for work, so they had no background in either rugby or the public-school system. The minutes of Queen's Park's first meeting confirmed that 'at half past eight o'clock a number of gentlemen met at No. 3 Eglinton Terrace for the purpose of forming a football club'.[3] This group of north Scotsmen wrote to Charles W. Alcock at the FA in London asking for a set of its laws and decided to adopt Association rules. The club's 'Rules of the Field' allowed some handling – like fair catches and touch downs over the goal line outside the goal.[4] The members decided that Queen's Park FC players would not be paid, successfully resisting the rise of professionalism by sticking to its motto *Ludere Causa Ludendi* – to play for the sake of playing. The club would remain amateur until, in 2019, members voted to turn professional. Within two years of its foundation, membership of Queen's Park FC had grown to 40, each paying a shilling entry fee.

'Their biggest problem at that time was they had no other forms of reference, they had very few opponents, so they developed very differently from the game in England,' Mitchell told me. 'In England, there was a culture of dribbling with a ball until you were tackled. Queen's Park hadn't had that experience so they realised that passing the ball was more efficient.' Like Sheffield FC before them, Queen's Park FC members played among themselves at the outset. Matches such as Reds versus Blues, Light versus Heavy Weights, North versus South of Eglinton Toll were all recorded in the early years.[5] There was a local rugby football team in Glasgow Academicals, founded a year previously in 1866. However, Queen's Park was reluctant to adopt the Rugby rules just in order to find opponents. The club rejected the chance to play a team from Ayr in 1868 due to costs, so the first match that Queen's Park appears to have played against an outside opponent was against Thistle Football Club of Glasgow Green, whose base was less than two miles from Queen's Park, just across the River Clyde. Queen's Park won by two goals to nil, while little is known about the Thistle Football Club, except that by 1873 it was defunct.[6]

Queen's Park's next match – and its first outside Glasgow – was against the Hamilton Gymnasium on 29 May 1869, apparently at great expense to the club. The visitors won this 15-a-side match by four goals and nine touches down, according to the *Hamilton Advertiser* on 5 June 1869 in one of Scotland's first Association match reports.[7] While the press may not have committed much space to this match, Queen's Park member – and later president – H.N. Smith was moved to write a 21-verse poem about the match.[8] The two sides met again at Queen's Park in August and the home side won again by a closer margin this time, 2-0.

In 1870, the club managed to arrange more matches. Firstly, Queen's Park dispatched Airdrie FC, a team with strong Irish connections, 4-0 in a 14-a-side match, before taking on other teams from around Glasgow. By the time Queen's Park played Airdrie FC again at the public park in Airdrie on Tuesday, 20 September, the sport had garnered enough interest to attract around a thousand spectators. Queen's Park was again victorious by three touches. Scotland's pioneer club remained unbeaten in its first three years of existence and had yet to concede a single goal. The club needed to expand its horizons.

## London calling

Notices appeared in early 1870 in *The Sportsman* announcing that a match between 'the leading representatives of the Scotch and English sections' would be played on 19 February at Kennington Oval 'under the auspices of the Association'. The announcements appeared between suggestions from Upton Park and the Civil Service Club over handling laws.[9] The Kennington Oval is now better known for its hosting of cricket Test matches. The venue has been a staple of England internationals since 1880 and was the scene for the burning of the Ashes following defeat to Australia in 1882. In 1870, the Oval was, as it is still to this day, home of Surrey County

Cricket Club. As a versatile space close to central London, it became something of a hub for nascent sports. It had hosted a match the year before when the Wanderers had lost 2-0 to West Kent, which opened the door for more clubs to play at the Oval.

The FA's Charles W. Alcock and Robert Graham were the contacts for those seeking to represent England, while James Kirkpatrick at the Admiralty, Somerset House, and Arthur (Lord) Kinnaird in Pall Mall recruited the Scots. The line-ups of that first informal international very much reflect the social class that the Association game was played in at the time. The eventual England team consisted of a majority of public-school boys, while the Scotland defensive pairing included two Members of Parliament – Wingfield Malcolm MP and Will Gladstone MP. Scotland's team also included players from the Colonial Office, the India Office and the Treasury. All bar one – lawyer Kenneth Muir Mackenzie – were born outside Scotland but claimed Scots roots. Alcock would later decry this team as 'counterfeit' and not truly representative of Scotland.[10]

The proposed date of 19 February 1870 had to be moved due to freezing conditions and the Oval was hit by a heavy frost. The game was rescheduled for Saturday, 5 March 1870, at 3pm. It would be an 11-a-side match with a half-time interval and change of ends if no goals were scored after 45 minutes. It was customary at this point in the game's development to change ends after each goal that was scored. Handling the ball was also prohibited. A crowd estimated to number up to 600 people braved the wind and rain to attend, which was impressive at this stage of the game's development. Scotland won the toss and captain Kirkpatrick opted to use the wind to his team's advantage. The teams kicked off at 3.15pm. By half-time, the game was still goalless, and the teams duly changed ends.

Match reports indicate that England laid siege to the Scotland goal in the second half. England captain Charles W. Alcock was determined on victory and committed his goalkeeper forward into the fray. In doing so, he left the English goal vulnerable and a long punt upfield from 17-year-old Harrow schoolboy Robert Crawford found its way into an empty goal. Crawford – who would go on to serve in the Afghan War and also receive a 12-month sentence for causing a servant to be flogged to death in Sierra Leone – had just made history as the first scorer of a goal in international football. There were just 15 minutes left for play. England attacked again and a minute from time Alfred Baker of the No Names Club sprinted forward to equalise. The game finished even at 1-1.

This unofficial match was the first of the so-called 'Alcock Internationals'. Alcock wanted genuine Scottish players to represent the Scotland team in the next international. He posted notices in Scottish papers and this time managed to secure at least one player who had played Association rules north of the Tweed. Queen's Park FC founder member Robert Smith, who is listed as club captain and treasurer at the club's inauguration, had moved to London by the time of the second Alcock International in November 1870 and was playing for the South Norwood club. Smith had retained his Queen's Park FC membership and, having taken part in the second Oval match – which resulted in a 1-0 win for England – he fed back to the club about the no-hands rule. Lacking opposition in Scotland while the Rugby code was picking up new entrant clubs, Queen's Park FC joined the Football Association.

Three more Alcock Internationals were played at the Kennington Oval between February 1871 and February

1872. There was a 1-1 draw, and 2-1 and 1-0 wins for England. In the final of these five, Sheffield FC's Charles Clegg became the first non-London-based player to represent an England XI. He even scored the winner.[11] By 1872, Alcock had led the creation of the FA Challenge Cup. As a member of the FA, Queen's Park was eligible to compete and the club was even given a bye to the semi-finals of the 15-club tournament, where they met Alcock's Wanderers team at the Oval on 4 March 1872. Robert Smith was joined by his brother James, who now also resided in the London area, in the Queen's Park team. The match ended goalless, but Queen's Park had to withdraw due to a lack of funds. The outing was a significant expense for the Glasgow club, too much to justify another lengthy trip south and Queen's Park withdrew, handing Wanderers a pass into the final.

The Association game was gaining traction in Scotland, with the formation of several teams that are still in existence. Kilmarnock FC was formed in 1869, although the club played a game more akin to the Rugby code at the outset. For this reason, its ground is known as Rugby Park.[12] Stranraer FC was formed a year later, and in 1872 Dumbarton FC and Rangers FC were founded. In the following four years, Hamilton Academical, Heart of Midlothian, Hibernian FC and Falkirk FC were also established. By 1872, there was popular demand for a proper, 'official' international between Scotland and England, with an authentic Scottish team. As the senior Association club in Scotland, it was down to Queen's Park to get the ball rolling. Due to the popularity of the Rugby code in Edinburgh, Glasgow made the natural option. Queen's Park secretary Archibald Rae put out a call for players in the press, and Hamilton Crescent – home of the West of Scotland Cricket Club and a multi-sports venue for cricket, rugby and athletics – was chosen to host.

In the end, the whole of the Scotland team that walked on to the Hamilton Crescent pitch on St Andrew's Day, 30 November 1872, were Queen's Park members – including the London-based Smith brothers, who became the first siblings to play together for an official international side. The two reserves were also Queen's Park players. The Scottish team's kit was Queen's Park's blue jersey, featuring a rampant red lion that had been sewed on to the shirt by Marion Wotherspoon, whose brother David was a forward in the Scotland line-up.[13] Charles W. Alcock had picked up an injury in the run-up to the match, so umpired alongside Queen's Park's poetic president H.N. Smith. The spectators – an estimated 2,500 who each paid a princely one shilling entry – were kept off the play area by ropes and stakes. Ladies got in for free. The game ended goalless, but the proof of concept would have an astronomical impact on the future of the game, both in terms of providing its popularity – and its profitability.

Scotland won nine of the first 13 games, with two draws and just two defeats. On 12 March 1881, Scotland was captained by the first black international footballer for a match against England at the Oval, which resulted in a 6-1 Scotland victory. The Queen's Park full-back Andrew Watson was born in Demerara, modern-day Guyana. His mother, Rose Watson, was from Guyana and his father was Scottish solicitor Peter Miller Watson, who used his wealth to send Andrew to Britain. His talent was discovered while a student at the King's College School in London. He later attended Glasgow University and played for local sides Maxwell FC and Parkgrove, where he played alongside another black player, Robert Walker. Watson played just three times for Scotland and won three Scottish FA Cup winner's medals with Queen's Park. He moved back to London to continue his engineering career in 1882 at a time when the Scottish Football Association would only select players based in Scotland to play for the country.

Nowadays, the Hampden Bowling Club pavilion sits on the site of the first Hampden ground, where Watson helped Scotland to a 5-1 win over the Auld Enemy. In 2019, a mural was painted on the side of the pavilion, visible to train passengers on their way from central Glasgow to the current Hampden Park, to mark Watson's feat. He is featured wearing the famous primrose and pink hooped Scotland shirt. These were the colours of racehorse owner, Lord Rosebery. He was honorary president of both the SFA and Edinburgh club Heart of Midlothian and an early patron of Scottish football. Scotland first wore the Rosebery colours in 1881 and they have been revived on occasions since. Watson is also celebrated in a special feature at the Scottish Football Museum in the bowels of Hampden Park stadium.

Scotland would only lose once to England during the entire decade. This success led to the creation of the Corinthian FC amateur team in England, and also attracted the attention of many leading clubs in England to the quality of Scottish players.

## The foundation of the Scottish Football Association

The first official international match had made it clear to Queen's Park of the benefits of creating an association, much like that of the FA in England. In February 1873, Archibald Rae wrote to Scottish clubs playing the Association rules to recommend the formation of the Scottish Football Association (SFA) and set up Scotland's own cup competition.[14] The founding meeting of the SFA was held at Dewar's Hotel on 13 March 1873, just five days after Scotland had lost a return match at the Oval 4-2 to England. The Scotland team for the second official international included six Queen's Park players – plus Robert Smith, listed as a South Norwood player. The only other Scotland-based player was W. Gibb of the Clydesdale Club. At the SFA's inaugural meeting, Queen's Park were joined by the Clydesdale, Vale of Leven, Dumbreck, Third Lanarkshire Rifle Volunteers (Third Lanark), Eastern and Granville clubs. While Kilmarnock sent notice of their intention to join.[15]

Sixteen teams were to enter the first Scottish Football Association Challenge Cup, all of whom contributed to the purchase of the trophy, now the oldest surviving trophy in Association football after the original English FA Cup was stolen and thought to have been melted down. The earlier Youdan Cup (1867) had been contested under Sheffield Rules, not Association. In 1873, Queen's Park FC moved from its parkland to the first of three Hampden Park grounds that the club would occupy during its history and switched from blue to black and white hooped shirts. 'The Spiders' duly won the first tournament in the 1873/74 season, beating Clydesdale 2-0 in the final. The following season Queen's Park beat Renton 3-0 in the final to retain the trophy and made it three on the trot in the 1875/76 season by beating the Third Lanarkshire Rifle Volunteers after a replay. The club did not even lose a match until 1876, a full nine years after its formation, going down 2-0 to Wanderers at the Oval. The club's first defeat in Scotland came against Vale of Leven in the fifth round of the Scottish FA Cup in December 1876. Queen's Park continued to enter the English FA Cup, twice losing in the final to Blackburn Rovers in 1884 and 1885, before withdrawing permanently after the 1886/87 season.

**Renton become the first 'Champions of the World'**
There were now two established cup competitions in England and Scotland. In 1888, FA Cup winners West

Bromwich Albion invited that season's Scottish Cup winners Renton – a village football team from Dunbartonshire – to play to determine who would be 'Champions of the United Kingdom and the World'. A one-foot-high pewter trophy was commissioned for the occasion, and now resides in the Scottish Football Museum. The match was held at Glasgow's Cathkin Park on Saturday, 19 May 1888, and between four and six thousand spectators turned up to watch. Renton took the lead early on before the game was postponed for 30 minutes to allow a thunderstorm to pass, by which time heavy rain had reduced the pitch to a quagmire. West Brom equalised but Renton, who boasted two Scotland internationals among its XI, went on to win 4-1. The club proudly displayed a plaque with the words 'Champions of the World' above its home pavilion but this proved to be the beginning of the end for Renton. Its players attracted the attention of talent scouts from the south and Renton FC had folded by 1922. Cathkin Park – home of Third Lanark from 1903 to 1967, when the club was dissolved – is not far from Hampden. Now open parkland, the terraces with their crowd barriers remain in situ, overgrown with trees and bushes. It's like a time capsule. To stand there, as I did during my research visit to Glasgow, you really get the sense of stepping back into the annals of Scottish football history in what is a beautiful, peaceful setting.

The professionalism debate that had engulfed English football and been resolved in 1885 was still raging in Scotland. English scouts were attending Scottish matches, and so concerned were the Scottish clubs that in Dumbarton a 'Vigilance Committee' was established to spot the spotters. Reports appeared of agents 'floating about' Dumbarton, with several of the players being 'interfered with'. One agent was set upon during his visit and, scared off, took the first train home for Lancashire.[16] The roughing up of a football agent could not deter Scottish players from the attraction of the English professional league and, within a year, many of Renton's best players had headed south, as did players from the Vale of Leven. These prized players, skilled at the 'combination' passing game, would become known as the 'Scotch Professors'. But when it came to professionalism, Scotland was haemorrhaging talent to the south. Something had to give.

## The Scottish Football League is formed

With the foundation of the Football League south of the border in 1888, Scots clubs started thinking of creating their own league. The Scottish Football League (SFL) was still staunchly amateur at the time of its launch for the 1890/91 season. This makes the Scottish system the second-oldest football league in the world. As in England, endless meaningless friendlies and sporadic cup matches were not enough to keep the paying Scottish public stimulated. Nor, as was often the case, were mismatches, such as when Arbroath beat Bon Accord 36-0. The 11 clubs that made up the inaugural Scottish Football League included Glaswegian sides Celtic and Rangers, Cambuslang, Cowlairs and Third Lanark; Dumbartonshire sides Dumbarton, Renton and Vale of Leven; Abercorn and St Mirren from Paisley; and Heart of Midlothian from Edinburgh. All 11 founding members came from the central corridor of Scotland; the northern and southern lowland clubs were not represented. Queen's Park was a conspicuous absentee. The club was concerned that a league system would lead to professionalism and force many sides to fold, which was indeed what happened – founder clubs Cowlairs and Cambuslang had disappeared within a decade.

It was professionalism that caused the Scottish Football League its first crisis. Just five games into the first season, Renton – whose chairman had driven the League's foundation – was expelled for playing a testimonial game against members of the suspended Edinburgh club St Bernard's. The Edinburgh club had not been admitted to the SFL due to concealed professionalism. Renton FC was reinstated after a legal fight with the SFA that the *Glasgow Evening Post* described as 'an unparalleled event in football history'.[17] Rangers and Dumbarton shared the first Scottish Football League title after a 2-2 draw in a play-off, the only time the title would be shared. The SFA's attitude towards professionalism mirrored that of the Rugby Football Union (RFU) in England. Players were banned from playing football in Scotland and lists of names were published. In 1884, just a year ahead of professionalism being permitted in England, 56 players had been banned from playing in Scotland, including 22 from Ayrshire and 14 from Edinburgh.[18]

At this time, Scottish clubs were still able to enter the English FA Cup, and in 1885, Queen's Park, Hearts, Rangers, Partick Thistle and Third Lanark all entered the tournament. In 1887, the SFA slammed the door on its members entering the English tournament. That same year, Cowlairs was accused of falsifying its accounts over player payments. A special general meeting of the SFA was held in March 1892 to discuss professionalism. Debating went on until 1am during what was a record sitting for the Association. An 'animated and prolonged debate' led to a vote against allowing professionalism by 71 to 54.[19]

Just 14 months later, Scottish clubs were back meeting at Carlton Place in Glasgow to discuss professionalism once more. By now the SFA had grown to a sizeable 182 clubs and reported an annual income of £1,384. It was here that Celtic's representative, Mr McLaughlin, highlighted the hypocrisy of the current system. Everyone knew that professionalism existed in Scotland, despite the SFA's best attempts to kill it, he argued. If golfers, cricketers and army volunteers could be paid, then why not footballers? McLaughlin argued that the SFA should take control of, and benefit from, professionalism, rather than risk losing its best players to England. Sunderland had just won the English championship with 14 Scots and just one local Wearsider on its books.

Divisions lay between city clubs and country clubs, who were fearful for their survival. Aberdeen had argued particularly hard for the word 'amateur' to be included and believed professionalism would have a detrimental effect on football in the north of Scotland. But McLaughlin argued that professionalism would benefit country clubs, as they would be guaranteed player loyalty for the full season. Vale of Leven supported Celtic's argument, but wanted to see a limit to money paid. Crucially, Queen's Park said that, although the club itself would remain purely amateur, it would support the move to professionalism. Season 1893/94 was therefore the first professional season for the Scottish football system, by which time 560 players at 50 clubs were registered professionals. It was at this point that Glasgow rivals Rangers and Celtic started their financial – and therefore sporting – dominance over the Scottish game, and the demise of the so-called 'village clubs' began. Also, in 1893, a second division was added including many members from the Scottish Football Alliance league of smaller clubs, and a third tier added in 1923. Professionalism did not stem the exodus completely. By 1910, nearly a quarter of England's First Division was made up of Scots-born players. One field where Scotland did reign supreme was at the fledgling international stage. The British Home Championship had been inaugurated in the 1883/84 season featuring Scotland, England, Wales and – at the time – a united Ireland team. Scotland won five of the first six competitions.

## Archibald Leitch, stadium pioneer

As the game took off in both Scotland and England, so the public flocked in ever-increasing numbers to football matches. This led to a requirement for purpose-built stadiums rather than roped-off parkland or cricket ovals. Rangers opened Ibrox Park in 1887, inaugurated with an 8-1 defeat to a Preston North End side nearing its prime. Celtic Park and Everton's Goodison Park followed in 1892. But it was the redesign of Ibrox Park in the late 1890s that would launch the career of Rangers fan and architect Archibald Keir Leitch. Leitch had been born in Camlachie, Glasgow, on 27 April 1865 and was named after his father, a blacksmith. He started out as a draughtsman, and his work took him to India and Ceylon, modern-day Sri Lanka, where he designed tea factories.

Ibrox Park had hosted two internationals and a Scottish FA Cup Final in its first five years. But the ground was dogged with issues in future cup finals in the early 1890s and by the end of the decade the club moved across the park to its current location. Rangers called on Leitch to create a stadium that matched its lofty ambitions. The result was a 40,000-capacity oval opened on 30 December 1899, complete with covered stands along the sides, including a pavilion. Additional curved, wooden stands open to the elements at either end were added later, bringing the capacity to 80,000. On 5 April 1902, Ibrox Park hosted an eagerly anticipated match against England. Around 70,000 spectators are estimated to have braved the heavy rain to come to the game but, tragically, some would not leave the match alive.

Leitch's west terrace was a steel frame constructed on concrete foundations. It contained wooden floor beams which rose to more than 12m (40ft) above the ground.[20] Despite the terracing being approved by the Govan burgh surveyor, nine minutes into the game, a shot caused excitement in the crowd and the pressure of the surge put strain on the new structure.

A section of the terrace collapsed, and hundreds fell to the ground. Leitch himself was at the match. Twenty-five spectators died, and 587 were injured. The game continued to a 1-1 draw with spectators in many other parts of the ground unaware of the unfolding disaster. The following month, the match was replayed at Villa Park and £1,000 was raised for victims. Unfortunately, it was not the last time that disaster would strike Ibrox. The resulting inquest blamed rain for weakening the beams. Glasgow architect John Gordon was called on to inspect the western terracing. He concluded that the 17 joists that had given way were made of poor-quality yellow pine, which is far easier to break than stronger red pine.[21] The Partick-based supplier of the beams was charged and later acquitted of culpable homicide. The tragedy could have been an early and terminal blow to Leitch's stadium building career, but instead lessons were learned, and Leitch went on to pioneer new forms of terracing that set the benchmark for much of what we still see today.

Leitch's mark was left around his native Glasgow as he went on to design Hampden Park and Celtic Park before heading south to develop Bramall Lane, Sheffield, Fulham's Craven Cottage and Stamford Bridge, home of newly formed

Chelsea FC. According to Leitch's biographer, Simon Inglis, at the height of his career in the 1920s, 16 of the 22 clubs in England's First Division had employed Leitch at some point. His work was on display at Arsenal's Highbury, Manchester United's Old Trafford, Aston Villa's Villa Park, Liverpool's Anfield, Everton's Goodison Park, and a host of other grounds.[22] Despite much of his work being lost in recent stadium redevelopments, his trademark red-brick stands can still be enjoyed today, such as the Johnny Haynes Stand at Craven Cottage, Fulham. Crucially for Leitch personally, Rangers rehired him several times, and his iconic Main Stand at Ibrox still stands. Leitch's passing in 1939 went largely unnoticed by the media, but 'Engineering Archie' is a critical pioneer in football's story, whose work is loved by fans across the world.

## Queen's Park FC today

We will be meeting many other Scots as we progress through this book. Scotland has never won a major championship but dominated the early British Home Championships, which ran for more than a century between 1883 and 1984. Queen's Park FC completed the sale of Hampden Park to the Scottish FA in August 2020, moving to the redeveloped Lesser Hampden ground with an initial capacity of 1,700. Also, in late 2019, the club voted to end 152 years of amateurism. The club, which developed talent including Scotland captain and Champions League winner, Andrew Robertson, can now offer permanent and part-time contracts. Queen's Park FC plays in Scotland's fourth tier, League Two. The club's legacy, along with providing Scotland's iconic deep blue shirts, is the genesis of the passing game. This passing style would be exported to the world, developed by coaches and ultimately reach its zenith in the Hungarian 'Golden Team' of the 1950s, Dutch *Total Voetbal* (Total Football) or the *tiki-taka* style of FC Barcelona in the early 21st century. But it all started on the public parks of Glasgow in the 1860s and 70s.

1 https://www.scotsman.com/lifestyle/lost-edinburgh-the-foot-ball-club-1-3438950

2 https://www.scotsman.com/news/revealed-how-edinburgh-gave-the-world-its-first-football-club-1-4376910

3 https://queensparkfc.co.uk/history/

4 http://www.qphistory.com/p/in-beginning.html

5 Morris, Terry, *Vain Games of No Value? A Social History of Association Football in Britain During its First Long Century* (Bloomington: AuthorHouse, 2016, p106)

6 http://www.electricscotland.com/history/sport/football/chapter7.htm

7 *Hamilton Advertiser*, 5 June 1869, p2

8 http://www.qphistory.com/p/1868-1870.html

9 *The Sportsman*, 5 February 1870 (p8)

10 Mitchell, Andy, *First Elevens* (Dunblane: Andy Mitchell Media, 2012, p19)

11 Brown, Paul, *Victorian Football Miscellany* (County Durham: Goal-Post, 2013)

12 https://www.scotsman.com/news/who-are-scotland-s-oldest-professional-football-clubs-1-4098282

13 Mitchell, Andy, *First Elevens: The Birth of International Football* (Dunblane: Andy Mitchell Media, 2012, p49)

14 http://www.qphistory.com/p/187374-was-another-momentous-season-for.html

15 https://web.archive.org/web/20080701213600/http://www.scottishfa.co.uk/scottish_football.cfm?curpageid=183

16 *Cricket and Football Field*, 29 September 1888 (p8)

17 *Glasgow Evening Post*, 9 May 1891 (p5)

18 Morris, Terry, *Vain Games of No Value* (Bloomington: AuthorHouse, 2016, p233)

19 *Derby Daily Telegraph*, 30 March 1892 (p4)

20 Brown, Paul, *Savage Enthusiasm: A History of Football Fans* (County Durham: Goal-Post, 2017, p90)

21 https://www.bbc.co.uk/news/uk-scotland-48028660

22 https://www.fourfourtwo.com/features/meet-archibald-leitch-man-who-invented-football-stadium

# 3.

# Wales

IT'S THE autumn of 2016. Welsh football has recently reached a historic peak as the national team ran all the way to the semi-finals of the European Championships, losing to eventual winners, Portugal. Down in the fifth tier of English football, the Vanarama National League, Wrexham AFC from North Wales are in Kent visiting Maidstone United. Around 150 Wrexham fans have travelled the 450-mile (724km) round trip and are – as ever, for Welshmen – in fine voice. At one point, the visitors break into their rendition of the Icelandic 'Viking thunderclap' chant to taunt their hosts about Iceland's surprise win against England in the second round of that tournament. The home fans remind the visitors that Wales lost to England in the group stage, as if that carries any weight against the eventual semi-finalists. Maidstone United take the lead; '1-0 to the part-timers!' goes the cry from the home fans, a reference to Wrexham's professional status. Wrexham is Wales's oldest football club and – after England's Notts County and Stoke City – is the world's third-oldest professional football club.

Yet Wrexham may very well have not existed at all. Like today's opponents Maidstone United, the current iteration is a phoenix club after being rekindled by a supporters' trust in 2011 before being taken over by actors Ryan Reynolds and Rob McElhenney in 2020.[1] The game ends 2-2. Honours even. That Wrexham found themselves down in the fifth tier of the English league system while fellow Welsh sides Swansea City and Cardiff City were competing in the top tiers is something of a comedown for the country's oldest side. So how did Wrexham come to become the pioneer of the Association game in Wales, a country often so closely associated with the Rugby football code?

## The formation of Wrexham Football Club

For a long time, Wrexham sold itself short. Its original foundation, as depicted on its former club crest, was thought to be in 1873, then evidence came to light in 2012 that changed everything. An eagle-eyed fan noted an entry in the *Wrexham Advertiser* from Saturday, 8 October 1864, which records the end-of-season meeting of the Denbighshire County Cricket Club at the Turf Tavern. Like the founders of Sheffield FC and Hallam FC in Yorkshire before them, the men behind the foundation of Wrexham Association Football Club started out as cricketers looking for a winter sport to keep them occupied and in good shape. The chairman, a Yorkshireman by the name of Edward Manners, is recorded as saying that there was a 'great want of amusement' in Wrexham during the winter. His proposal? To purchase a football and set up a training session, adding that he expected 'a good many down to the field next Saturday'.[2]

Manners didn't waste any time knocking his team into shape. By 22 October that year, the team had played a ten-a-side match next to the Turf Tavern against a side from the Prince of Wales Fire Brigade. The firemen won what appears to be a best-of-three-goals game by scoring twice.[3]

By January 1865, notices were appearing regularly in the *Wrexham Advertiser* from the 'Wrexham Football Club' for players, meeting every Saturday afternoon at 2.30pm.[4] By late September 1865, the 'Wrexham Football & Athletic Club' was advertising its opening game of the season to be played 'on the Race Course' on Saturday, 7 October at 2pm.[5] The message was signed by Edward Manners, who replicated his duties at the Denbighshire County Cricket Club by acting as the club's honorary secretary and treasurer.

Manners appears to have thrown himself into the sporting society within Wrexham. He was born in Knaresborough, Yorkshire, in 1831 and had settled in Wrexham with his work. North Wales was to be the cradle of Welsh football for the next half-century. In South Wales, the Rugby code would dominate.

Like many places in the world, a kicking game – *cnapan* or *criapan* – existed in Wales before Association football arrived. By the 1850s and 1860s, kicking games were being played in Welsh public and grammar schools. As in many other parts of the world, students wanted these games into adulthood once they had left school, and major footballing clubs that would adopt the Rugby code emerged in the south of Wales during the 1870s. The march of rugby in the south of the country was assisted by Wales's coal boom, as it became increasingly attractive for migrants. A large influx of migrants to South Wales came from neighbouring counties in England, where the Rugby code was popular, as it is today with major professional clubs like Bath, Bristol and Gloucester. The factory and mine bosses also saw diversions such as rugby as a good way to keep their workers occupied and away from partaking in other activities, such as antisocial behaviour and politics.[6] Similarly, Wrexham's proximity to the English border meant it would be influenced by the round-ball game. Football games were recorded in the schools of North Shropshire and Oswestry in England, close to the Welsh border, in the 1860s.

The small town of Ruabon, some six miles south of Wrexham, also appears early in the Welsh footballing story. It was here that the Druids Football Club was formed in 1872 from a merger of three local teams: Plasmadoc FC, Ruabon Rovers FC and Ruabon Volunteers FC. For a small town to be home to three clubs would suggest a healthy football culture existed in Ruabon for some time prior to the formation of Druids FC. Druids FC would feature as a prominent side in early Welsh football, winning the Welsh Cup eight times and the Welsh Senior League three times by 1904. The club was the first Welsh side to enter the FA Cup in 1876. Perhaps most famously, the club lost to Blackburn Olympic on the Lancastrians' historic 1883 FA Cup run. It would not be until Cardiff City in 1927 that a Welsh club would win the FA Cup.

The man who had overseen the merger between the three Ruabon clubs to form Druids FC was the solicitor Samuel Llewelyn Kenrick, although he rarely used his first name. Llewelyn Kenrick was a product of the Ruabon Grammar School, whose alumni also include former Wales, Manchester United and FC Barcelona striker, Mark Hughes, and the football commentator, Bryn Law.[7] Kenrick would go on to become known as the 'Father of Welsh Football' and was pivotal in the development of the Welsh national football association and early tournaments. It was an advertisement in *The Field* publication that propelled Kenrick to form a Welsh football association. The advertisement proposed an international football match between Scotland and Wales. Kenrick responded, promising a 'Cambrian XI', of which six players would come eventually from the Druids team, four others from North Wales and just one would come from the south.[8] The match took place on Saturday, 25 March 1876 in front of a crowd of 12,000 in Glasgow. This was something of a novelty for the Scots, after four years of playing internationals solely against England. Having won the toss and playing downhill in the first half, it took the Scots 30 minutes to break through. Chasing the game, the Welshmen left themselves exposed to Scotland's superior passing game. Scotland ran out 4-0 winners.[9]

Shortly after, the Cambrian Football Association was renamed the Football Association of Wales (FAW), with Kenrick appointed as its chairman and secretary.[10] Kenrick masterminded the launch of the Welsh Challenge Cup for the 1877/78 season, which featured 19 teams from North Wales, including Druids FC, Newtown, Bangor, Carnarvon, and 11 teams from Wrexham itself. The first Welsh Cup Final was held at Wrexham's Acton Park on 30 March 1878, as the Racecourse Ground was not available. Wrexham FC ran out winners of what is the third-oldest football tournament still running. The game was hotly contested during a mighty gale. Tempers flared before Wrexham scored in the dying seconds to win the first-ever Welsh Challenge Cup.[11] Kenrick was the losing Druids captain that day. Kenrick himself played much of his football in England but, after two defeats against England, helped Wales gain its first win against its neighbours, a 1-0 victory at Blackburn, in his last international match at the age of 33.

The Welsh had learned Scotland's combination game and adopted the SFA's by-laws so could, according to the sporting publication *Bell's Life*, be viewed as the SFA's protégé.[12] The Welsh now needed a home for their international side. Wales established Wrexham's Racecourse Ground as its national home, hosting Wales's first home international in 1877 – a 2-0 reverse to Scotland. The ground is recognised by the *Guinness Book of World Records* as the world's oldest international football stadium that still hosts international matches. According to Clint Jones, who runs the Welsh football website, the94thminute.com, the vast majority of Welsh fans are very aware of the Racecourse Ground being the oldest international stadium and it has a somewhat mythical status among them – not just because of it being Wales's first international ground, but because of all of the past games which have been played in the old stadium. 'Naturally, the older fans can fondly remember regular games being played at "Y Cae Ras" from the 1970s and 1980s. Such magical moments like Wales's 4-1 demolition of England in May 1980 and Mark Hughes's scissor kick against Spain in April 1985 will live long in the memory of those fans,' Jones tells me.

Due to required ground improvements, fewer internationals are being played in Wrexham. In 2019, a friendly with Trinidad and Tobago held at the Racecourse Ground was just the fifth held in Wrexham this century. 'As a result of this, and the stories of past games told by the older fans, it has added to the Racecourse Ground's almost mythical status amongst younger fans, due to there being so few games played at Wrexham nowadays,' Jones adds. While the south of Wales revelled in the oval-ball game, the north was – for now – the round-ball hotbed. Football in England had turned professional in 1885, attracting players from across the border and limiting the influence of amateur clubs such as Druids. One of the players born and raised in Denbighshire but tempted to move to England, where he was to excel with both major Manchester clubs, was Wales's first footballing icon: Billy Meredith.

## Wales's first soccer icon

William Henry Meredith was born in the mining town of Chirk, ten miles south of Wrexham, in 1874. Meredith was driving pit ponies at the age of 12, playing football as a pastime. Chirk's football team was enjoying something of a high when Meredith joined them aged 18 in 1892. The club had won three of the previous six Welsh Cups and, in 1893, Meredith featured in the Welsh Cup Final at the end of his first season with Chirk. Wrexham won 2-1 that day, but Meredith was already on the radar of English clubs. With Chirk hit by a coal miners' strike, Meredith started turning out for both Chirk – winning the 1894 Welsh Cup – and for Northwich Victoria, a club from Cheshire, England, that subsidised his income.

Meredith's exploits caught the eye of Manchester City, who secured his signature in 1894. His second match was the first-ever Manchester derby against Newton Heath – who would later become Manchester United – and within a few months he had turned professional. He played out on the right wing, was renowned for his dribbling style, and bagged his fair share of goals from that position. His shot was so fierce he is even reputed to have smashed a crossbar.[13] Billy Meredith was fast becoming Wales's – and arguably football's – first superstar. He captained the blue half of Manchester to its first major honour, scoring the only goal in the 1904 FA Cup Final against Bolton Wanderers. This was the first trophy that either Manchester club won.

He had played 339 games and scored 129 goals for City before moving across town to Manchester United in 1906 after a match-fixing scandal the year before soured his relationship with City. The maximum weekly wage for a professional footballer at that time was £4, but Meredith was accused of attempting to bribe Aston Villa's captain Alex Leake with £10 as City needed to win at Villa to have a chance of securing the 1904/05 title. The FA threw the book at Meredith and he was suspended for a year, denied a benefit match and would not receive payment from City. The club was also penalised when Meredith blew the whistle on City's payment above the minimum wage. The FA demanded City break up the side and 17 players received fines, and some club directors were banned indefinitely. Meredith's career recovered fairly quickly. In 1907, he was instrumental in Wales's first British Home Championship title win. He scored in a 3-2 victory over Ireland, was captain in a 1-0 win against Scotland and helped Wales secure a 1-1 draw with England. The following year, he was part of Manchester United's first title-winning team, followed by the FA Cup in 1909, in which he was named man of the match.

Meredith's Methodist upbringing was instrumental in the character formation required of a sporting icon at this time. He was a lifelong teetotaller, so bought into the Victorian ethos of health as a Christian virtue. It also empowered him with a sense of purpose and leadership. He was involved with the Association Footballers' Union (AFU) – the first organised attempt at a trade union for footballers in England – and in 1907, Meredith arranged the first meeting of the Players' Union. Professionalism was already well established in England but the members of the Players' Union sought greater rights for footballers, including unlimited wages, increased transfer rights and a percentage of transfer fees. They were dubbed 'The Outcasts' by some, but their efforts paved the way for the Professional Footballers Association.[14]

The National Football Museum in Manchester has a whole cabinet dedicated to Meredith memorabilia. He can be seen in either a suit or his playing gear, his distinctive moustache sitting proudly, his gaze piercing. Meredith went on to play until the age of 49. He died on 19 April 1958, just two months after his beloved Manchester United team was nearly wiped out in the Munich air crash. He is buried in Chorlton-cum-Hardy in Greater Manchester. Meredith himself did very well out of the game, promoting leading brands' products and running his own sports shop. He even had his own brand of football boots.[15] He was a pioneer in the mobilisation of players to derive a better cut of the profits enjoyed by football club owners, and he paved the way for sports sponsorships that would later become the norm. But there was one divide he couldn't bridge – that of north and south in Wales.

## North and south

As we learned earlier, rugby had a strong grip on the south due in part to the championing of the sport among the public schools in the region and the influx of migrants from the rugby-playing west of England. In the last quarter of the 19th century, rugby's dominance in the south was unchallenged. In the early years of the 20th century, however, inward migration from the Association-playing north of Wales and England's Midlands was starting to build demand for the round-ball game in the south. Professional clubs began to spring up. Domestically, a league system was established in the 1890s. In the north, agreement had been reached at the Lion House in Wrexham in March 1890 between nine clubs to create a Welsh Football League.[16] In the south, a South Wales Association League was also up and running in the 1890s. Future leading club Cardiff City was founded as Riverside AFC in 1899 and was the first southern Welsh club to win the Welsh Cup, in 1912, the same year that Swansea Town – now Swansea City – was formed. In 1900, the first Welsh international to be played in the south of Wales was held at Cardiff Arms Park. Billy Meredith scored the home team's goal in a 1-1 draw with England.

Meanwhile, rugby maintained its grip on the public consciousness in the south, something that was cemented by Wales's 3-0 victory over a powerful New Zealand All Blacks side at Cardiff Arms Park in 1905. This match, arguably the most influential in Wales's rugby history, helped cement the oval ball's status in the south of Wales and beyond. According to Clint Jones, in recent years, Wales's success on the football pitch, coupled with the FAW's promotion of Welsh language and ancient culture, has led the round-ball game to become seen more in line with the growing independence movement, while rugby is perceived as more 'Unionist' and British. National identity and footballing code would also be a key element in the Association game's next shore – Ireland.

1  https://www.bbc.co.uk/sport/football/54973357

2  *Wrexham Advertiser*, 8 October 1864 (p5)

3  *Wrexham Advertiser*, 29 October 1864 (p5)

4  *Wrexham Advertiser*, 14 January 1865 (p4)

5  *Wrexham Advertiser*, 30 September 1865 (p1)

6  Johnes, Martin, *A History of Sport in Wales* (Swansea: University of Wales Press, 2005, p24)

7  https://www.ysgolrhiwabon.co.uk/community/concise-history-ysgol-rhiwabon/

8  Brown, Paul, *The Victorian Football Miscellany* (County Durham: Goal-Post, 2013, p76)

9  *Dundee Courier*, 28 March 1876 (p3)

10  Brown, Paul, *The Victorian Football Miscellany* (County Durham: Goal-Post, 2013, p76)

11  *Wrexham Advertiser*, 6 April 1878 (p5)

12  *Bell's Life in London and Sporting Chronicle*, 5 March 1881 (p12)

13  Johnes, Martin, *A History of Sport in Wales* (Swansea: University of Wales Press, 2005, p34)

14  https://www.nationalfootballmuseum.com/halloffame/billy-meredith/

15  Johnes, Martin, *A History of Sport in Wales* (Swansea: University of Wales Press, 2005, p35)

16  *Oswestry Advertiser*, 5 March 1890 (p2)

# 4.

# Ireland

GIVEN THE close links between Belfast and Glasgow through trade, it is perhaps something of a surprise that football arrived comparatively late in the island of Ireland. But it has Glasgow in part to thank and, like Sheffield FC and Wrexham AFC before it, Ireland's first football club was the result of cricket club members looking for a winter pursuit. Ulster Cricket Club played what is probably the first exhibition match of Association football in Belfast on 11 December 1875. While there are reports of matches as far south as Cork in 1877, it was in the north where soccer first put down solid roots in Ireland.[1]

Advertisements appeared regularly in the *Northern Whig* newspaper in the autumn of 1876 posted by James M. Calder, secretary of the Windsor Football Club, calling for players for practice matches. Windsor FC played the Rugby code as well as Association rules. The club would be instrumental in the arrangement of the first significant soccer match in Belfast in October 1878, which involved Scottish pioneer club, Queen's Park. Sixteen years after the formation of the Football Association in London, six years after the Scottish Football Association, and two years after the Football Association of Wales was formed, Ireland saw the foundation of its first dedicated soccer club, Cliftonville Association Football Club, in 1879.

At this time, Ireland was still one country ruled from Westminster and the nearest outpost of the British Empire. Ireland had been exposed to foreign rule ever since the Anglo-Normans first set their sights on it in 1171. By 1871 in the northern counties of Ulster, more than 60 per cent of the population was made up of Protestants. Many of these were descended from English and Scottish migrants, encouraged to settle as part of the 'Ulster Plantation' of the early 17th century. This is when James I, the new king of both England and Scotland, ordered the settlement of agricultural lands in the north of Ireland. Not only did this create divisions along sectarian lines, which would explode into violence at regular intervals throughout history in the north of Ireland, but it also split communities down sporting lines. British games, such as cricket, rugby and Association football, were to exacerbate these divisions for decades in what was to become the Irish Free State after the Civil War of 1922/23 and later known as the Republic of Ireland.

While soccer had a socio-economic role in Britain, in Ireland the game took on a political edge for the first time. Association football would come to be seen by Irish nationalists as a 'garrison game', an imperialist import.[2] While not all Republicans were opposed to the sport, some of its prominent leaders were.[3] Indeed, the Gaelic Athletics Association (GAA) – which was founded in 1884 – disciplined any member found playing or watching Association football, right up until 1971. But by the late 19th century the foundations had been laid already for the spread of the game and, as in Britain, the combination of new labour laws that gave workers more leisure time and an expanded railway network enabled the Association game to grow in Ireland.[4]

## The foundations of Cliftonville Association Football Club

The story attached to the man credited with introducing football to Ireland, John McCredy McAlery, is that he was in Edinburgh on honeymoon in 1878 when he first saw a match taking place. McAlery was to be pivotal in the development and promotion of the game in Ireland.

McAlery is credited with inviting Glaswegian clubs Queen's Park and Caledonians to play an exhibition match at the Ulster Cricket Ground on Thursday, 24 October 1878, although local media cites the 'Grand Football Match' to be arranged 'under the auspices of the Windsor and Ulster Football Clubs'.[5] Indeed, an article in the *Freeman's Journal* the week before states that Windsor FC had been seeking to introduce Association rules to help improve their rugby forward play at the club following alterations to Rule 18, which demanded players to release the ball upon being tackled.[6] Queen's Park took part in order to evangelise the Association game. The Spiders won the fixture 3-1 in front of a crowd of around 400 locals.[7] Admission cost 6d for men, while ladies could watch for free.

On 20 September 1879, McAlery posted an advertisement in the *Belfast News Letter* inviting local men to join practice at the 'Cliftonville Association Football Club (Scottish Association Rules)'.[8] He was 30 years old at the time. Born into a farming community in Rathfriland, McAlery had been drawn to the growing city of Belfast to pursue a career in the drapery business. In 1870, at the age of just 21, he helped establish the Cliftonville Cricket Club, a sport at which he was particularly adept. He was clearly a driven man with an entrepreneurial spirit because he was soon opening his own business on Belfast's Royal Avenue.

McAlery wasted no time in arranging matches for his new club. Just seven days after his original call for players, on 27 September 1879, the *Northern Whig* newspaper carried a notice of Cliftonville's first match with J.M. McAlery listed as a back in the team's match against 'Quidnuncs'.[9] Keen students of Latin will note that the visitors' name means 'The What Nows?' The Quidnuncs were made up of rugby players and they ran out 2-1 winners at the Cliftonville Cricket Club ground. By mid-October, McAlery had arranged a match with the Caledonian Club of Glasgow, making a return almost exactly a year after its first appearance in Belfast against Queen's Park. McAlery was hands-on as club secretary, player, groundsman and even some-time security guard trying to stop spectators scaling the hedge that surrounded the ground to avoid payment. He also encouraged the formation of other clubs in Ireland, so that his team had someone to play against.[10] McAlery's groundsmanship was critical in the Caledonians fixture, as it took place in terrible conditions. This bad weather appears to have affected the turnout, which must have seemed like something of a personal blow to McAlery, perhaps even more than the 9-1 defeat to the visitors. The Cliftonville club was soon entertaining other Scottish teams, including Ayr and Portland of Kilmarnock, but – according to the club's first season report – had struggled to recruit local players to take part in practice matches.[11] Yet McAlery had planted a seed that started to grow.

## The foundation of the Irish Football Association

Organised Association rules football was just a few years old in Ireland, but McAlery was ready to follow the example of England, Scotland and Wales by founding a national governing body for the sport to agree a set of consistent rules and promote the game's development across the country. On 18 November 1880, the Irish Football Association (IFA) became the fourth such national football organisation. The meeting at the Queen's Hotel in Belfast was arranged by the Cliftonville Football & Athletic Club and brought together teams from Belfast and nearby counties. These included Avoniel, Banbridge Academy, Distillery, Knock, Moyola Park, Oldpark and Alexander FC from Limavady, who contributed to the purchase of the original Irish Cup and was the first team from outside Britain to defeat Everton in 1886. McAlery would be the honorary secretary of the IFA, while the first president was Major Spencer Chichester, patron of the Moyola Park club. In line with their Home Nations counterparts, a Challenge Cup competition was quickly established. The first edition saw Moyola Park defeat Cliftonville 1-0 on 9 April 1881 in front of around a thousand spectators. Moyola Park's captain Morrow scored with just 15 minutes remaining to bag the County Londonderry club the first Irish Association Challenge Cup.

Like Kenrick with his first Welsh team, McAlery was keen to get in on the international action to gauge where Irish football stood compared to the other established nations. A match was arranged with England for Saturday, 18 February 1882 at Bloomfield Park, Belfast. McAlery would assume his traditional role as captain skippering from the right side of defence. The IFA team attracted a 2,500-strong crowd but the Ulster weather once again conspired against McAlery, and the game was played in heavy winds accompanied by rain and hail. England were ahead within three minutes with a goal from Aston Villa's Howard Vaughton. By half-time, England led 5-0. While the wind abated in the second half, Ireland failed to score and withered as England ran riot. The final score was Ireland 0-13 England. Vaughton had bagged five himself and his Villa team-mate Arthur Brown had four. The game remains England's largest victory and either Irish national team's biggest defeat to this day. *The Sportsman* was scathing of McAlery's defence: 'The goal-keeping and back play of the Irishmen was weak in the extreme.'[12]

The scoreline devastated McAlery, but it set a benchmark of how far Irish football had to improve in order to compete at the Home Nations level, a problem the island would solve within three decades. McAlery took charge again for Ireland's second international match against Wales in Wrexham a week later. The result was 7-1 in favour of the Welsh. McAlery, by now in his mid-30s, switched his focus towards the administration of the game rather than the playing. He retained his position as secretary of the IFA until 1888 and acted as an international referee. Within two years of McAlery's leaving the IFA, the Irish League was founded.

## The foundation of the Irish League

In September 1890, the inaugural season of the Irish League kicked off. The league consisted of eight teams, seven of which came from Belfast and the outlier was Milford FC of County Armagh, who would leave an indelible spot on the game during its short existence. More on that shortly. The teams would play each other twice, meaning a 14-game winter season for each club with two points awarded for a win.

The Irish League's opening weekend was a sign of what was to come. Linfield won 8-0 at Cliftonville's Solitude ground while the match of the weekend must have been Clarence's 5-4 win over Glentoran.[13] Linfield prevailed as champions in the inaugural season, winning 12, drawing one and suffering just one single defeat. The secret to Linfield's success was its passing game, which contrasted to the dribbling game which was still popular. It even led to some successful runs in the English FA Cup, which Irish clubs could enter right up to the First World War. The game's popularity continued to grow rapidly across the island of Ireland and by 1910 the IFA had 420 members.

## Paying the penalty

In 1891, the IFA left what could be its most important legacy on the sport. William McCrum, a 25-year-old goalkeeper for the Milford FC club from Armagh, frustrated at the amount of foul play entering the game, petitioned the organisation to introduce a penalty spot kick in 1890. McCrum was no ordinary keeper. He was from a wealthy family and was educated at Trinity College in Dublin. He'd been key in the foundation of Milford Football Club, which was the only club outside Belfast to feature in the first edition of the Irish League. McCrum pitched his idea to IFA general secretary, Jack Reid, who sat on the International Football Association Board (IFAB) and therefore had some say over the rules of the game. Opponents of the proposal cited the disruption to the game that a penalty kick would entail but there was also a prevalent sense of denial – particularly from the English public-school figures high up in the game's administration – that gentlemen would purposefully cheat to seek an advantage.

The so-called 'Irishman's Motion' was put on ice until a farcical situation emerged in an FA Cup quarter-final between Notts County and Stoke City at the Trent Bridge cricket ground in Nottingham that put it back on the agenda. County led 1-0 in the final minute and a County player deliberately handled a last-minute, goal-bound shot on the line. An indirect free kick was awarded to Stoke, as that was all the laws of the time would allow. County players blocked the goal line and prevented a Stoke equaliser. By the time the IFAB met again in the summer of 1891 at Glasgow's Alexandra Hotel, McCrum had the support of the English FA and his proposal was passed as Law 14. From now on, any player intentionally tripping or holding an opponent, or deliberately handling the ball within 12 yards of his own goal line, would incur a penalty kick, taken from any point 12 yards from the goal line. The kicker would face just the goalkeeper, who could not advance more than six yards from the goal line. The ball would be in play once kicked, and it was to be placed on a line, not a spot – that would come in 1902. For Reid, who was present representing the Irish delegation, and McCrum himself it must have felt like an incredible victory.

Despite its opponents – including Victorian all-round sports star and Corinthian, C.B. Fry, who refused to believe that a gentleman would deliberately commit a foul – the penalty kick prevailed. Corinthian FC stood by its beliefs, and keeper Thomas Rowlandson famously stepped aside when faced with penalty kicks. The first penalty in the Scottish League was awarded on 22 August 1891 to Renton and on 14 September 1891 in England to Wolves. Both were successfully converted. Meanwhile, Milford FC did not make much of an impression on the Irish League, losing all 14 games in its first season, but Milford does welcome visitors with the sign 'Milford: Home of the Penalty Kick'.

## Meanwhile, in Dublin

While Belfast was fast establishing itself as Ireland's industrial heartland, Dublin, 160km to the south, was the administrative and academic centre, and the seat of British power on the island of Ireland. It had been since the Anglo-Norman conquest seven centuries earlier. Like England,

Scotland and Wales, Ireland had its own folk football before the early forms of what would become soccer and rugby were played. Trinity College in Dublin was playing the Rugby code in 1854, and there are reports of soccer matches in Cork and Sligo, and the Scottish FA had tried to arrange a match in Dublin before the Belfast exhibition.

In the 1870s, the Gaelic Athletic Association (GAA) had not yet been established. One of its founder members, Michael Cusack, was a huge fan of rugby and cricket, which was played in Ireland across social classes. When the GAA was founded in Thurles in 1884, one of its objectives was to create a separate Irish identity to British identity as part of a wider nationalist awakening. Gaelic football took inspiration from elements of both rugby and soccer, together with folk football, and the GAA was sponsored by Archbishop Croke, whose name lives on in the Croke Park stadium, the home of the GAA. Early on in Dublin, soccer was the game of the elite and the educated. The first football club, the Dublin University Association Football Club of Trinity College, which is still in existence, was founded in 1883, a year before the GAA.

In the following years, new clubs emerged, such as Freebooters Dublin, Castleknock College, Montpelier and Leinster Nomads. In 1890, the famous Bohemians FC was founded by students who played at Phoenix Park, many of whom went on to qualify as doctors. As more clubs emerged, the Leinster Football Association was founded in 1892 at the Wicklow Hotel. It was affiliated to the IFA in Belfast. A Challenge Cup and a league were established in the 1890s and the Association game was becoming formalised. Two clubs that still exist – Shelbourne and Shamrock Rovers – were formed during the latter half of the 1890s. Professionalism emerged in this period, with many players from Dublin travelling up to be paid handsomely by northern clubs.

By 1901, Bohemians had its own ground at Dalymount Park, beating fellow Dubliners Shelbourne FC 4-2 in an exhibition match in front of 5,000 spectators. Dalymount is still Bohemians' home, though much changed. Archibald Leitch even designed the club's former main stand. In 1902, the Bohemians became the first Dublin side to join the Belfast-heavy Irish Football League. Shelbourne joined in 1904. But by now, Irish clubs were branching out. Freebooters of Sandymount, Dublin, toured Belgium in 1903, demolishing a select Bruxelles XI 13-0 before moving on to Antwerp to dispatch Beerschot AC 5-2 and wrapping up a high-scoring tour with a 4-1 victory over a Belgian universities combination. British Army divisions were also active – the Irish Cup was even won by the Gordon Highlanders, a Scottish military division – and clubs began to emerge in Cork and the Midlands.

## Ireland's first footballing superstar

Just as Wales had Meredith, Ireland found a national hero in Patrick O'Connell. Dubliner O'Connell's achievements both on and off the pitch are nothing short of remarkable. However, his story was mostly forgotten until in 2018 his descendants and some keen football historians got together to retell his story in a biopic film. Born in 1887, Patrick O'Connell started playing football as a youngster in the streets of north Dublin, near to Croke Park, the home of the Gaelic Athletic Association. O'Connell started his playing career at a strong amateur team called Liffey Wanderers in the early 1900s, going on to captain the side. Belfast Celtic – a representative of the Catholic community based near the Falls Road – offered O'Connell the chance to turn professional, so he headed north.

Playing for Belfast Celtic put O'Connell on the scouting map of English clubs, and he moved to Sheffield Wednesday in 1909. It was during his time in England that O'Connell earned a call-up to the Irish national team. At this point, the Irish had never beaten England on English soil or won the British Home Championship. Under O'Connell's captaincy, Ireland achieved both. The 1914 British Home Championship-winning team was fairly representative of the island of Ireland, without what was often perceived as the Belfast-based bias. It included Bill McConnell and Ted Seymour from Dublin club Bohemians, Billy Lacey from Wexford and Billy Gillespie from Donegal. O'Connell's role in this victory caught the attention of Manchester United, and he was transferred there in 1914 for a substantial fee of £1,000. His appearances at United – the first Irishman to captain the club – were limited by the onset of the First World War. After the war, he played for Dumbarton in Scotland before coming to Ashington in County Durham as player-manager, then moving on to Spain to become part of an early tranche of British and Irish managers to take up roles on the continent. Real Oviedo and Racing Santander improved and won silverware under O'Connell. His career in Spain culminated with taking Seville's Real Betis from the second division to the first and winning its one and only Primera Liga championship in 1935. This remarkable achievement is remembered fondly by *Béticos*, the club's fans.

Alan McLean is a founder member of the Patrick O'Connell Memorial Fund, which was set up to celebrate O'Connell's memory and restore his unmarked grave in Kensal Green, North London. He told me about the significance of O'Connell's legacy in Seville. 'If you go to the green and white half of Seville, even today, and mention Patrick O'Connell – or, as he's known in Sevilla, "Don Patricio", you will hear people react very, very spontaneously to that as to the hero that he was to Real Betis and he's still remembered there to this day,' McLean explains. McLean says that O'Connell's biggest achievements are overlooked because they coincided with pivotal moments in world history when media and national attention was elsewhere. When his playing career was at its peak, the First World War broke out. When he was at FC Barcelona – where he moved after securing the title for Betis – the Spanish Civil War erupted.

As one of the key symbols of Catalan national pride, Franco's fascists set about targeting FC Barcelona. Club president Josep Sunyol i Garriga was killed by Franco's troops in the early days of the war, and the regime later froze FC Barcelona's bank accounts. Franco wanted to make an example of Barça. To save the club from extinction, O'Connell accepted an offer from a Mexico-based businessman for the club to tour Mexico and North America. Proceeds were wired back to a private bank account in Paris. O'Connell returned to Spain after the Civil War ended, followed by just four of his players. He then went on to rebuild FC Barcelona, which became champions in the 1944/45 season. Patrick O'Connell died in 1959, but the Memorial Fund set up in his name has now secured a blue plaque at his Dublin house, a bronze bust at Real Betis, a mural in Belfast, and a 90-minute documentary film.

**The great divide**
Patrick O'Connell had long left Ireland by the time the country descended into civil war in the early 1920s. Sectarian violence was nothing new in Irish football. In May 1912 fights were breaking out between Presbyterians and Catholics in Derry. By September of the same year, tensions spilt over in a game between Belfast Celtic and Linfield. A fist fight between Catholics and Protestants soon escalated

during the half-time break to the point that missiles were thrown, such as nuts and bolts from the shipyards – known as 'Belfast Confetti'[14] – and shots were fired. Both sides carried flags and symbols of their communities. Crowd trouble also marred the international between Ireland and Scotland at Dalymount in 1913, resulting in a member of the crowd being hospitalised and the mob breaking nearly all the windows in the clubhouse. The Dublin-based clubs had already become frustrated with the Belfast-based IFA, especially around the selection of players for international duty. Early protests from the regional Leinster FA, which was second only in size to the Ulster FA, led to brief divisions before the complete break-up of the island. The IFA was run by influential Protestants at the time.

'The [First World] War in some ways is the biggest dividing factor,' Dublin-based football historian and writer Gerard Farrell informs me. 'When the war breaks out, football continues on, but is gradually suspended by 1915. There is no Irish League. Football is regionalised, so there's a Belfast and area league and a Leinster league. It showed the Leinster Football Association that they didn't necessarily need the IFA for the day-to-day running; they could run their leagues and cups and run committees and disciplinary panels and so on. The Irish Cup is also regionalised in the early rounds, so Bohemians played Shelbourne repeatedly in the first round of the competition.' But divisions had been boiling over for years before the Great War broke out on the continent. 'There is violence at football matches that begins to take on a sectarian tone,' Farrell explains. 'There are interesting newspaper reports at the time about games being interrupted by the sound of "revolver music", as it's referred to, there are fights and pitch invasions at representative games between Ulster and Leinster in Dublin. There is a lot of inter-club rivalry [in Belfast] that spills out into violence between the likes of Belfast Celtic and Linfield. That also happens in Dublin as well when some northern teams are coming down although not with the intensity or frequency as happens in Belfast.'

The 1916 Easter Rising in Dublin damaged relations further and by 1921 three Dublin clubs – Bohemians, St James's Gate from the Guinness Brewery, along with Shelbourne – had pulled out of the Irish League.[15] When Belfast club Glenavon played Shelbourne of Dublin in the IFA Cup Final of 1921 in Belfast and the match was tied, the IFA ruled the replay be held in Belfast in contradiction to the rules. Glenavon had concerns about travelling to Leinster. Shelbourne refused, demanding Dublin – which was under curfew at the time – as the venue and thus surrendered the chance to win the cup. Set in a backdrop of an island that was fracturing, the clubs and associations of the south met at Molesworth Hall in Dublin on 1 June 1921 to form the *Cumann Peile na hÉirean* – the Football Association of Ireland (FAI).

The League of Ireland was established on 30 August 1921. Football writer Benjamin Roberts has written extensively about Northern Irish football. In his book *Gunshots & Goalposts*, he highlights that widespread dissatisfaction with the IFA meant that, by 1922, the organisation had lost around a quarter of its members in just one year, falling from 387 to 282.[16]

Association football across the island of Ireland was now split into the Belfast-based IFA and the Dublin-based FAI. However, the FAI was not yet internationally recognised and some clubs even flirted with rejoining the IFA to arrange overseas friendlies. Reunification talks with the IFA broke down so, as a new state, the organisation applied as the Football Association of the Irish Free State (FAIFS), responsible for football across the 26 counties of what is now the Republic of Ireland. The IFA found itself governing in just the six counties which remained under British control in the north.

## The Irish Free State's international debut

FIFA recognised the Football Association of the Irish Free State in 1923. The new country could now put a team together in time for the 1924 Olympic Games in Paris. The squad included seven players from the St James's Gate club, six Bohemians, five from Athlone Town, two from Shelbourne and one player from the short-lived Brooklyn FC. The Irish Free State committed £100 to the Olympic Football Fund, the Leinster Association gave £50, and other individual clubs and members raised just over £100. On arrival in Paris, the Irish Free State team placed a wreath at the tomb of the unknown soldier at the Arc de Triomphe, presenting the Irish tricolour on French soil for the very first time.

The team entered the tournament at the second round, with 28 May 1924 being the birthdate of international football for what is now the Republic of Ireland team. The opponent that day was Bulgaria at the Stade de Colombes and nearly 1,700 Parisians came to watch. The Irish team dominated play and missed a hatful of chances or were denied by Bulgarian keeper Ivanov – he even blocked one shot with his head! In the 75th minute, St James's Gate striker Paddy Duncan ran on to a pass from Bohemians' Johnny Murray to fire home what is now the Republic of Ireland's first-ever international goal. In the next round – the quarter-finals – at the Stade de Paris, the Irishmen took the Netherlands to extra time, drawing 1-1 after 90 minutes. The Dutch were expected to win easily but 'displayed a chronic incapacity to shoot'.[17] Sparta Rotterdam's Ocker Formenoij had given the Dutch an early lead, only for Athlone man Frank Ghent to equalise just after the half-hour mark. The Dutch were well on top over the second half and extra time, with Formenoij scoring just before the change of ends. The Irish couldn't claw their way back into the game.

Regardless of the result, an independent Ireland team was on the world stage, and the Irish team followed up the Olympics with friendlies against Estonia in Paris, which the Irish won 3-1, and hosted a USA team that featured some Irishmen at Bohemians' Dalymount ground. It was a fitting fixture for the Free State's first home match, and one which the Irish won 3-1, with a hat-trick for Ned Brooks on his home ground. Brooks had also turned out for the IFA while a Shelbourne player in 1920.

The Olympic experience was an eye-opener for footballers in the Irish Free State, having witnessed the great Uruguayan side that took the gold medal, a feat Uruguay would repeat in 1928 en route to winning the inaugural World Cup in 1930 on home soil. While many Irish players made solid careers in England and Scotland, some did go further afield. Former Bohemians players in New York City formed the New York Bohemians in the 1920s, even donning the famous red and black.

## McAlery's legacy

The 2016 European Championships was the first time that the two Irish football associations both sent teams to an international tournament. Both benefitted from the 24-team set-up, and made it through to the second round. This journey all started back in the 1870s thanks to the efforts of Windsor FC's secretary, James Calder, J.A. Allen of the

Caledonian club and, of course, John McAlery. McAlery appears to be particularly protective of his role as pioneer of the Association rules game in Ireland. When an article suggested Calder had introduced the sport, McAlery wrote a letter to the editor stating that 'alone, I did it'.[18] McAlery lived well into his seventies and died on 3 December 1925. In 2013, the Cliftonville Football Club that he founded and the Ulster History Circle honoured him with the unveiling of a blue plaque at the club's Solitude stadium. The plaque reads simply: *John McCredy McAlery 1849–1925 Introduced Association Football to Ireland 1879 Founded Cliftonville FC.* There's only so much you can fit on a blue plaque, but it serves as a small and fitting acknowledgement to McAlery's huge legacy.

1   https://www.historyireland.com/20th-century-contemporary-history/alone-he-did-it-john-mcalery-and-the-origins-of-association-football/
2   Roberts, Benjamin, *Gunshots & Goalposts: The Story of Northern Irish Football* (Eastbourne: Avenue Books, 2017, p32)
3   https://www.balls.ie/football/type-footballer-michael-collins-133688
4   Roberts, Benjamin, *Gunshots & Goalposts* (Eastbourne: Avenue Books, 2017, p31)
5   *Northern Whig*, 23 October 1878 (p1)
6   *Freeman's Journal*, 18 October 1878 (p7)
7   *Northern Whig*, 25 October 1878 (p8)
8   *Belfast News Letter*, 20 September 1879 (p1)
9   *Northern Whig*, 27 September 1879 (p8)
10  https://cliftonvillefc.net/club-history-chapter-1/
11  Roberts, Benjamin, *Gunshots & Goalposts* (Eastbourne: Avenue Books, 2017, p27)
12  *The Sportsman*, 22 February 1882 (p1)
13  *Belfast News Letter*, 8 September 1890 (p3)
14  Roberts, Benjamin, *Gunshots & Goalposts* (Eastbourne: Avenue Books, 2017, p8)
15  http://www.fai.ie/domestic/news/fai-history-the-early-years
16  Roberts, Benjamin, *Gunshots & Goalposts* (Eastbourne: Avenue Books, 2017, p47)
17  *Freeman's Journal*, 5 June 1924 (p6)
18  https://www.historyireland.com/20th-century-contemporary-history/alone-he-did-it-john-mcalery-and-the-origins-of-association-football/

# 5.

# France

IN 1872, the artist Claude Monet left Paris to visit his hometown of Le Havre, Normandy, in north-west France. Here, he set about capturing the harbour in a series of six canvases to depict the setting at different times of the day. Arguably, his most famous piece from this series is *Impression, Soleil Levant* (Impression, Sunrise). This image depicts a busy working harbour at dawn, with rowboats in the foreground and further vessels gradually disappearing into the blue-grey mist in the distance. A low orange orb of the sun casts a fiery hue across the sky and on the water. Monet's brushstrokes make the cold Atlantic Ocean appear to move. As its title suggests, it was an early work of the impressionist movement, which included Pierre-Auguste Renoir, Paul Cézanne, Édouard Manet and a host of other avant-garde men and women from Paris and beyond. But it wasn't the only artistic impression left on Le Havre in 1872. This is also the year that French football was born.

Nestled on the Normandy coast, the strategically important port of Le Havre sits on the mouth of the River Seine. Given its proximity to England and a few hours' reach of the ports of Southampton and Portsmouth, it's no surprise that it became an important base for the Nazis during the occupation of France in the Second World War. While the Allies had made inroads into France in the summer of 1944 following the D-Day landings south of the Seine, Le Havre itself was still in German hands in September. Rejecting the Allied offer of surrender, the Nazis vowed to fight on. The Allied response was to send hundreds of bombers to level the city centre over a week-long barrage and force the Germans into submission. The September bombings were not the first aerial bombardment Le Havre had received – there had been raids as early as 1941 – but over the course of the war more than 5,000 people lost their lives and the city was left as a smouldering ruin.

Also lost along with the lives and property during the bombing campaign was much of Le Stade Municipal du Havre, then home of Havre Athletic Club, France's first football team. After the war, the port of Le Havre was rebuilt by Auguste Perret in a post-war modernist style and celebrated its 500th birthday in 2017. The UK newspaper *The Independent* then reported Le Havre had gone 'from laughing stock to hipster heaven'.[1] Perret's Le Havre is now a UNESCO World Heritage site. Monet would not recognise his hometown now, but it would be very interesting to know what he made of it.

When Monet painted *Impression, Soleil Levent*, France was smarting from defeat in the Franco-Prussian War at the advent of the 1870s, but in the coming four decades, French sportsmen and writers would go on to take a leading role in administrating football, overseeing the creation of the modern Olympics and the establishment of FIFA. It was a French stockbroker that would ultimately go on to create the World Cup. But France's long footballing journey to two

World Cups and two European Championship triumphs starts in Le Havre.

## How football came to France

The Olympique de Marseille team that lost the 1991 European Cup Final to Red Star Belgrade featured English winger, Chris Waddle. Waddle and his compatriots at Monaco, Glenn Hoddle and Mark Hateley, had been drawn abroad in part because English clubs were banned from European competition after the Heysel tragedy in 1985. The ban would last until the season following the Italia 90 World Cup. This contingent was the latest English involvement in French football that started by bringing both the round- and the oval-ball games to France in the 1870s. As with many countries around the world, a kicking game existed in France centuries before the Association or Rugby codes. In the Middle Ages, a game called *choule* or *soule* involved a leather sphere stuffed with hay that was contested violently, often resulting in injuries. The game appears to have been particularly popular in Brittany and Normandy.

When Havre Football Club, as it was first known, was established by English Protestants living in the port city in 1872, only nine years had passed since the creation of the Football Association. So, it appears the club played a 'combination' of the Association and Rugby rules. The club later broke into two sections – one for soccer and one for rugby – with some players turning out for both codes. And it wasn't just the Brits; the locals joined in too. The English living in Le Havre also liked to play cricket, and it's this sport that inadvertently leads us to possibly the first written record we have of football in Le Havre, from the *Hampshire Advertiser* in the south of England on 22 February 1873. It records a match played at the Antelope Cricket Ground in

Southampton the week before between the English residents of Le Havre and the Portswood Park Football Club. The newspaper notes that it cannot recall any time previously where an overseas-based team had crossed the Channel to play an English one.[2] The secretary of the Havre Football Club was a Reverend George Washington, a British minister in Le Havre, who received Portswood Park Cricket Club's invitation to play a cricket match in Southampton. In his response, Washington asked to play a football match. Portswood Park duly accepted, and history was made.

The report focuses mainly on the after-match dinner arrangements and various toasts rather than the game itself. The match report, however short, demonstrates the very early scoring system that was being deployed at the time. Portswood Park scored one goal, 11 touch downs and 11 rouges to Havre's single rouge. One-sided it may have been – with Rev. Washington reportedly *battu, mais content* (soundly beaten, but happy) – but it was a truly historic occasion. Although Havre Football Club was made up of British expatriates, it was probably the first time a football team had to come from overseas to play an English team in England at this new fledgling sport. Indeed, Southampton's role in the early spread of the Association game would be particularly influential, not just for France, but also for Brazil and Bilbao, as we will discover elsewhere in this book.

This Havre Football Club would later become Havre Athletic Club (HAC) to reflect its multi-sport nature as tennis and hockey were later added, but at the outset it does appear to have been a fairly small society. As Protestants, there was no chance of these players turning out on a Sunday, the only rest day at the time, so players turned out in the middle of the day, when their businesses closed for lunch. Games were therefore very short. The club members naturally had to play amongst themselves at the outset as there was no one else to play against. By all accounts, Rev. Washington appears to have been one of the club's better players before the Langstaff family took the club forward.

By 1891, Havre Athletic Club was ready to ditch its white blouses for a proper uniform. As a nod to the club's English roots and the ultimate compromise between sporting and academic rivals, HAC adopted the colours of the English university at which the players had studied, namely the light blue of Cambridge and the dark blue of Oxford. HAC still dons these colours to this day, giving it the nickname 'Les Ciel et Marine' (The Sky and Navy Blues). The club is also known as 'Le Club Doyen' (The Dean Club), in recognition of its position as the oldest club in France. We shall see this term surface again during the course of this book. But by the 1890s, the game was well and truly up and running in other parts of France, most significantly, in the capital.

## Parisian fields

Two hundred kilometres south-east of Le Havre, the British community was busy doing in Paris what it was doing in countless other cities across the world – creating sporting social clubs, such as the Paris Football Club, formed in 1879 but dissolved seven years later. Another such club, founded on 1 March 1890 in a back room of Le Copernic bar on Avenue Kléber, was the Standard Athletic Club. This multi-sport club still exists, and its crest features the distinctive British royal standard: three lions in two quarters, representing England, a lion rampant representing Scotland and a harp for Ireland. For 40 years until 1930, the club was active in France's major official football competitions. Elsewhere in the capital, the International Athletic Club was a short-lived society for rugby and Association rules football that existed in Paris between 1888 and 1894. In 1892, International AC was hammered 10-1 by fellow Parisians, White Rovers, at Bécon in the north-west of Paris. A full 20 years after the foundation of Havre Athletic Club, these initial inter-club Association rules matches were taking place in the capital, a movement that would prove a catalyst to spreading the game across France.

White Rovers was another short-lived club (1891–1899) formed by British émigrés living in Paris at a café on the Rue Paquier. Englishman William Sleator was the club's treasurer, and the club's first match was against a YMCA XI.[3] The first English club to visit Paris was Marylebone FC in April 1893, who beat a mixed Paris XI 3-0, before beating White Rovers 4-1 and trouncing Standard Athletic Club 7-0. Marylebone FC returned the following April. The standard had improved markedly, with Standard AC reducing the size of defeat to 3-0 and White Rovers claiming a 0-0 draw. Standard AC would bounce back to win the first French Football Championship, held in April and May 1894 under the auspices of the French sports' governing body, the *Union des Sociétés Françaises de Sports Athlétiques* (USFSA). The USFSA was formed in 1887 by a merger of two independent sports bodies, one headed by Georges de Saint-Clair, secretary of the Racing Club de France, and the other by Pierre de Coubertin, who went on to establish the modern Olympiad.

The USFSA had originally favoured the Rugby football code due to its more elite and amateur status across the Channel in England, but realised it needed to get involved in the Association code before it grew out of its control.[4] The Paris-based American, James Gordon Bennett Jr, publisher of the *New York Herald*, donated the trophy for the Championship of the USFSA. The knockout tournament featured six Parisian clubs; Standard AC gained a walkover against International AC in the first round, while White Rovers thrashed Cercle Athlétique de Neuilly 13-0. Club Français and Cercle Pédestre d'Asnières gained byes to the semi-finals. White Rovers and Standard AC won their semi-finals and met in the final at the Vélodrome de Courbevoie in Paris, where Standard AC triumphed 2-0 in a replay after an initial 2-2 draw. Most of the names on both team sheets were British.[5]

In the 1895/96 season, the championship switched to a league format, with Club Français triumphant. On Christmas Day 1896, Club Français welcomed the English Ramblers, a travelling team of public school and university footballers, at the Champs de Mars, potentially the first time that a French team made up of predominantly Frenchmen took on a visiting team from abroad. The English Ramblers were 5-0 up by half-time, adding another three goals in the second half without reply.[6] The gulf between the early Parisian scene and even the amateur English sides was wide in France's first footballing decade. White Rovers finished runners-up the first four editions of the French Football Championship and would never triumph before ceasing activities in 1899. In the same year, Le Havre became the first club from outside Paris to win the tournament, retaining it a year later.

By the late 1890s, cup competitions began to emerge. Club Français won the first five editions of the *Coupe Manier*, a national competition reserved for clubs with three foreign players or less, due to the large number of British players at the leading clubs. In response, an industrialist named Dewar donated an eponymous trophy – *Le Coupe Dewar* – open to any club, which ran up until the First World War. Standard AC won four of the six editions held between 1899 and

1904. Racing Club, a multi-sports outfit whose club colours were the sky blue of the University of Cambridge, launched its football branch in 1896. In 1900, when de Coubertin brought the second edition of the Olympic Games to Paris, Racing Club's stadium, Le Stade Croix-Catelan, hosted some athletics while the Vélodrome de Vincennes held the football tournament. It was very much a prototype tournament with just three teams taking part: a French side selected by the USFSA, a Belgian team from the University of Brussels, and Great Britain represented by East London amateur side, Upton Park. Only two matches were played, with Upton Park beating the French side 4-0 before France took apart the Belgian students 6-2. Upton Park was awarded the gold medal for Great Britain.

The take-up of football in France remained slow as it was not generally permitted or encouraged in French schools and colleges, hindering its development. A French national team was established in earnest four years later for a match against Belgium at the Stade du Vivier d'Oie near Brussels. The French tricolour kit from that match was an inverted style from its famous current design. The debut shirt was white with the USFSA's two intertwined rings, blue shorts and red socks. Just 12 minutes into the game, at just after 5pm on 1 May 1904, Louis 'Didi' Mesnier scored the very first goal in *Les Bleus'* illustrious history. The game finished 3-3. The French team selector that day was a journalist named Robert Guérin and he was about to change football forever.

## The foundation of FIFA

Aged just 28, Guérin was a journalist with *Le Matin* newspaper and was secretary of the USFSA's football section. Together with Carl Anton Wilhelm Hirschmann from the Dutch FA in the Netherlands, Guérin was keen to galvanise international competition. They gathered together seven international FAs in Paris on 21 May 1904 to create the *Fédération Internationale de Football Association* (FIFA). There had been calls for several years from early European footballing pioneer countries for an international body to ensure consistency of the rules and promote friendlies between countries. For example, in May 1902 – 30 years after the very first official match between the teams of the English and Scottish FAs – the Dutch association wrote to other countries pushing for an overseeing organisation. Present at FIFA's founding at 229 Rue Saint-Honoré, the USFSA's headquarters in Paris's exclusive *Premier Arrondissement*, were the heads of the football associations of France, Netherlands, Belgium, Denmark, Spain, Sweden and Switzerland. Guérin would be the new organisation's first president.

During Guérin's two-year tenure, eight more associations joined, including the Football Association in England.[7] Article 9 of the 1904 statute stated that the body had the right to organise an international championship and, a quarter of a century after FIFA's creation, the initial World Cup was a French-driven affair. In the meantime, though, it would be FIFA's responsibility to organise the de facto football world championship of the time – the football tournament at the Olympic Games.[8] FIFA joined the IFAB as a full member in 1913 and was given the same voting power as the original four founding associations put together.

### The French game grows

A year after France's international debut, the country hosted the Swiss in front of 500 spectators at the Stade Vélodrome du Parc des Princes, on the site of the current eponymous stadium, which was redeveloped in 1972. The

USFSA provided shirts, but not shorts, so Club Français forward Georges Garnier wore his black shorts while Louis Mesnier wore the white of his club, FC Paris.[9] France notched its first international victory, coming away with a 2-1 win after a fairly bruising encounter. But the country was a series of emerging – and sometimes competing – organisations. Charles Simon was the head of one of those organisations – the *Fédération Gymnastique et Sportive des Patronage de France* (French Gymnastic and Sports Federation – FGSPF). In 1907, Simon founded the *Comité Français Interfédéral* (French Interfederal Committee – CFI) to bring them all together. Out of this organisation came the first truly national championship, where the four champions of the different member organisations would play for the *Trophée de France*. The first final in 1907 was held in Bordeaux, with local side FC Simiotin losing to Parisian FGSPF side l'Etoile des Deux Lacs. The USFSA would not join the CFI until 1913, so the first editions did not feature its members.

Corinthian FC made just one tour to France during this nascent period for football in France. The Easter tour of 1908 saw the English amateurs play three matches in just four days. In the first game at Colombes, the Corinthians beat the Comité de Paris 5-1 on 17 April before thrashing their compatriots at the Standard Athletic Club 9-0 the following day. A 7-2 victory over the Outcasts XI two days later meant that Corinthians left Paris with a 21-3 goal aggregate. French teams fared even worse at the London Olympics of 1908. France entered two teams in the tournament at White City, West London. France B lost 9-0 to Denmark while France's first team got a walkover after scheduled opponents Bohemia withdrew. That France 'A' team then went on to lose by an incredible 17-1 margin to Denmark, with Sophus Nielsen scoring a hat-trick within six minutes on his way to a record ten individual goals in that match. France declined to play their bronze medal match after such a dramatic defeat and did not send a team to the Stockholm Olympics of 1912.

To help grow the domestic game, English clubs were invited to take part in the Dubonnet Cup, which was held annually at the Parc des Princes between 1910 and 1912. The huge bronze trophy was modelled on ancient Greek pottery and weighed a staggering 51kg. It was donated by a prominent French sportsman and guarded by gendarmes with fixed bayonets. In the first edition, Swindon Town beat Barnsley 2-1 in front of 5,000 spectators braving driving rain. The following year, Clapton Orient (now Leyton Orient) beat fellow Londoners Millwall 3-0. In the final edition, Fulham trounced Queens Park Rangers 4-1, again in torrid conditions for May. Rangers had played Blackburn Rovers on the Saturday afternoon and travelled from London overnight to play the Dubonnet Cup in Paris on the Sunday. Meanwhile, in the domestic game, USFSA member Olympique Lille won the final *Trophée de France* in 1914 before the outbreak of war put a halt to football until 1917, when the *Coupe de France* was born. The driving force behind the *Coupe de France* was former l'Etoile des Deux Lacs player and administrator, Henri Delaunay. When he was aged just 19, he had been impressed by the 1902 FA Cup Final at Crystal Palace between Sheffield United and Southampton, which had attracted 80,000 spectators. He would have to wait a further 14 years before he would present his ideas to the governing body of the time, the CFI.[10]

Despite the war still being in full force and key CFI leaders, including Jules Rimet, still fighting in the trenches, the first edition of the knockout *Coupe de France* was launched in 1917 with 48 entrant clubs. The tournament was initially named the *Coupe Charles Simon*, after the sportsman and administrator, who was killed in action in June 1915. Parisian club Olympique de Pantin – who would later merge with Red Star in 1926 – beat FC Lyon 3-0 in the first final on 5 May 1918 in front of 2,000 spectators at the Stade de la Légion Saint-Michel in the capital. The tournament may have helped unite the formerly disparate country, as pressure from supporters and clubs to create a single governing body led to CFI's transformation into the *Fédération Français de Football Association* (FFF) on 7 April 1919. Of 24 bodies, only one – the USFSA – voted against the transformation. Jules Rimet was duly declared president and Henri Delaunay became secretary general. 'Our great family is finally formed,' Delaunay wrote. 'We will understand each other very well because we will all speak the same language.'[11]

## Jules Rimet: the 'Father of the World Cup'

While England describes itself as the home of Association football, if there were to be a home for the FIFA World Cup Trophy then it would be Theuley-les-Lavoncourt in the Franche-Comté region of eastern France. It is here that a small monument recognises local man Jules Rimet, born the son of a grocer on 14 October 1873, one year after the Englishmen of Le Havre had formed France's first football club. Rimet himself went on to become a stockbroker in Paris and never excelled at sport. He was, however, a keen spectator and organiser, founding the Red Star club in 1897 at the age of 24. Red Star, based in the northern Parisian suburb of Saint-Ouen, was a multi-sports club, including football, and it was Monsieur Rimet's ambition that it be open to people of all backgrounds. This is significant because the French upper and middle classes at the time looked down on the Association game as a thug's game.

Rimet was a key figure in the creation of France's first nationwide league competition, the Football Association League in 1910, and became the organisation's first president. The First World War put a halt to football in France, during which as an officer Rimet won the *Croix de Guerre* medal. Rimet helped found the FFF and was immediately elected its first president. The FFF's affiliation with FIFA gave him a platform to realise his bigger ambition – a global tournament. As a proven organiser, Rimet was placed in provisional charge of FIFA during the 1920 Olympic Games in Antwerp, Belgium, where he first touted his vision of a 'World Championship'. In March of the following year, he succeeded the Lancastrian Daniel Burley Woolfall, who had died in October 1918, as full-time president of FIFA.

The Olympic football tournament, which had been in place since 1900, was the only global tournament for the sport and was devoutly amateur. This is why the Upton Park Football Club from East London represented Great Britain in the inaugural 1900 tournament in Paris as top-flight football had already been professional – in England, at least – for 15 years. By the mid-1920s, tensions had been building between the International Olympic Committee (IOC) and FIFA over the running of the tournament. Fellow Frenchman Pierre de Coubertin, founder of the modern Olympics, opposed access to professionals to the games and, following the war, the Football Association had also withdrawn from FIFA, as it did not want to associate with Britain's recent enemies, such as Germany. Rimet believed FIFA was able to run its own international competition. Rimet was supported by Henri Delaunay, now FIFA's secretary, whose own legacy was to suggest a European nations championship. The UEFA European Championship trophy is named after Delaunay. The two made a formidable team.

At FIFA's 1928 Congress in Amsterdam, the organisation's members voted in favour of establishing a World Cup tournament to be held every four years. By virtue of its back-to-back gold medals at the 1924 and 1928 Olympic football tournament, Uruguay was selected to host the first tournament in 1930 over Italy, the Netherlands, Spain and Sweden. Uruguay also offered to pay passage for participants. The Home Nations declined to enter, as did many European sides, despite Uruguay's offer. Rimet had to work hard to convince France, Belgium, Yugoslavia and Romania to make the long sea journey to the River Plate. The art deco trophy designed by Frenchman Abel Lafleur to hand to the tournament winners stood, as BBC commentator Kenneth Wolstenholme described famously in 1966, 'only 12 inches high. It is solid gold.' Rimet himself carried the trophy in his own luggage onboard the SS *Conte Verde* to Montevideo, where he would hand the trophy to the eventual champions, hosts Uruguay, in the just-completed Centenario stadium, constructed especially for this tournament. The winged statuette was originally called 'Victory' but renamed the Jules Rimet Trophy in 1946 in honour of the FIFA president, who went on to serve the organisation until 1954. The trophy was given to Brazil in perpetuity after its third World Cup win in 1970 and the new – and current – FIFA World Cup Trophy was presented to winners from 1974. The original Jules Rimet Trophy was held at the Brazilian Football Confederation's headquarters behind bulletproof glass but was stolen in 1983 and never recovered.

## The French international journey

The Paris Olympic football tournament of 1924 saw the start of Uruguay's international dominance outside of

South America. The competition was held across the French capital, including at the newly built Stade de Colombes (later renamed Le Stade Yves-du-Manoir after a French rugby star). France entered in the second round, exploding on to the scene with a 7-0 thrashing of Latvia at Stade de Paris, with a hat-trick from Marseille's Édouard Crut. However, French expectations were crushed in the quarter-finals at the Stade de Colombes when the hosts were thrashed 5-1 by eventual winners Uruguay. The Stade de Colombes itself would go on to host three matches – including the final – at World Cup 1938. It was home to Racing Club de France, host to several *Coupe de France* finals, and was often the home ground of the French national football and rugby sides until the redevelopment of the Parc des Princes in the early 1970s. At the time of writing it is scheduled to host field hockey matches at the Paris 2024 Olympics, one century after its first games. Four years later at the 1928 Olympic Games in Amsterdam, France raced into a 2-0 lead within 17 minutes against a strong Italian side but eventually succumbed 4-3. Italy went on to win the bronze medal.

The 16-man squad for the 1930 World Cup included five Racing Club de France players, four from FC Sochaux, two apiece from Red Star Paris and Amiens AC, one from Olympique Antibes and one from Excelsior AC Roubaix. They were accompanied by coach Raoul Caudron, a physio and a French referee on the SS *Conte Verde* from Villefranche-sur-Mer. Three players from the Yugoslavian team were also based at French clubs. The French were drawn in Group 1 alongside Argentina, Chile and Mexico. Despite the long journey, France dispatched Mexico 4-1 in the first match at the Estadio Pocitos, home of Peñarol. FC Sochaux's Lucien Laurent made history with a 19th-minute volley to score

France's first goal at a World Cup tournament; indeed, the first-*ever* goal scored in a World Cup. Two days later, France lost 1-0 to eventual finalists, Argentina. Luis Monti popped up with a late winner. Another second-half goal cost France against Chile in the last group game, meaning the French finished third in the group and were therefore eliminated. Within two years, the French game would turn professional. France's long wait for an international trophy would finally end in 1984 with a Michel Platini-inspired team winning the European Championship on home ground. *Les Bleus* would then win the World Cup – again at home – in 1998. Lucien Laurent was a guest of honour that day and lived until 2005, when he died aged 97. France won the Euros again in 2000 and its second World Cup in 2018.

## The pioneer Le Havre Athletic Club today

Le Havre Athletic Club now plays in the French second division, Ligue 2, at the Stade Océane, which was completed in 2012 and was a host venue for the FIFA Women's World Cup in France in 2019. Rather like Southampton in England, HAC has something of a reputation for the quality of its youth development. Graduates include Paul Pogba, Riyad Mahrez, Dimitri Payet, Benjamin Mendy, Lassana Diarra, Steve Mandanda and Ibrahim Ba. Since its halcyon period of the late 19th and early 20th century, Les Ciel et Marine has added just one piece of major silverware – the 1959 *Coupe de France* at the Stade de Colombes, defeating FC Sochaux 3-0 in front of General Charles de Gaulle. Yet the club has not forgotten its English roots.

The club anthem is even set to the tune of 'God Save the Queen' and celebrates the origins of the club as the first in France, the sons of Oxford and Cambridge and its ciel et marine colours.

France was the first country to explore the Association game in continental Europe, albeit limited to Normandy before the Paris clubs emerged in the late 1880s. Le Havre probably provided the first match between a continental side and an English side in their Southampton friendly of 1873 ... Not only that, but Frenchmen were also the driving force behind the organisation of international football: De Coubertin with Olympic soccer, Guérin with FIFA, Rimet and Delaunay with the World Cup and European Championships. French sports magazine *L'Equipe* would later donate the first European Cup trophy. French silverware may have been late in coming, but the tournaments would not exist at all without French men of vision.

1  https://www.independent.co.uk/travel/europe/le-havre-architecture-auguste-perret-what-to-see-niemeyer-le-volcan-muma-gallery-a8040531.html

2  *Hampshire Advertiser*, 22 February 1873 (p3)

3  http://www.scottishsporthistory.com/sports-history-news-and-blog/the-father-of-french-football-a-tailor-from-worcester

4  https://www.fff.fr/articles/la-fff/histoire-du-football-francais/details-articles/230-544116-1887-les-premiers-pas-de-lunion

5  http://www.rsssf.com/tablesf/fran-prewwi.html#1894

6  *The Scotsman*, 26 December 1896 (p7)

7  https://www.fifa.com/about-fifa/who-we-are/the-president/robert-guerin/

8  https://www.fifa.com/mensolympic/archive/london1908/

9  https://www.fff.fr/articles/la-fff/histoire-du-football-francais/details-articles/232-544119-1905-debuts-victorieux-a-paris

10 https://www.fff.fr/articles/la-fff/histoire-du-football-francais/details-articles/210-544078-1918-au-son-du-canon

11 https://www.fff.fr/articles/la-fff/histoire-du-football-francais/details-articles/211-544081-1919-la-federation-est-nee-

# 6.

# Switzerland

ON MY first visit to Zürich, I thought I had dropped into some sort of a utopia. It was a balmy summer evening, people were milling about the banks of the city's eponymous lake or partaking in sports on the water, while in the distance the horizon was flanked by the snow-capped Alps. It is here that world football's governing body, the *Fédération Internationale de Football Association* (FIFA), has its headquarters. Europe's top football organisation, the Union of European Football Associations (UEFA), is also based in neutral Switzerland, at Nyon. The Swiss national football team's fortunes have fluctuated over the years. Still, it has always failed to puncture the latter stages of tournaments in recent decades. For any modern follower of the game, it may come as a surprise that this small landlocked country played a key role in the development of the sport in the latter decades of the 19th century and early parts of the 20th, most notably among its neighbouring countries, but also in South America.

The Lausanne Football and Cricket Club was founded in 1860 by English students based in the area and was probably the first 'football' club to be founded on mainland Europe. Given the formation of the club predates the creation of the

Association rule book by three years, we can only speculate as to what form of football the Lausanne boys practised. One British newspaper report from 1879 records a football match under Rugby rules between Geneva and Lausanne, describing both institutions as long-established clubs.[1] The club lasted long enough to become a founder member of the Swiss Football Association – the *Schweizerischer Fussballverband* (SFV) in German and *Association Suisse de Football* (ASF) in French – in 1895 and competed in the first two championships. Another founder member of the SFV was Switzerland's oldest surviving football club, FC St. Gallen. Founded on 19 April 1879 at the city's Hörnli restaurant, the club practised every day between 1pm and 2pm, and in the evening until dusk. The club did not always apply the Association rules in their entirety. For example, on occasions, the size of the goals was halved. St. Gallen entertained foreign opposition early on and gradually absorbed smaller clubs from across the city as they cropped up.

As Swiss football gathered momentum, an 11-1 win for Ouchy-based Villa Longchamp over Yoccard of Lausanne in October 1889 attracted a number of spectators, and was even reported in England.[2] Joining Lausanne Football and Cricket Club and FC St. Gallen at the foundation of the SFV were nine other clubs: the aforementioned La Villa Longchamp Ouchy FC, Neuchâtel Rovers FC, Yverdon FC, Exelsior Zürich FC, FC Basel, Anglo-American Club Zürich, Châtelaine Genève and Château de Lancy of Geneva, and Grasshopper Club Zürich, founded by English student Tom E. Griffith in 1886. Grasshopper Club Zürich is Switzerland's most successful club. The origin story of its naming is unclear, but it appears that the founders were inspired by the insect's speed and agility. Its light blue and white halved shirts reflect the heraldry of its home canton but also the shirt of Blackburn Rovers. Grasshoppers' balls, shirts and caps were sent directly from England.

Despite the religious conservatism of the country, and even the death of a boy in 1895 from a head injury in the Thergal canton, Switzerland was going football crazy.[3] Even traditional sports such as gymnastics and shooting were being challenged, although some clubs – such as Grasshoppers – opened divisions for other sports. A championship – Serie A – was up and running by 1897 and by 1900 the SFV had admitted some other now-familiar names from the Swiss game, including Young Boys of Bern and FC Servette. Grasshoppers would dominate this early period, winning the inaugural title and then claiming back-to-back titles in 1900 and 1901. By 1904 the SFV had amassed 26 member clubs. Due to its position at the heart of Europe, Swiss teams were regularly hosting German and Italian teams – and winning. In the same year, the ASF-SFV became a founding member of FIFA. The association's official representative was the Basel-based businessman Victor E. Schneider. Schneider was elected FIFA vice-president and also selected the first Swiss international side to play against France the following spring.

As an organisation, FIFA moved around until 1932, after its first World Cup. FIFA chose neutral Switzerland for geographical and political reasons: Zürich was at the heart of Europe, easily accessible by train from all directions – indeed, its first office was on the *Bahnhofstrasse*. The Swiss would play a key role in football's development wherever they went. It was the son of a Swiss-Italian, Edoardo Bosio, who founded Italy's first football club in Turin. The Swiss Hans Max Gamper-Haessig went on to co-found FC Barcelona and Catalanise his name to Joan Gamper. Gamper was born in Winterthur in 1877. He had already excelled in other sports, including swimming, cycling, athletics and tennis, and played rugby as well as Association football. Gamper played in Switzerland for FC Zürich, FC Basel and his hometown team FC Winterthur.

And the Swiss didn't stop there. Swiss men formed their own breakaway club to escape the limitations of Milan Cricket and Football Club (now AC Milan) with the creation of Football Club Internazionale Milano, the only club never to have been relegated from Italy's Serie A.

Elsewhere in Italy, one of Juventus's early presidents was the Swiss Alfred Dick. Dick led a group of dissidents from Juventus in 1906 to form Torino Football Club. One suggestion is that Torino gets its famous *granata* maroon colour from Dick's favourite club, Servette FC from the Swiss capital. Further south, Swiss grain merchant Gustav Kuhn founded FC Bari.

Swiss-based advocates would form clubs in Bulgaria, Slovakia, Russia and Hungary, and their reach would also extend far further afield. Swiss merchants founded Medellin's Sporting FC in Colombia, while on returning to Rio de Janeiro following his education in Lausanne, Anglo-Swiss Oscar Cox founded Fluminense in 1902.

## Football becomes engrained in Swiss culture

By the turn of the 20th century, the Association game was being taught and played in schools across Switzerland. The first national team match took place on 12 February 1905 in Paris, resulting in a 1-0 defeat for the Swiss. Servette FC travelled to Turin in Italy for what was probably the first international club tournament in continental Europe – the *Torneo Internazionale Stampa Sportiva* – featuring German side Freiburger FC, US Parisienne of France and the recently formed Torino from the host city. Servette beat

Freiburger 5-3 in the semi-final before dispatching Torino 3-1 in the final. It must have been a special moment for Alfred Dick to see his two favourite teams contest the final. English amateur side Corinthian FC did not visit Switzerland until relatively late. Even then, Corinthians only played two matches in April 1909, hammering both Geneva and Lausanne 6-0. The following month, a team of English amateurs thrashed a Basel XI by nine goals to nil. Swiss football was trailing far behind the mother country; in 1910, the Swiss played an England Amateur XI and lost 6-1, then 4-1 the following year. The two countries would not contest a full international until 1933. During this first decade of the 20th century, Young Boys of Bern became the first Swiss team to win three consecutive titles. Swiss clubs continued to tour neighbouring Italy and Germany to take part in competitions, such as Servette's return to Turin for the Sir Thomas Lipton Challenge Cup in Turin in 1909, and compatriots FC Zürich to the same tournament two years later. Swiss players also proliferated the early Italian club scene.

Football continued in Switzerland during the First World War and was indeed critical to the recuperation of prisoners of war and casualties resident in the neutral territory during the conflict. The war had a massive impact on the Swiss tourism industry as guests from regular source markets, such as Britain and Germany, no longer headed to the country. The war left hundreds of hotels empty. As wounded soldiers arrived in Switzerland with the aid of the Red Cross, so the British, German and French governments paid for their upkeep. The hotels offered up their inventory, and they became comfortable, safe places of recuperation for troops.[4] Sports were key to the recovery of injured soldiers, and football competitions sprang up between hotels. In 1916, a team of British prisoners beat FC Bern 9-3. Flat fields in the Alpine country were gold dust, and by the end of the war, many of Switzerland's football pitches had been turned into fields to grow crops. After the war, Switzerland did not send an Olympic team to Antwerp for the 1920 Olympics, but did defeat its war-hit international neighbours, Italy and Germany, in friendlies. At home, the Swiss domestic scene was flourishing, with 64 clubs in the west of the country, 48 in the centre and 74 in the east. 'The growth of the game in Switzerland has been steady, and it was one of the first Continental countries to take kindly to it,' reported the *Nottingham Journal* in December 1921.[5] Football was now widely popular among the Swiss public.

By 1924, the Swiss had a strong squad to send to Paris for the Olympic Games. Switzerland's prospects were helped by the absence of both the Great Britain and Denmark teams over disputes with FIFA over what made a player a 'professional'. The 22-man squad was drawn from nine clubs from across Switzerland, and Real Madrid's Swiss player Adolphe Mengotti was also selected. The team was under the guidance of Servette FC's English manager, Teddy Duckworth. The former Blackpool player drew seven of the Swiss national squad from his Servette team. The Swiss got off to a flyer, smashing Lithuania 9-0 at Vincennes in the first round, with FC Zürich's sole squad member Paul Sturzenegger hitting four and Grasshoppers' Max Abegglen bagging a hat-trick. In the second round, the Swiss needed a late Walter Dietrich goal to scramble a draw against the Czechs and force a replay. Again, it was a late goal from a Servette player – Dietrich's club team-mate Robert Pache – that sent the Swiss through in the second match.

On to the Stade Bergeyre for the quarter-final against the Italians. After a goalless first half, the scoring was condensed into a 15-minute period at the start of the second. Sturzenegger notched the first on 47 minutes before Bologna's Giuseppe Della Valle equalised five minutes later. On the hour mark, Max Abegglen scored again, and the Swiss held on in front of a crowd of more than 8,000. The Italian team coach was Vittorio Pozzo, who had learned football as a student in both Zürich and Winterthur in his youth. Pozzo would go on to coach the Italian national side – the *Azzurri* (Blues) – to two World Cup titles in the 1930s. Abegglen was Switzerland's star again in the semi-final against Sweden at Stade de Colombes, scoring a brace as the Swiss won 2-1 to book their final with Uruguay. The South Americans were little known outside their continent on this, their first trip to Europe. The Uruguayan team had won many fans throughout their progress with their flare and quick-passing game. They had already blown away Yugoslavia 7-0, the USA 3-0, France 5-1, and edged the Netherlands 2-1 in the semi-final. The team featured some names that would go on to be considered among the greatest of their époque, such as Héctor Scarone, Pedro Petrone, Pedro Cea and 'The Black Marvel', José Leandro Andrade.

And so it was that on 9 June 1924 at the Stade de Colombes, Uruguay burst on to the world scene, playing the Swiss off the park to win 3-0 in front of 40,522 spectators. The press would dub the encounter as 'epoch-making and unforgettable'. British newspapers relayed the enthusiasm of the French media, which exclaimed that the Uruguayans had adopted the Scottish passing game and branded it with their own 'Latin genius'.[6] The Swiss went home with their country's first international honour, the Olympic silver medal, and Duckworth would try again in Amsterdam in 1928.

Between the two Olympic tournaments of the mid-1920s, the Swiss FA launched a cup competition – the Swiss Cup – to run alongside the Serie A league championship. As it had with the league in its first season, Grasshoppers won the first edition of the Swiss Cup in 1926, beating FC Bern 2-1. Duckworth's team at Amsterdam in 1928 included more Grasshoppers players than his own at Servette, despite Servette having dispatched the Zürich club 5-1 in the Swiss Cup Final that year. But, unlike four years previously, this time Switzerland's campaign would only last 90 minutes; the side was demolished 4-0 by Germany in the opening round, including a hat-trick from 'King' Richard Hofmann.

The Swiss decided not to send a team to the inaugural World Cup in Uruguay but would achieve the quarter-final stage at the 1934 and 1938 editions, held in neighbouring Italy and France. While Uruguay held the first World Cup in the summer of 1930, Switzerland played host to the *Coupe des Nations* (Nations Cup), an early forerunner of the European Cup. The nine-day-long knockout competition held in Geneva pitted champions and cup winners from FIFA member nations – except the Home Nations. Swiss, French, Italian, German, Austrian, Hungarian, Dutch, Belgian, Spanish and Czechoslovakian teams took part in the tournament.

Host club Servette were thrashed 7-0 by Austrian side First Vienna in the first round, before recovering in the consolation round by beating Belgians Cercle Brugge 2-1. Servette then hammered a strong Bologna side 4-1 before losing in the semi-final to eventual winners, Újpest from Hungary. Újpest beat Slavia Club 3-0 in the final refereed by Englishman Stanley Rous. Rous went on to simplify the laws of the game in the 1930s and pioneered field positioning for officials to get a better view of proceedings.

He also went on to serve as FIFA's sixth president between 1961 and 1974.

## FC St. Gallen today

What of Switzerland's pioneer club? FC St. Gallen has struggled to keep up with the clubs that went on to dominate Swiss football in Young Boys, FC Basel and FC Zürich, but it has two titles to its name, nearly a century apart in the 1903/04 and 1999/2000 seasons. FC St. Gallen joined the Club of Pioneers in 2014 on the occasion of its 135th anniversary. The club received its certificate prematch ahead of beating Switzerland's second-oldest club, Grasshoppers, 3-0. FC St. Gallen is the fifth oldest of the Club of Pioneers after Sheffield FC, Wrexham, Queen's Park and Kjøbenhavns Boldklub. The Swiss legacy in football extends far beyond its borders and even its continent.

1   *The Field*, 1 November 1879 (p42)

2   *Liverpool Echo*, 19 October 1889 (p4)

3   *South Bucks Standard*, 26 April 1895 (p6)

4   https://www.bbc.co.uk/news/world-europe-36391241

5   *Nottingham Journal*, 20 December 1921 (p4)

6   *Western Daily Press*, 12 June 1924 (p18)

# 7.

# Scandinavia

ON 26 June 1992, Denmark lifted the European Championship trophy after defeating newly reunified Germany in the final. A rare John Jensen goal on 18 minutes and another from Kim Vilfort 12 minutes from time at the Ullevi Stadium in Gothenburg sunk the Germans, many of whom had won the World Cup as West Germany just two years before. Yet Denmark had not even qualified for the tournament. The Danes had stood in at the last minute for a talented Yugoslavia side that would have been one of the favourites to win the tournament. But as the Balkan region descended into war and the country broke up, Yugoslavia was disqualified, and Denmark took its place. That summer marked the high watermark for Scandinavian men's football – the Danish side winning a Swedish tournament. Sweden, the biggest of the Nordic countries with nearly twice the population of Denmark, Finland or Norway, hosted the World Cup in 1958 and lost the final to Brazil after being undone by a 17-year-old Pelé. The Swedes have also finished third in two World Cups (1950 and 1994) and won gold at the London Olympics of 1948. Sweden's clubs have performed best of the Nordic countries on the international stage. IFK Göteborg won the UEFA Cup in 1982 and 1987, and Malmö appeared in the 1979 European Cup Final, losing to Nottingham Forest.

For their part, the Danes – who had a golden generation in the 1980s and early 90s with the talented Laudrup brothers, Preben Elkjær, Jan Mølby, Allan Simonsen, Jesper Olsen and many others – were early pioneers of the game on the continent. Norway has not fared too well, apart from brief spells of brilliance in the 1930s – when it beat hosts Germany in front of Adolf Hitler on its way to Olympic bronze in 1936 – and in the 1990s, when it qualified for the World Cups of 1994 and 1998, and Euro 2000. Iceland's recent success, beating England en route to reaching the quarter-finals of Euro 2016 and qualifying for the World Cup in Russia in 2018, is the zenith of its history. The Finns, on the other hand, had never qualified for a major tournament until they secured a place at the delayed Euro 2020.

## Football arrives in Denmark

Many fervent Anglophile Danes of the 19th century sent their sons to the top schools in England. This exposed Denmark's finest young minds to the emerging ball sports of the time, including Association rules football, which they may well have seen themselves – or heard of being played – on Danish docks by British sailors. Football may have already been in the Danish schooling system. One of the students at the Sorø Akademi school, 100km west of the capital, had been sent a ball from England as early as 1877.[1] As in England, cricket was the key summer game in Denmark among the upper classes, and players were looking for a winter sport. Other factors came into play that would determine football's spread in Denmark: regular trade between Britain and Denmark, and the growth of railways across Denmark transported ideas as well as goods and people.

On 26 April 1876, four men – Frederik Levison, August Nielsen, Carl Møller and E. Selmer – met at Levison's house to form Kjøbenhavns Boldklub (KB). This sports society adopted football three years later. The purpose of the club was to 'provide its members with healthy exercise and a pleasant diversion'.[2] On Sunday, 7 September 1879, at Klampenborg in Copenhagen, a football game more similar to rugby than the Association game was played. A large body of men scrapped over a ball, much to the bemusement of the watching Danish public. The club had written its laws down on paper as the young men could not afford to get them printed. In 1880, lawyer Frederick Markmann became KB's new chairman. Something of a visionary, Markmann wanted to promote football within schools alongside the club's summer sport, cricket. Markmann's translation of the Football Association rules in 1887 brought consistency to the growing number of football games played in academic establishments.[3] Yet more football clubs began to crop up around Copenhagen, often playing at the common ground at Fælledparken. KB's dominance was clear at the outset of Danish football. When the first domestic football tournament was held in Copenhagen in 1888, KB won its three matches by an aggregate of 40-0.

Fremskridtsklubbens Cricketklub was founded in 1886 by liberals of the Venstre Reform Party before switching to its current name, Boldklubben (BK) Frem, when football was added to the roster a year later. In February 1889, Akademisk Boldklub (AB) was formed from a merger of a students' cricket club and a polytechnic football club. AB beat BK Frem in its first match a month later 2-0 at Blegdamsfælleden. In May of that year, Markmann contacted 86 associations with a total of 4,000 members with the aim of creating a national association to oversee the development of Danish football and cricket. On 18 May 1889, the *Dansk Boldspil Union* (Danish Ballgame Union – DBU) was formed with 21 Copenhagen-based clubs and five from Jutland. The DBU became the first national football association outside Britain and Ireland, with Markmann – by now an assistant in the Ministry of Finance – as its first chairman. A seven-club tournament was held to celebrate the birth of the DBU but by now KB's dominance was diminishing. On 16 March 1890, BK Frem became the first team to beat KB. Later that year AB played against Swedish side Halmstad, winning 3-0, marking the first match between clubs from different Scandinavian nations.

New Copenhagen clubs B93 and Østerbros Boldklub (OB) joined in the first half of the 1890s, by which time teams were moving out of the Fællenden common land and establishing their own stadiums. The game was still amateur and would remain so for almost another century, but players often turned out for more than one club. These players were mostly educated and influential men, and they may have helped football to appear on the school sports curriculum in 1896. This was a massive boost to football in Denmark, as it exposed people from all classes to football – not just the traditional high end of Danish society. Growing bolder, the DBU embarked on its first overseas tour in 1897. The players paid half of the cost of the trip to Hamburg, travelling by third-class railway and standing on the deck for the crossing from Korsør to Kiel in driving wind and rain.[4] The trip was worth it – the DBU XI defeated Hamburg-Altona 5-0 in front of 5,000 spectators.

The DBU wanted to assess the standard of the Danish game against the very best and invited Scottish pioneer club, Queen's Park FC, to play two matches in Copenhagen against a select DBU XI as part of its International Festival.

True to the Danish tradition of amateurism in football, which would last until 1978, visiting teams would also need to be amateurs. 'The Spiders', being among the few leading Scottish clubs living the amateur ethos, also became the first Scottish club to play on the continent – albeit with £100 assistance from the Danish organisers for their passage.[5] The Glaswegians won the first match 7-0 in front of a crowd of 7,000 spectators and the second game 3-0. The Scots returned two years later to play the DBU and won 6-1 and 8-1 in front of the Danish royal family. Neither tour raised more than a paragraph or two in the British press; by the time of Queen's Park's third tour of Denmark in 1903, the *Dundee Evening Telegraph* merely remarked that the Danes 'had made progress in the game'.[6] Indeed, they had, losing just 1-0 to the fast-passing Scots in the first fixture. The Danes also put up a better fight against England's premier amateur club Corinthian FC, but still lost heavily as the London club wrapped up its 1904 Scandinavian tour in Copenhagen with 4-1 and 4-0 victories against a local combined XI. The gulf between the Danes and the top British professional clubs was vast. Newcastle United and Southampton both toured Copenhagen, with the Magpies defeating KB 6-1, a combined Copenhagen XI 6-2 and a Danish XI 3-1. Southampton had visited the year before – the first professional club to do so – beating both B93 and a Copenhagen XI comfortably. The Saints and Newcastle United then played an exhibition on their May tour of 1904, with the Magpies winning 4-0.

The year 1904 was also pivotal for the DBU. Its application for affiliation to the Football Association in England was rejected in February, yet former Sorø Akademi student and now DBU executive Ludvig Sylow headed to Paris in May 1904 to co-found FIFA with six other countries' associations. Danish footballing confidence was growing, and that April it sent a team to the Intercalated Games in Athens, taking on teams from Greece and Turkey to win gold, defeating Athens 9-0 in the final. Southampton returned to Copenhagen in 1906 and lost to a local XI side for the first time. Ilford, Chelsea, Middlesbrough and Celtic all visited, with the Bhoys suffering a 2-1 defeat to a Copenhagen XI. The combination game that Queen's Park FC had promoted in the Danish capital just a few years previously had now undone their fellow Glaswegians.

Danish football was now on the march, and in the autumn of 1908 the first official Danish national side sailed for London to take part in an eight-team Olympic football tournament at White City. Seven of the 17-man squad were drawn from the KB club, including captain Kristian Middelboe, a sturdy defender who would later head up the DBU. The Danes were coached by former Woolwich Arsenal and Manchester City goalkeeper, Charles Williams – the first keeper recorded to have scored a goal in the First Division in his City days – and dispatched a France B-team 9-0 in their first match. A day later, Great Britain, captained by Tottenham Hotspur striker Vivian Woodward, thrashed Sweden 12-1. Denmark would top that score later in the week with an incredible 17-1 victory over France, with BK Frem striker Sophus Nielsen becoming the first player in history to score ten goals in an international. Nielsen, whose nickname was 'Krølben' – 'curl leg' – ended the tournament as top scorer. The semi-final does not seem to have captured the London public's attention, with just a few hundred in attendance. Nielsen, Middelboe, Williams and their comrades now faced Woodward's Great Britain side in the final, witnessed by 8,000 spectators – including nobility from around the world. The crowd had had to wait for a delayed kick-off due to an overrunning lacrosse final. *Sporting Life* noted that the Danes were 'quick, nippy and most determined in their methods' and praised their stoic defending, if not their ability in front of goal.[7] Despite having scored 26 goals already in just two matches, the lack of finishing cost the Danes, who lost by two goals to nil. The team sailed home with the respect of the British public and the silver medal. Revenge of sorts would follow in 1910 when, in front of the Crown Prince of Denmark, a Danish national XI beat an amateur XI from England 2-1.

A year later, the Danes had built a national stadium, the Idrætsparken near Denmark's spiritual football birthplace at Fælledparken, the first such stadium built especially for football in continental Europe. Matches held included a 3-2 defeat to Sheffield Wednesday, and a record attendance was set later that year when 11,233 turned out to watch Glasgow Rangers. The Idrætsparken was demolished in 1990 to make way for the new Parken Stadium. Ironically, the final match at Idrætsparken was a Euro 92 qualifying tournament defeat to Yugoslavia, the team Denmark would replace at that competition on its way to its first piece of major silverware.

## Sweden's football journey

The Danes headed to the Stockholm Olympic Games in 1912 full of confidence. The fifth modern Olympiad was a 102-sport tournament including an Association football competition managed by the Swedish Football Association. The Swedish Ballgame Association *(Svenska Bollspells Förbundet – SBF)* was founded in 1904, the same year it had been involved in the foundation of FIFA alongside its neighbours across the Øresund strait in Denmark. In 1906, it would change its name to *Svenska Fotbollförbundet* (SvFF), to reflect the organisation's focus on football. 'Fotboll' was less than two decades old in Sweden by the time the guardian of the national game was founded.

The main protagonist driving this new sport was Wilhelm Friberg, the son of a sailor who grew up in the Majorna district of Gothenburg. Compulsory gymnastics had been introduced into schools in 1880 in a drive to promote physical as well as intellectual wellbeing. Alongside gymnastics, popular sports in Sweden at the time also included athletics and – in winter – skating. Friberg left school in 1881 aged 16 to become a clerk at a mechanic's workshop, where the director would later reflect that Friberg 'cannot help but spend too much time on sports'.[8] In early 1880s Gothenburg, sports began to get organised with the foundation of ice skating and sports clubs. Together with a friend, Walfrid Silow, Friberg rented a property, cleared the grounds and built an ice-skating rink. It was here on 4 December 1887 that Friberg and 11 others gathered together to form the *Örgryte Idrottssällskap* (ÖIS) – a sports society that Friberg would chair for nearly 40 years. The society's colours would be red for love and blue for faithfulness. While the ÖIS included several sports, it wasn't until 1891 that the club took up football, with some help from Scottish instructors. The first match recorded in Sweden using Association rules was played on 22 May 1892 in the Heden district of Gothenburg. Friberg's ÖIS squared up against the now defunct Idrottssällskapet Lyckans Soldater for a game of two 30-minute halves. Six Scots took part in the match that ended 1-0 to Örgryte, including two named John Lawson and William Scott. Reports record that the Scots were far better players than the Swedes. A stone memorial marks the spot where the match took place – now a public park. It features three simple lines depicting goalposts and the words *To the men of the first football match in Sweden. Örgryte IS – Lyckans Soldater. 22 May 1892.*

Sports clubs continued to emerge in Gothenburg, Malmö and the capital, Stockholm – port cities with exposure to British sailors and the growing Danish football culture. Among these new establishments were the future *Tvillingderby* (Twin Derby) clubs of AIK and Djurgårdens IF in 1891. On 1 February 1895, the *Idrottsföreningen Kamraterna* (Comrades' Sporting Society) – IFK – was founded in Stockholm. Swedish football journalist David Berg tells me this was a significant moment in the development of the Association game in Sweden. 'IFK were active in a lot of sports, and soon other IFKs were founded all around Sweden. IFK Göteborg and IFK Norrköping are two of the most successful teams in football and you can find at least one IFK team in almost every Swedish town or city,' he says. Enough sports clubs were playing football by the middle of the decade that by 1896 the first football championship – the *Svenska Mästerskapet* – was held at a military field in the west Swedish port of Helsingborg. This knockout competition would become an annual event contested mainly between the clubs of Gothenburg and Stockholm. Friberg's Örgryte IS side beat IS Idrottens Vänner 3-0 in the first final and dominated the first four tournaments before Stockholm's AIK interrupted its winning streak. ÖIS would win nine of the first 12 editions of the tournament. By the turn of the century, the Stockholm clubs had formed their own local league competition, the *Svenska Bollspelförbundets Tävlingsserie* (Swedish Ballgame Association's Match Series).

The Swedish game lagged well behind the Danes in the early years of the 20th century, due in part to the conditions of the pitches. Many Swedish grounds were made of gravel and were flooded in winter to create ice rinks.

Corinthians visited in 1904 in a trip arranged by Charles Wreford Brown's wife. The Corinthians notched six goals without reply in Gothenburg before heading to Stockholm for a double-header with a combined Swedish XI. The leading English amateurs hit double digits in both games, trouncing their hosts 11-0 and 14-1. Berg doesn't feel that the Corinthians' visit was that significant to the game's popularity in Sweden as the sport was developing fast, and there had already been overseas instructors – in ÖIS's case, for example, from Scotland – almost 15 years beforehand. 'With that said, it must certainly have been a great honour to have the Corinthians to visit, and probably they learned a lot by playing a better team,' Berg adds. 'So, the Corinthians might have had an impact on the tactical and technical development of the game here, but I don't think their visit was that important to make people play football all around Sweden.' As in Hungary earlier in the year, Corinthians contributed a trophy – The Corinthian Bowl – for Swedish clubs to contest. It ran between 1906 and 1913, with Örgryte IS once more the main force, winning all but one edition – to Djurgårdens IF – in 1910. In 1907, Corinthians' sister club Casuals, who often followed Corinthians tours to check on the progress of countries they had visited, played three games in Gothenburg, hammering a Stockholm XI 7-0 before retiring to a winter resort for the weekend. Casuals dispatched a Copenhagen side before facing Örgryte IS, who were reportedly the strongest side they met on the tour, although Casuals still ran out 6-1 winners.[9]

Between the first Corinthians tour of 1904 and the Casuals' follow-up of 1907, the Swedish FA and numerous leagues were established, and Sweden put a national side together for the 1908 Olympics in London. The team would feature four Örgryte IS players, including goalkeeper Oskar

Bengtsson, and players from six other clubs from around
the country. The team was managed by Ludvig Kornerup,
a Dane who had lived in Scotland before moving to Sweden
where he chaired the SBF and later the SvFF. He later moved
on to become vice-president at FIFA. In the opening match –
effectively a quarter-final – Sweden suffered a 12-1 reverse to
the hosts in front of just 2,000 spectators at White City. The
team was invited to play the bronze medal match against the
Netherlands because France – shocked by their 17-1 defeat to
the Danes – refused to play. The Dutch won 2-0. Back home,
football gathered pace with the creation of the *Svenska Serien*
(Swedish Series) league in 1910. This tournament would
be played on and off until the creation of the *Allsvenskan*,
the current national Swedish league system, in 1924. The
winners of the *Svenska Mästerskapet* cup competition were
still regarded as Swedish champions up until Brynäs's
victory in 1925. From 1931 onwards, *Allsvenskan* winners
were considered national champions, with GAIS clinching
the title that year. No Stockholm club would ever win the
*Svenska Serien*, with ÖIS, IFK Göteborg and GAIS ensuring
that the title remained at all times in Gothenburg.

The first chairman of the Swedish Football Association
in 1904 was the prominent horseman, Clarence von Rosen.
He is credited with promoting several sports in Sweden,
and reintroducing equestrianism to the Olympic Games.
von Rosen was succeeded as chairman of the Swedish FA
by Friberg in 1908. The *Allsvenskan* trophy had been named
after von Rosen until reports emerged around the year 2000
alleging that he had had personal connections with leading
Nazis. A new *Allsvenskan* trophy was created and named
in honour of the former Swedish head of UEFA, Lennart
Johansson, with Hammarby being the first club to win
it in 2001.

## The Nordic Olympic experience

The Olympic Games held in Stockholm in 1912 were three years in the planning. Swedish officials, impressed by London's 1908 games, gained royal support for a Swedish host bid. For the first time, more than one stadium was used for the Olympic football tournament, with three venues in action for the 11 European teams of amateurs entering. One of those stadiums, the Råsunda Idrottsplats, would also host the 1958 World Cup Final. Four Nordic sides – hosts Sweden, 1908 silver medallists Denmark, and Norway and Finland – took part. The Finns were officially the Grand Duchy of Finland and part of the Russian Empire at the time. The Finnish FA joined FIFA in 1907, and its national side had debuted with a 5-2 home defeat to Sweden in October 1911. The Finns were something of a surprise package in the tournament, defeating Italy 3-2 in extra time in the first round and sticking one to the Russians with a 2-1 win in the quarter-finals before succumbing to Great Britain 4-0. The Finns were then thrashed 9-0 by the Dutch at Råsunda in the bronze medal play-off.

Norway's football story probably started in the 1880s as a youth pursuit in Bergen, with its oldest football club, Odds Ballklubb, spinning out of a multi-sports organisation in Skien, 100km south of the modern capital Oslo, in 1894. Odds took its name from the legendary Norwegian giant and famed bowman Örvar-Oddr, whose story appears in *The Sagas of Icelanders*. Fittingly, Odds BK took an arrow to be its symbol. The club's chairman, Ludvig Forvald, was probably the first to introduce the Association rules game into Norway. The Norwegian Football Federation – the *Norges Fotbollforbund* (NFF) – was founded in the Hotel Bristol in Oslo by members of the Lyn, Grane and Spring clubs. A small national league was up and running – albeit with just six teams – by 1914.

Both Norway and Denmark were awarded byes in the first round at the 1912 Olympics and met in the second round. The Danes' superiority was apparent as they swept aside the Norwegians 7-0, Ole Anthon Olsen of B93 bagging a hat-trick. Olsen scored another double as Denmark swept aside the Netherlands 4-1 in the semi-final. Once more, Olsen scored twice in the final against Denmark's Olympic nemesis, Great Britain. But the British amateurs scored four before half-time to win 4-2 and retain the gold medal they won four years earlier in London. After the 1912 tournament, Denmark's Nils Middelboe – younger brother of Kristian – signed for Chelsea, becoming the West London club's first-ever overseas signing.[10] Middelboe stayed true to his amateur status, however, drawing a wage as a lawyer in London rather than earning from his sport. Twenty-five thousand people – including the Crown Prince of Sweden – came to the Olympiastadion in Stockholm to witness the final. Denmark left a Swedish football pitch with medals rounds their necks, and not for the last time … Although the Danes had lost once again to a team from England, they achieved some kind of revenge in June 1914. A side sent by the Football Association to tour Scandinavia lost by three goals to nil in Copenhagen in front of 20,000 spectators, a new record for a Danish crowd.

Although Scandinavian countries were neutral throughout the First World War, they were still disrupted by the conflict. At the 1920 Olympics in Antwerp, Belgium, the Norwegians caused one of the greatest upsets up to that point in world football on 28 August, defeating Great Britain 3-1 in front of 5,000 people. British press put the defeat down to injury and the age of the British amateurs –

which included three Corinthians – but credited Norway for its strong approach. The Danes also exited in the first round in Brussels to Spain. Meanwhile, Sweden defeated Greece 9-0, with IFK Göteborg's Herbert Karlsson – who would go on to enjoy a successful career in the American Soccer League – striking five times. In the quarter-finals, Sweden lost 5-4 in extra time to the Netherlands while Norway lost 4-0 to eventual finalists Czechoslovakia. There would be no Scandinavian team on the Olympic podium this time. A year later, B 1903 striker Carl Hansen signed for Glasgow Rangers for £20, becoming the first Dane to move abroad to turn professional. Rangers had been impressed by Hansen in a 2-1 friendly match win at Idrætsparken and snapped him up. The 'Great Little Dane', as he was known, scored his first goal in a 2-0 win in thick fog at Ibrox two minutes after half-time in an Old Firm derby against Celtic.

Sweden was Scandinavia's only representative at the 1924 Olympic Games in Paris. Denmark, along with Great Britain, had withdrawn its players over the definition of what constituted 'amateurism'. Sweden opened their tournament with a thumping 8-1 victory over 1920 gold medallists, Belgium, including a hat-trick from Sven Rydell. Rydell went on to become the Swedish national team's leading goalscorer for almost a century. Zlatan Ibrahimović finally beat Rydell's tally of 49 international goals in 2014. Rydell notched another in the Swedes' 5-0 victory over Egypt, before the team fell short 2-1 in the semi-final with Switzerland. Sweden secured the bronze medal after a 3-1 rematch victory against the Netherlands after the two had drawn their first match 1-1. The bronze medal was Sweden's first international honour.

Denmark's national champion had been decided by a series of knockout matches each year since 1913, but in

1927 a group system was inaugurated, proved unpopular, and was cancelled after just two years in favour of a two-league system of ten teams with promotion and relegation. This *Mesterskabsserien* would run from 1930 until German occupation brought Danish domestic football to a standstill in 1940. The Danes, still at odds with FIFA over the definition of professionalism, would not take part in the 1928 Olympic football tournament, and nor would any of the other Nordic countries. But on 18 June 1933, Denmark's 3-2 win away to Sweden in Stockholm was the first time a radio transmission took place for a Danish match. Football was well and truly ensconced into Scandinavian life.

## The pioneers today

On the 50th anniversary of Kjøbenhavns Boldklub, co-founder E. Semler gave a speech. In surmising, he wished that KB would always be 'an adornment among the ball clubs'.[11] The club boasts 15 national championships, won between 1913 and 1980, and the Danish Cup in 1969. On 1 July 1992, the two historic clubs of Kjøbenhavns Boldklub and Boldklubben 1903 merged to create the new Football Club København (FCK), occupying the then recently built national stadium, Parken. Boldklubben 1903's licence was used to play in Denmark's top-flight Superliga, while Kjøbenhavns Boldklub became the reserve side. In its short modern history, FC Københavns has already established a fierce cross-city rivalry with Brøndby IF, itself a relatively new club, having only been formed in 1964.

Claus Bermann runs the Danish-language groundhopping website VisitFootball.dk. He tells me Brøndby IF was the most successful Danish club in the 1980s and 90s, and a pioneer club in Danish professional football. FCK was the newcomer in 1992 and born with clear and spoken ambitions to become a leading football club in Denmark. This immediately sparked tension in the Danish capital, with no love lost between the two sides. 'Since then the Copenhagen derby has evolved to a spectacular show outside the pitch, with two very strong and creative sets of supporters,' he says. 'In recent years FCK has proved to be the stronger side on the pitch, with the current upper hand in the Danish capital.' Kjøbenhavns Boldklub joined the Club of Pioneers in 2018, joining Norway's first football club, Odd Ballklubb. Odd BK has won the Norwegian Football Cup 12 times, more than any other Norwegian club, although it has won it just once since 1931 – in 2000. Odd plays in Norway's top division, the Eliteserien.

In Sweden, following its illustrious beginnings, Örgryte IS went into decline from the 1930s. The club has only won one national title – in 1985 – since the First World War, and in 2011 found itself down in Sweden's third tier. ÖIS is one of three main clubs in Gothenburg after IFK Göteborg – with whom it has a huge rivalry – and GAIS. The club now plays in Sweden's second tier, the Superettan.

1 https://idrottsforum.org/mcdowell140514/

2 http://www.kb-boldklub.dk/om-kb/profil/klubbens-historie/semlers-50-aars-jubilaeumstale/

3 https://www.dbukoebenhavn.dk/om-os/historie/klubber/k/kb/kb-75-aar/

4 https://www.dbu.dk/om-dbu/dbu-s-historie/1889-1920/

5 https://idrottsforum.org/mcdowell140514/

6 *Dundee Evening Telegraph*, 6 June 1903 (p5)

7 *Sporting Life*, 26 October 1908 (p8)

8 http://ois.se/historia/

9 *The Sportsman*, 10 April 1907 (p8)

10 https://thesefootballtimes.co/2019/02/15/nils-middelboe-the-buccaneering-danish-banker-who-became-chelseas-first-foreign-star/

11 http://www.kb-boldklub.dk/om-kb/profil/klubbens-historie/semlers-50-aars-jubilaeumstale/

# 8.

# Belgium

FOR MANY visitors to Belgium, Antwerp might fly under the radar. The historic bustles of Bruges and Ghent draw the weekenders while Brussels hums to the tones of business people and bureaucrats. Yet in the late 19th century and for the first three decades of the 20th, the port city of Antwerp, nestled against the broad Scheldt river, was the centre of Belgian – and briefly, global – sport. In 1920, just two years after the end of the First World War, which had devastated much of the country, Antwerp hosted the sixth modern summer Olympiad. Belgium's second city boasts a rich history as a sports pioneer. It was in Antwerp that Belgium's first golf club was established in 1888. Thirteen years previous, the country's second cricket club was founded and in 1875 the second tennis club was formed. And Antwerp beat Brussels and Liège in soccer, too; this is where Belgium's first football club – now known as Royal Antwerp Football Club – was founded in 1880.

## The Great Old
Antwerpen-Centraal station is one of the most elegant railway buildings you will ever see. I trundled in from Amsterdam

one cold Saturday afternoon in winter and found myself in this incredible transport hub. Layers of trains like Matchbox toys arrive and depart in a modern interior crowned with a cathedral-like hall and modern Gothic exterior. From here, it's a 20-minute tram ride out to the Bosuilstadion, Royal Antwerp's home since 1923, when it was inaugurated with a prestigious friendly against England. Belgium held the visitors to a 2-2 draw that day in front of 38,000 spectators. The winter night I visited the Bosuilstadion was clear and crisp. The floodlights spread a brilliant grey-white blanket across the red curved-iron roof. I had arrived too early, as I often do. Growing up in England, where matches often sell out – or, at least, the cheaper tickets do – I have never quite come to terms with the fact that this simply doesn't happen in many other leagues. Especially so in Belgium's second tier, which is where Royal Antwerp played when I visited; the club has since been promoted back to the Belgian First Division A.

The eastern stand of the Bosuilstadion – a barn-like curved-iron roof – is an old-school marvel. Instead of seats, there are rows of wooden benches. Not the most comfortable place to park one's behind but certainly a novel departure from the generic and ubiquitous plastic bucket seat. The wind blew right through us. The iron rattled. I loved it. This was my first experience at a Belgian football match, so it was something of a culture shock for me to hear the fans from this Flemish-speaking region singing half their songs in English. 'Come on, you reds!' sung with a guttural tone. A single flare lit up the night – a one-man *tifo*.

In 1926, Belgium adopted a *Matricule* system. It lists the order in which clubs register with the Royal Belgian Football Association. As Belgium is a trilingual country, this organisation is known as the *Koninklijke Belgische*

*Voetbalbond* (KBVB) in Flemish, *Union Royale Belge des Sociétés de Football Association* (URBSFA) in French and *Königlicher Belgischer Fußballverband* (KBFV) in German. Royal Antwerp is Number 1 in the *Matricule* system, and, as early as its 25th anniversary in 1905, the club gained the nickname 'The Great Old'.

Stéphane Lievens is a Brussels-based groundhopper. He informs me that the *Matricule* system is unique in the world and is a source of pride for many clubs, especially the older ones. '[Royal Antwerp] is respected as the oldest club but also hated by a few, like Club Brugge fans and, of course, their big Antwerp rivals, Beerschot, who were one of the strongest clubs in Belgium before World War II,' Lievens adds.

## The foundation of Royal Antwerp

Antwerp has a businesslike air. One can sense that here, rather like Brussels, things get done. With its fortunes so reliant on the North Sea, it is perhaps little surprise that football found its way here across the Channel from England. British port workers were kicking balls in Antwerp in the 1860s. It is known that the game was played in Brussels at English schools as early as 1865 and in Liège at the Cockerill factory. The foundation of the Antwerp Football Club mirrors that of many other clubs as it spun out of a wider athletic society. An accurate date cannot be found for the foundation of the Antwerp Athletics Club, but 1880 is the accepted year. This athletic club played both the Association and Rugby football codes in the winter, as well as tennis and cricket in the summer, although the latter would struggle and ultimately fizzle out during the 1890s. Cyclists Emile Van Migem and Charles Pfeiffer spotted football being played, and they, together with some local friends and

English students, formed the Antwerp Athletics Club. By 1887 a dedicated Antwerp Football Club had been created.[1] It appears the club played against the crews of visiting British ships, but by 1889 it had a regular rival with the foundation of the Brussels Football Club. They started playing each other several times a year.

In 1890, Antwerp Football Club branched out internationally. Firstly, in March the team travelled to Breda in the Netherlands to take on Rotterdam's VV Concordia, losing 1-0. The following month a Belgian XI in Antwerp was beaten far more convincingly by Clapton FC from East London, losing 8-1. Significantly, this is the first time a continental European side hosted a visiting English club. Clapton would return in 1893 to thrash Antwerp by a seven-goal margin. Football started to gather momentum in the early years of the 1890s. Brugsche FC in Bruges and Racing FC in Brussels were founded in 1891. FC Liégeois from the south and the Brussels Football Association Club followed in 1892. The Antwerp Football Club, together with its sister tennis and cricket clubs, moved to new grounds at Transvaalstraat in 1893. At the ground's inauguration on 3 December, Antwerp Football Club became the first Belgian club to charge an entry fee for a match, with spectators paying 0.50 Belgian francs. Antwerp drew 2-2 with Dutch visitors Victoria Rotterdam.

During the 1890s, more English teams would tour Belgium, including Harwich & Parkston (1892), University of Cambridge (1893), Old Westminster (1894), and London sides Olympian FC, Plumstead and Enfield all toured in 1897. Another frequent visitor was Kent club, Tunbridge Wells FC, who won four games by considerable margins in 1896 in Brussels and Bruges, returning undefeated in 1897, 1899, 1900 and 1901.

## Belgian football gets organised

By the mid-1890s there was a growing consensus among the existing Belgian clubs for the formation of a competitive league and a governing body. The secretary of Racing Club de Bruxelles, Louis Mühlinghaus, was a vocal advocate. On 4 August 1895, the executive committee was formed with its inaugural meeting held at the Le Courrier brewery in Brussels. This meeting led to the foundation of the Belgian Union of Athletics Sports (UBSSA) on 1 September that year. The Union featured ten football-playing clubs with Mühlinghaus as general secretary of the football section and the mining engineer Baron Édouard de Laveleye as the football sector president. The Baron would also form the Belgian Olympic Committee and help attract the Games to Antwerp in 1920.

The first national championship ran between the autumn and spring of 1895/96, with Antwerp Football Club as hot favourites. But the team disappointed and FC Liégeois made history as the first recognised champions of Belgium, with Antwerp finishing second. The Liège outfit saw Racing emerge as its major rival for honours during the nascent years of the championship, with Antwerp failing to launch a serious bid until the 1899/1900 season. That year, the club, by now playing in the city's velodrome and no longer tied to its tennis partners, lost to an own goal at Leuven, leaving Racing to take the title. At the end of that season, the team faced its most serious challenge yet in its short history. Another team in Antwerp was established in September 1899 – Beerschot Antwerpen Club. In May 1900, former Antwerp player Alfred Grisar managed to persuade many of the first team to defect to the newly formed Beerschot AC team. Such was the blow to Antwerp Football Club that it volunteered to take part in the second division for the 1900/01 season. Beerschot played a key role in developing the international game. The club's honorary chairman, Jorge Díaz, organised a tournament held on 28 April 1901 in which representatives from Belgium and the Netherlands competed for the *Coupe Vanden Abeele*. The Belgian team won, but fielded four Englishmen, so the match is not recognised by FIFA. The team wore white with tricolour bands of the national flag – black, yellow and red – on the arms.

FIFA itself was not founded until three years later in Paris, with Mühlinghaus representing the Belgian FA and becoming the organisation's first general secretary for its first two years. It is believed that Mühlinghaus was the first to propose the idea of an international football competition. Belgium's first official match was staged on 1 May 1904 against France at Racing Club de Bruxelles's Stade du Vivier d'Oie. The game ended 3-3. The main stand from that era still remains, although the ground itself is now a protected monument used solely for hockey matches.

At the Paris Olympics in 1900, a group of students from the Université de Bruxelles had represented Belgium, where they came up against English amateurs Upton Park and a French side selected by the national sporting body, USFSA, from Parisian champions, Club Français. The Brussels students ended up playing just one exhibition match against the French XI at the Vélodrome de Vincennes in Paris in front of 1,500 people. This exhibition tournament was a tiny foreshadow of what would follow. FIFA took over organisation of the Olympic football tournaments from 1908 onwards. The Belgians did not send a team to the football tournaments at the London Olympic Games of 1908 and withdrew shortly before the Stockholm 1912 draw. The First World War would disrupt and devastate

Belgium, its people and its economy for four long years but, as part of its national rebuilding, Antwerp hosted the 1920 Olympics. The new Olympisch Stadion in Beerschot – later home to Beerschot AC – hosted a number of games in the tournament, including the final and Norway's surprise first-round victory over Great Britain's amateurs. Other host venues included Royal Antwerp's then home, Stadion Broodstraat; Stade Joseph Marien in St Gilles, Brussels; and the Jules Ottenstadion in Ghent. Belgium's coach was the Scotsman Willie Maxwell. The former Third Lanark and Sunderland player had first moved to Brussels in 1909 to take charge of Leopold FC. Within two years, he was Belgium's national team coach and it was under Maxwell that Belgium headed to its home tournament.[2]

Belgium's first-round opponents, Poland, had to withdraw due to war with neighbouring Russian Soviet forces, giving the hosts a bye to the quarter-finals. Robert Coppée of the strong Royale Union Saint-Gilloise side emerged as the local hero of the tournament, and he bagged a quarter-final hat-trick against Spain at the Olympisch Stadion in a 3-1 win. A 3-0 victory over the Netherlands in the semi-final led to a controversial final with Czechoslovakia. Coppée slotted home from the spot in the opening ten minutes, with Beerschot's Henri Larnoe doubling the hosts' lead on the half-hour mark. At this point, the Czechoslovakians appear to have lost their cool with the English officials, including the 65-year-old referee, John Lewis, and linesman Charles Wreford Brown – the former Corinthian and England international. One of the Czechoslovakian team was sent off for kicking a Belgian, prompting the whole team to walk off in protest and the match was abandoned. Belgium was awarded gold having completed just two matches. The Czechs were disqualified and Spain now had an unexpected place in a silver-bronze play-off against the Dutch. Four years later in Paris, the Belgians were dumped out of the Olympic tournament 8-1 in the second round by Sweden, in a match that included two hat-tricks. In 1928 in Amsterdam, Belgium endured another high-scoring second-round exit, this time to a strong Argentina side, 6-3. The Argentinians had raced into a 3-0 lead within the first ten minutes.

Despite a poor run in international tournaments since its home Olympics, the Belgian FA was one of just four European countries to send a team to the inaugural FIFA World Cup in Uruguay in 1930. The 16-man squad sailed for Montevideo under the leadership of Club Brugge (then called Royal FC Brugeois) player and coach, Hector Goetinck. Two Belgian officials also made the long trip to South America, Henri Christophe and John Langenus, who would referee the inaugural World Cup Final. The Belgians were pooled with the USA and Paraguay, with just one team progressing from the group to the semi-finals. In their first match against the Americans at Nacional's Estadio Gran Parque Central, the Belgians were stunned by the athletic American side. The USA led 2-0 at half-time with goals from McGhee and skipper Florie, before superstar Bert Patenaude bagged the third on 69 minutes; 3-0 was a disastrous start of the tournament for Belgium. Four days later, the USA beat Paraguay by the same margin, guaranteeing their passage to the semi-finals and meaning Belgium's match with Paraguay was a dead rubber. In the end, Paraguay won 1-0, meaning Belgium exited its first World Cup without even scoring a single goal.

## The Belgian pioneers today

At the time of writing, The Great Old is back in the top flight of Belgian football. The club won the last of its four

national championships in 1956/57 season, and has three
Belgian Cups in its trophy cabinet, most recently lifting the
cup in the 2019/20 season. Following the 1992 cup win,
Royal Antwerp went on a run to the European Cup Winners'
Cup Final at Wembley the following year, where it lost 3-1
to Parma. It was the last time a Belgian club appeared in a
European final to date, despite the rise and rise of the Belgian
national side to top the FIFA rankings. The Bosuilstadion
has been updated in recent years to accommodate the club's
ascent back to the top flight of Belgian football.

1   http://www.rafcmuseum.be/clubhistoriek/clubhist.php
2   https://www.scottishsporthistory.com/sports-history-news-and-blog/the-
    scot-who-made-belgium-world-champions-willie-maxwell

# 9.

# The Netherlands

IT WAS a freezing night in December. My mission was to show a Dutch friend and her cousin, Jeroen, the delights of London's pubs followed by their first-ever football match in England. The only fixture in London during their brief visit was Millwall versus Gillingham, hardly the big-ticket fixture they may have hoped for. The Dutch may speak perfect English, but they learned some choice new words that evening! As well as being a football coach back in the Netherlands, Jeroen was a former defender with FC Lisse, where he marked Patrick Kluivert in one match. He also played for the Netherlands' oldest football club, Koninklijke (Royal) Haarlemsche Football Club (HFC). On the first Saturday of each new year, HFC plays an exhibition match against a team of retired Dutch internationals. This tradition has run since 1923, interrupted only by extreme weather conditions, a fire in 1974 and the Second World War when Nazi Germany occupied the Netherlands. Jeroen had played for Koninklijke HFC for one season, including one of the testimonial matches.

'My opponents in that game were Ben Wijnstekers and Simon Tahamata,' Jeroen tells me.

Wijnstekers was a cultured right-back for Feyenoord in the late 70s and early 80s. As well as being among Feyenoord's highest appearance makers in the country's top flight – the Eridivisie – Wijnstekers was capped 36 times by the national team, the *Oranje* (Orange). Tahamata played with Ajax, Standard Liège and Feyenoord as a winger and won 22 Dutch caps. 'After the game there was a dinner with all the families and I had the privilege to sit at the table with Simon and his family,' Jeroen continues. 'He was a generous person who was really interested in my family and work.' Jeroen describes Koninklijke Haarlemsche Football Club as a special club. And it is.

## Football in the Netherlands

The Netherlands is one of the 'bridesmaids' of world football: three times losing finalists in World Cup finals and with just a solitary European Championship (1988) to its name, despite an almost endless conveyor belt of exceptional footballing talent coming through since the 1960s. But where did it all begin for Dutch football?

Football in the Netherlands owes its existence in large part to Willem J.H. 'Pim' Mulier. In 1870, Mulier was sent to join his elder brother at boarding school at the coastal village of Noordwijk. It was here that young Pim saw his first 'English-speaking Englishmen' playing cricket and football. When Mulier returned to his family in Haarlem in 1875 he struggled to describe to people the 'famous big ball' that he had seen and he couldn't get hold of one to demonstrate the game. Bert Vermeer sits on Koninklijke HFC's Archives Committee and has studied Mulier's own writing and other contemporary accounts of his life. 'Finally, he discovered in a shop window a ball, that he described as "brand new, bright yellow with an orange leather strap, a paradise on a string".

He bought it and subsequently went off with a couple of his friends, desperately looking for a place to play,' Vermeer tells me. 'Armed "with the ball, some wooden sticks and a plank" and a small green English booklet on the rules of the game, he took his friends to the surrounding pastures and an open space in Haarlem's local forest Haarlemmerhout.'

Four years later, in the winter of 1879/80, those same boys formed a football club: Haarlemsche – spelled in the old-fashioned Dutch way – Football Club. Mulier wrote to Haarlem's mayor to request the rent of a field. He signed the letter 'President of the HFC'. The local authorities finally designated a piece of grazing land by the self-explanatory name of *Koekamp* (Cow field) for Pim and his friends. The Koekamp was a piece of pasture with three large poplars in the centre where horses and cows were grazing. The boys were allowed to rent the place on condition that they would financially compensate the principal tenant for the abuse of the soil.

## Football comes of age in the Netherlands

Until 1883 the game that HFC played was a form of rugby, which at that time was a wild, disorganised fight between groups of boys over a ball. Many parents complained bitterly about the number of torn shirts. From 1883 onwards, HFC started playing according to English Football Association rules and in 1886 played its first competitive match at Koekamp against a team made up of nine Englishmen and one Dutchman from Amsterdam simply named 'Sport'. Sport won 5-3. While HFC was the original football club founded in the Netherlands, the very first competitive match on Dutch soil took place in the town of Enschede between Enschedese Football Club (EFC) and Lonneker on 6 September 1885. Jan Bernard van Heek, whose textile career had taken him to Burnley, England, where he had learned about football, initiated the match. Over the following years, HFC found a new pitch in the south of Haarlem.

In the first years, Mulier encountered resistance from high society and the authorities to his matches. But reflecting on those early days in 1919, Mulier explained that football's arrival in 1880 made young men feel free. As was to be the experience of the football pioneers in neighbouring Germany, leisure activities up to this point in the Netherlands included the passive pursuits of long hikes, gymnastics and reading. This more exhilarating pastime – football – seems to have been a welcome change and the club's membership multiplied. In the early years, sports like cricket and football were principally only accessible to young men of the higher ranks of society. Cricket predates football in the Netherlands by some years and, as elsewhere in the world, many football clubs would spring out of cricket clubs as a winter pursuit. Only from around 1910 onwards did participating actively in sports become more common in the other layers of Dutch society.

## Pim Mulier: football pioneer

As Mulier passed a couple of years at boarding schools in England, he learned how to organise sporting events. Later, Mulier emerged as a leading pioneer of sports in the Netherlands, where he not only introduced soccer, but also promoted sports like cricket, tennis, athletics, speed skating and long-distance skating. He promoted football in major cities like Amsterdam, Rotterdam and The Hague, but encountered only little interest in the beginning. But in the winter of 1880/81, a club was formed in Amsterdam, and in 1883, the football club Excelsior was founded in Haarlem. In 1884, Concordia was founded, followed by VVA in 1887, both in Amsterdam. Olympia of The Hague and a club in the town Wageningen were founded in 1886. In December 1887 HFC beat Olympia of Haarlem 5-0. In those days new football clubs sprung up suddenly and vanished even faster or merged, such as RAP of Amsterdam that was a combination of the Run, Amstels and Progress clubs.

In the first-ever Dutch football season, 1887/88, HFC played matches against VVA, RAP and Excelsior. In 1888/89 HFC, Concordia, VVA, HVV and RAP played inter-club matches in a mini competition. By 1889/90 the group was composed of HFC, RAP, HVV, Olympia and Concordia. After several attempts, Pim Mulier managed to convince ten other clubs of the need to create a national football association, which came to fruition on 8 December 1889. Of these 11 founder clubs, only three still exist – Mulier's HFC, HVV of The Hague and the Rotterdamsche Cricket en Football Club Olympia (1896). After a merger in 1904 with Volharding of Rotterdam (1895), the new entity became VOC (Volharding Olympia Combinatie). This organisation was the predecessor of the current KNVB (*Koninklijke Nederlandse Voetbal Bond*) – the Royal Dutch Football Association. The organisation did not start out with the regal title. That was bestowed upon the organisation by Queen Wilhelmina on the occasion of its 40th birthday in 1929. During this time, membership of the association had growth from 250 in 1889 to more than 65,000. HFC had to wait a further 30 years to receive its royal prefix from Dutch Queen Juliana on its 80th anniversary in 1959. The KNVB acknowledges 15 September 1879 as the official date of the foundation of HFC. Mulier's account of having been in Haarlem at that exact date has been questioned by Dutch football historians as he would have been at boarding school in eastern Holland at the time. No official document of

HFC's founding has ever been found. But even suggested alternative dates of 1882 or 1883 would not change the fact that Mulier's Haarlem-based organisation is the first and oldest football club in the Netherlands.

Vermeer points out that Daniel Rewijk, the Dutch author of Mulier's bibliography *Captain van Jong Holland* (Captain of Young Holland), does not give Mulier all the credit for being the founder of sports in the Netherlands. He refers specifically also to Frits van Tuyll van Serooskerken, who was more than ten years older than Mulier. In an article in the national daily *Nieuws van den Dag* of December 1878, van Tuyll complained that physical culture in the Netherlands confined oneself to dull indoor gymnastics. According to van Tuyll, sports were indispensable for every form of education. Rewijk underlines that there were more pioneers of sports than van Tuyll and Mulier alone. In 1887, Dutch sports paper *Nederlandsche Sport* translated some English footballing terms into Dutch, which helped the game to be better understood within the Netherlands.

## Sparta Rotterdam

In 1888, the first of the Netherlands' major clubs was formed. Sparta Rotterdam, based in the western Rotterdam suburb of Spangen, started life as a cricket club. It is the Netherlands' oldest professional football club; Dutch football did not turn professional until the 1950s with the launch of the Eredivisie league championship. By the 1890s, English teams began to tour. Harwich & Parkeston from the East Anglian coast had already played in the Low Countries, having beaten Antwerp in 1892. It makes sense for an English port connected to the Hook of Holland to establish footballing connections and competition between the two became an almost annual event. In 1893, the club sailed to Rotterdam to take on

Sparta, dispatching them 8-0. Another year later, the Essex team was back, but the margin of victory this time was just 1-0, although this was a 20 minutes-a-half match due to the English team arriving late in the fog. The Harwich side stayed in Rotterdam to play an All Rotterdam XI, which included seven Sparta players and the rest from Victoria. Despite the Dutch soup apparently disagreeing with them, the Harwich players composed themselves to win 5-2. Other teams came to the Netherlands in the 1890s, including Maidstone United, Felixstowe and the English Wanderers. Sparta joined the new league in the 1893/94 season and was the main club in Rotterdam until it was eclipsed by Feyenoord in the 1920s. Sparta's stadium, nicknamed 'Het Kasteel' (The Castle), was the Netherlands' first purpose-built football stadium when it was completed in 1916.

## Dutch football gets competitive

HFC won Mulier's pioneer league in 1890, 1893 and 1895, although these national titles are not recognised by the KNVB. Season 1897/98 was the launch date of the first 'official' championships, which saw play-offs between winners of regional leagues to establish a national champion. That season, the Dutch National Football Association met in The Hague and agreed to launch a knockout cup competition – now known as the KNVB Beker – based on the English FA Cup system. On 9 May 1899, RAP Amsterdam beat HVV Den Haag 1-0 in extra time to win the first edition.

In the first decade of the 20th century, the Football Association in London, driven by secretary Frederick Wall, was keen to sponsor evangelists of the game abroad. The Netherlands was a key target market, partly because of its proximity and also because, following the South African

War at the turn of the century, relations between Britain and the Netherlands were strained. Soccer ambassadors Corinthian FC won two games in The Hague in 1906, and Chelsea toured a year later. Bolton Wanderers – newly promoted champions of the Second Division – toured in 1909, winning five matches comfortably. The final game, a 10-1 win against FC Dordrecht, opened the door for Bolton player, Jimmy Hogan, to become coach of Dordrecht and, briefly, the Dutch national side. Hogan would go on to make his name in the Danubian football scene of Vienna and Budapest in the coming decade.

## The birth of the Dutch giants

Over a period of 13 years from the turn of the new century, the three modern giants of Dutch football – Ajax Amsterdam, Feyenoord of Rotterdam and PSV Eindhoven – were formed. Named after an ancient Greek warrior, Ajax was founded on 18 March 1900 after a short-lived FC Ajax had been founded six years earlier. The club spent its first decade in the second tier of Dutch football before reaching the top flight in 1911 under Irishman Jack Kirwan, for just three seasons before its first – and only – relegation. As an indicator of the quality of the Dutch game before the First World War, in 1913 Ajax even lost a friendly 3-1 at home to lower-league English amateurs, Tunbridge Wells FC.

On 8 July 1908, at the De Vereeniging café in Rotterdam, four young sportsmen formed the Wilhelmina club.[1] Four years later, the club settled on the name Rotterdamsche Voetbal Vereeniging Feijenoord (Rotterdam Football Club Feijenoord) and, after several kit changes, selected its now famous red and white shirts and black shorts. It was not until 1974 that the club changed its spelling to the current 'Feyenoord'. Based in the south of the city, Feyenoord quickly gained a reputation as the working-class football club at a time when Dutch football was still very much a gentleman's game. Dutch football journalist Jurryt van de Vooren tells me: 'When football started in the Netherlands, it was not played by the poor people, only by the rich, and they didn't allow poor people to become part of the club. The higher society would decide who could become members and, besides, the poor people didn't have time to play football as they were working.'

The third of the big three – Philips Sport Vereniging (Philips Sports Union) – was founded in Eindhoven on 31 August 1913 after a party marking the centenary of Dutch independence from Napoleonic France at the Philips electronics company. The roots of the club had been set in train three years earlier when a group of employees played within the grounds of the Philips village before the football team was absorbed into the wider PSV on 22 October 1913. It joined the Dutch league a year later and within a decade had made it into the first division, where it has stayed since 1926.[2] For its first 15 years, the club was only open to Philips employees but opened up to people without a connection to the company in 1928. 'Most of the southern clubs in the Netherlands after the First World War were members of the Catholic Football Association. Everything was in their own society, they were never meeting each other, so football helped break down barriers,' van de Vooren adds. Yet, PSV Eindhoven was something of a latecomer to the top table of Dutch football. Until the mid-1970s the club had only won four championships. It has won a further 20 since then – nearly half the championships played since 1975. The pinnacle came in 1988 with European Cup glory in Stuttgart against Benfica. HVV of The Hague (1878) claimed ten national titles in the years up to 1914, but they include the two championships in 1891 and 1896 that, according to the KNVB, are not official titles. The club wears one star on its shirts for having won ten national championships and is the only club outside the 'big three' to boast ten titles.

## Birth of the Oranje

The KNVB had been keen to internationalise football. As early as 1902, it had written to other national associations to arrange international fixtures and tournaments, and to ensure the consistency of rules across football-playing countries. Dutch efforts – spearheaded by the banker Carl Anton Wilhelm Hirschmann – helped lead to the foundations of FIFA in 1904 at a meeting that Hirschmann would attend. The Netherlands played its first game against neighbours Belgium in Antwerp on 30 April 1905 for a trophy – the *Coupe Vanden Abeele*. The cup, reminiscent of a bulbous vase, was named after Frédéric Vanden Abeele, who was the father of Beerschot Athletic Club's secretary. The cup ran for 14 editions until 1925. A five-member panel at the KNVB had picked the team. While the Belgians had won an unofficial 'Low Countries derby' 8-0 in 1901, the 1905 encounter at Beerschot's ground in Antwerp marked the first official match between the two neighbours. The Dutch ran out 4-1 victors. The Dutch had donned a white shirt for that inaugural match. Not until 1907 did the national side adopt orange, the colour of the Queen, for the first time. However, the Dutch royal family was not at all interested in football. Queen Wilhelmina did not attend a football match until 1916 – and then, quite by accident – when football was part of a wider sporting event at the national stadium.

The Dutch were keen participants in the early Olympic football competitions, taking part in all the European-based competitions held between 1908 and 1928. At London in

1908, the Netherlands' first international tournament, the team was coached by former Everton player, Edgar Chadwick. The first scheduled match at White City never happened. Opponents Hungary withdrew from the tournament due to domestic unrest in Bosnia, handing the Dutch a walkover. In the semi-finals, Henry Stapley scored all four of Great Britain's goals as the hosts comfortably condemned the Dutch to a bronze medal match witnessed by just 1,000 spectators. HVV Quick's Gerard Reeman and Edu Snethlage scored in the Netherlands' 2-0 victory over Sweden to secure the Netherlands' first international honours. Four years later in Stockholm, the Olympic football podium was exactly the same as at White City, with Great Britain – essentially an English amateur side – winning gold, Denmark silver and the Dutch again took bronze. Englishman Chadwick was still in charge, drawing players from 13 clubs – including Ajax – indicating how quickly the game was evolving and changing domestically in the Netherlands. The Dutch were drawn against hosts Sweden in the first round and surrendered a two-goal lead to draw 3-3. Utrecht's Jan Vos settled nerves in the first minute of extra time by notching what turned out to be the winner.

Then, during the First World War, football really took off in the Netherlands. 'There was a big social revolution at the start of the First World War,' Jurryt van de Vooren explains. 'Although the Netherlands was neutral, young men had to join the army in case of invasion. These young men would pass much of the time playing football – for many Dutch men this was the first time they had ever played football and they liked it, so after the war they started up their own clubs. It is during the First World War that we see football move from being the game solely of the rich towards becoming the national sport as it is now. We have never had a class war in Dutch society, but in football we have.' It was déjà vu for the Dutch in 1920 at the Antwerp Olympics as the team finished in third place once more. The country had remained neutral during the war that had just ravaged its neighbours and hosts to the south. The Netherlands opened its account with a comfortable 3-0 first-round win against Luxembourg at Union Saint-Gilloise's ground in Brussels. The opening goal was scored by Be Quick forward Jaap Bulder, whose brother Evart was on the bench. The Bulders were just one of many sets of brothers to represent the Netherlands at the highest level. The Dutch headed to Antwerp for the quarter-final showdown with Sweden, which was a lively 4-4 draw that took a strike five minutes from the end of extra time to resolve. The Netherlands lost comprehensively to Belgium in the semi-final and entered a silver and bronze medal play-off after the Czech team was disqualified for walking off the pitch in protest during the final. The Dutch lost that play-off to Spain, playing its inaugural tournament, with legendary striker Rafael Moreno Aranzadi – 'Pichichi' – scoring Spain's third in a 3-1 win.

In 1924 at Paris, the Dutch would again falter at the semi-final stage, but there would be no bronze this time as the Swedes reaped their revenge for defeat four years earlier. By 1928, it was Amsterdam's own turn to host the Olympics. It would prove to be the last Olympic football tournament before the launch of the FIFA World Cup in Uruguay in 1930. It was at the FIFA congress in Amsterdam on the eve of the Olympic tournament that Jules Rimet launched a vote on holding a World Cup tournament that would be free of the amateur restrictions of the Olympic tournament. This controversy over professionalism had seen the British Home Nations and the Danes refuse to participate in Olympic football competitions. For the first time at a tournament, the

Dutch squad would include players from the eventual big three, with representation from Ajax, Feyenoord and PSV. The Dutch would play the reigning champions Uruguay in the opening round, whom the Dutch had met in an ill-tempered semi-final in Paris four years earlier. Jurryt van de Vooren describes the mayhem as Dutch fans rushed for tickets. 'The Netherlands was drawn against Uruguay – the champions of 1924 – in a first-round knockout and everyone realised there would only be one match of the Dutch football team in their own Olympics. Only one pre-sell place was available and there were riots and there were thousands of people waiting for tickets; there were fights as drunk sailors came out of the pubs.' No one was killed but a number were hospitalised.

In the end, 27,730 fans would attend the match on the evening of 30 May 1928 and, indeed, the Dutch were eliminated by the eventual champions by two goals to nil; Scarone and Urdinaran with the goals. The referee was Belgian John Langenus, who would go on to officiate the inaugural World Cup Final two years later. With an established league and decent international standing, the Dutch lodged a bid to host the first FIFA World Cup, only to withdraw. The Dutch did not attend the 1930 tournament in Uruguay due to the expense and time required to sail to the River Plate.

## Koninklijke HFC today

In the early days of established competition, HFC flitted between the first and second divisions but the game itself was taking off, gaining sponsorship from Hak Holdert, later owner of the Dutch newspaper *De Telegraaf*, for a knockout tournament, the *Holdert Beker*, which was the predecessor of today's national cup. Although HFC never won the national championship title, it did win the *Holdert Beker* in 1904, 1913 and 1915. HFC reached the final in 1904 having beaten among others the Vlissingsche Voetbal Vereniging (VVV) 25-0. HFC's striker was Eddy Holdert, Hak's younger brother, who scored 13 goals. No player has ever scored so many goals in a Dutch cup match since. After just 30 years of existence, HFC became nicknamed 'The Good Old' – rather like Belgium's first club, the 'Great Old' Royal Antwerp. In the early years of glory when the first team played in the highest ranks of the amateur league, the abbreviation HFC attained a second meaning: *Hollands Fijnste Combinatie* (Holland's Finest Combination). Both nicknames are still in use, not only by the club but also by the national press. In May 1907, HFC hosted an international match between Holland and Belgium in front of 10,000 spectators. Belgium won 2-1. In the same month, HFC played a home game against Chelsea, losing 7-3, and hosted the Netherlands' 7-0 win over Belgium in 1910, attended by 11,000. This gives some indication of football's growing popularity in a society where other leisure pursuits, including cricket, rugby, tennis and a form of baseball called *kastie*, were prevalent.

HFC has had something of a turbulent ride throughout its history. The club almost folded as early as 1899 but was saved from liquidation by a single benefactor, Martinus 'Tinus' Loosjes. Arsonists irrevocably damaged the historic wooden grandstand and clubhouse in 1974. By 1986 the club was in the first class of the amateur regional subdivision – the Haarlemse Voetbal Bond (HVB) – the second class was the very lowest tier in the country at the time. Membership was alarmingly low, but the club managed to recover and climb the leagues. HFC played in the old top flight for the majority of seasons between 1888 and 1936. The club currently plays in the semi-professional third tier of Dutch football, the Tweede Divisie, and has an impressive youth academy, meaning its players attract the scouts of both the major clubs and amateur clubs alike.

1   https://www.feyenoord.com/the-club/about-feyenoord
2   https://www.psv.nl/english-psv/club/history-1/history.htm

# 10.

# Argentina

ON 13 May 1980 at Wembley Stadium, Diego Armando Maradona, the 20-year-old emerging starlet of the reigning world champions Argentina, swapped shirts with England striker Kevin Keegan. Keegan had scored the third of England's goals in a 3-1 win in an evenly balanced match. For a few brief moments, as he trudged off the Wembley pitch, exhausted and barely able to hide his disappointment, Diego Maradona is photographed in the iconic Admiral England shirt of the early 1980s. This photo was taken two years before the conflict between the UK and Argentina over the Falkland Islands – or Islas Malvinas for Argentinians – and six years before Maradona's infamous 'Hand of God' and sublime second goal helped knock England out of the Mexico 86 World Cup. I saw the image of Maradona in the England shirt on Instagram. Some of the comments in Spanish were, as you can imagine, interesting; the English are one of Argentina's bitterest footballing rivals. One popular chant to get people off their seats at Argentine football stadiums is *El que no salta es un inglés*, which loosely translates as 'If you're not jumping, you're English'. And yet, if it were not for the English initially and, later, one particular Scot, the game would not have arrived in the River Plate until a lot later than it did.

In the 19th century, when the British Empire was at its peak, Argentina – whose independence from Spain Britain had recognised in 1825 – was very much under British commercial influence. What Britain's opponents in Argentina called *El Pulpo Inglés* (the English Octopus) had its tentacles spread across the land: railways, mines, farms, telecommunications and other infrastructure. For its small population, the British community wielded extraordinary influence in helping Argentina become one of the world's richest countries before the First World War. Argentina is a melting pot in which the English speakers did very well. The Italians, famously, make up the bulk of the European diaspora in Argentina, along with the Spanish. Both were often driven to Argentina in the 19th century by poverty in their respective peninsulas. The Italians were so numerous that they defined both the accent and the language. Between 1880 and 1914 four million people arrived in Buenos Aires from around the world, each contributing to a new dialect, *Lunfardo*.

While the Italians and Spanish immigrants to Argentina often came from poverty, the Brits often came with money and ambition. They often took up residence in upmarket Belgrano or Palermo, and established the very Anglo district of Hurlingham. Harrods' only store outside London at that time opened in 1912 in Buenos Aires. Anglo-Argentines are now estimated to number around 100,000, still a small number in a population of 45 million.[1] The English-speaking population was large enough to justify its own English-language publications, including the *Buenos Aires Herald*, which ran presses for 140 years from 1876 until its closure in 2017. With these British immigrants came their sports – cricket, polo, hockey and the emerging football codes of the Association and Rugby rules. The British influence would decline, particularly after the First World War. By then, the game was already half a century old in Argentina, with an established league, club hierarchy and Football Association. By the 1920s, it would start to build its own powerful footballing brand outside South America.

## Football comes to Argentina

The *Asociación del Fútbol Argentino* (AFA), Argentine football's governing body, puts 1840 as the date when the game that would become the country's favourite sport entered Argentina. Armed with a cow's bladder for a ball, and stones to mark out the pitch, the English looked for ways to pass their spare time in their new life in the Americas.[2] A crude form of the kicking game had arrived in Argentina nearly a quarter of a century before formal codification back at the Freemasons' Tavern in London. Cricket was more widely played, not just in Argentina but throughout British communities in the Americas. The Buenos Aires Cricket Club (BACC) was formed as early as 1831.[3] And it was the Buenos Aires Cricket Club in Palermo that hosted the first Association rules football match on Argentine soil on 20 June 1867. The game was arranged by Yorkshire siblings and keen sportsmen, Thomas and James Hogg. Like Sheffield FC a decade before them, the two teams of eight players that took to the pitch for the 100-minute match were distinguished by the colour of their caps. The *Blancos* (Whites) beat the *Colorados* (Reds) 4-0.[4]

This match marks the real birthdate of not just Argentine soccer, but possibly of the whole sport in South America, although the British community that formed the Lima Cricket Club in Peru in 1859 may also have been practising a form of football from the outset. Yet, despite its showpiece debut, the game would not appeal to the mainstream population for more than a decade. While Thomas Hogg viewed football as the easiest and cheapest pastime for young people, the British community continued to keep the game within their exclusive clubs.[5] The Buenos Aires Football Club, founded by the Hogg brothers and fellow Britons Walter Heald, as secretary, Thomas Jackson and Thomas Barlow Smith, actually adopted the Rugby code until 1875, when it went back to Association rules. Many of the records from the Buenos Aires Cricket Club were destroyed in a fire in 1946. A small stone monument in what is now the Bosques de Palermo (Palermo Woods) urban park in Buenos Aires marks the significance of the venue as the location of the first cricket, rugby and football matches in Argentina. It reads: *Lugar Historico. Aquí se instaló el primer campo de deporte del Buenos Aires Cricket Club.* (Historic Site. Here stood the first sports field of Buenos Aires Cricket Club.) Nearby, the city's planetarium now stands. But Argentina's astronomical rise from park kickabout to world dominance was yet to begin.

## The father of Argentine football

As in England, Argentina's top schools would play a key role in the country's early football education. It all started with the St Andrews Scots School in Buenos Aires, who offered the Glaswegian teacher Alexander Watson Hutton a new start in the New World. He arrived in February 1882 and four years later his friend William Waters followed, bringing with him footballs and inflators, which caused confusion at customs.[6] Watson Hutton had worked as a teacher while completing his studies at Edinburgh University. In this same decade, the 'father of Spanish football', William Alexander Mackay, was also studying at Edinburgh University and was active in the Edinburgh University Association Football Club, founded in 1878. The Irish football pioneer John McAlery would also have visited Edinburgh around this time and caught the football bug. So, Watson Hutton will have been exposed to a strong footballing culture in Scotland which, as we have seen with Queen's Park, was very much based around an attractive passing game. Watson Hutton's start in life in Glasgow's Gorbals area had not been good. He had lost most of his family to ill health before he was ten and was taken in by the Daniel Stewart Hospital School. Perhaps because of his background, Watson Hutton believed that physical education should play a key role in all students' lives. Watson Hutton and St Andrews were quite soon at loggerheads on this topic. Feeling he was not getting the support he needed to expand the school's physical education programme, he left to set up his own academy – the English High School – all within two years of landing in the Argentine capital. We get some sense of Watson Hutton's determination as an educator and as an entrepreneur, because the English High School took off at an incredible pace, growing to more than 500 students in its first two years.[7]

By 1891, the first football championship was played in Buenos Aires. The initiative was driven by Scotsman Alec Lamont, a teacher at St Andrews.[8] It was the first league championship outside Britain or Ireland – just three years after the launch of the Football League – and ran between April and September. In the league system, the five teams played each other twice. Those teams were Old Caledonians, St Andrew's Athletic Club, Buenos Aires and Rosario Railway, Belgrano FC and Buenos Aires FC. Hurlingham FC withdrew. At the end of August, Old Caledonians and St Andrew's had tied at the top with six wins, a draw and a defeat each. In a play-off between the two, St Andrew's – captained by the aforementioned William Waters – triumphed 3-1, with a hat-trick from Charles Douglas Moffatt.[9] Yet the league was disbanded after just one edition.

In February 1893, Watson Hutton gathered together representatives from several clubs, among them Quilmes Atlético Club, Old Caledonians, St Andrew's, Lomas, Flores and, of course, his own English High School (later called Alumni Athletic Club), to found the Argentine Association Football League (AAFL) – reviving the same name as the previous attempt at a competition. The growing popularity of the sport was causing problems for the nascent league. Players were turning out for two clubs, creating conflicts of interest. The local *criollo* population was also starting to take an interest. Thomas Hogg's vision of a cheap and easy game for young people was soon flourishing in the *barrio*. These players from the slums were to bring their own interpretation to this foreign game and make it their own. In Argentina, this character is known as the *pibe de barrio*, the boy from the neighbourhood. The exact origins of the word *pibe* are disputed, but it could come from Italian regional dialects. The culmination of the mythical *pibe* was the Golden Boy himself – *el pibe de oro* – Diego Armando Maradona. The British also continued to form clubs that still exist. One such is Quilmes Atlético Club – founded in 1887 as Quilmes Rovers Athletic Club – which has a strong claim to be the *decano* (doyen) of Argentine football and is the only existing club to have joined the AAFL at its revival in 1893.[10]

In the northern city of Rosario, a new football culture was also emerging, with the British-owned Central Argentine Railway company launching its football club. That club, the Central Argentine Railway Athletic Club (CARAC) – now Club Atlético Rosario Central – played its first games in 1890 against a visiting British ship's crew.[11] In 1903, Club Atlético Newell's Old Boys was formed in Rosario. Isaac Newell had left Strood, Kent, England in 1869 as a 16-year-old and founded his own school – the *Colegio Comercial Anglicano Argentino* (the Anglican Argentine Commercial College) – in 1884. Football was part of the curriculum from the get-go. Isaac's son Claudio became director of the college in 1900. Three years later he founded the football club for current and former students. Newell's started off in the white and blue colours of the college but soon after migrated to red and black halves – the red for Isaac's native England and the black for his wife's homeland of Germany.[12] Both Newell's and Rosario Central would feature in the inaugural regional league – *La Liga Rosarina* – in 1905. During this campaign Newell's beat Rosario Central on its way to the title, marking the first encounter of what is now one of the world's fiercest rivalries. Newell's is where Lionel Messi, Gabriel Batistuta and Mauricio Pochettino all started their illustrious careers. There is even a campaign to have a statue of Isaac Newell put up in his hometown of Strood, Kent.

By the 1880s, the first *criollo* clubs began to emerge. On 3 June 1887, 50km south-east of the capital, Club de Gimnasia y Esgrima La Plata (Gymnastics and Fencing) was founded. The club is the oldest on the American continent that practises professional football, although it did not add football to the roster until the turn of the 20th century. Club Atlético River Plate was founded in May 1901 by a merger of two clubs, Santa Rosa and Las Rosales, in the Buenos Aires port *barrio* of La Boca. The club would later move out of the area, leaving it to its eventual bitter rivals, Boca Juniors. In 1905, Genoese immigrants in La Boca founded Boca Juniors – still known as *Los Xeneizes* (The Genoese). According to legend, the founders chose its iconic blue and yellow kit after agreeing to take the colours of the flag flying from the next ship to sail into port. That ship came from Sweden. Boca Juniors versus River Plate – *el Superclásico* – is now arguably the fiercest rivalry in world club football.

As the *criollo* population took to the round-ball game with gusto, so the British communities in Argentina retreated inwards. It would be the local professional middle classes, not the British communities, that would advance the sport in South America. Yet it would still need the injection of British clubs to fire up the imagination. In June 1904, Southampton FC was the first British team to visit the River Plate, sending a 13-man squad on a nine-week tour. Saints won all six games handsomely, beating the leading club of the time, Watson Hutton's Alumni, 3-0. They then beat a British Players XI 10-0, Belgrano AC 6-1, an Argentina Select side 8-0 and a Liga Argentina XI 5-3. In their one match in Montevideo, the Saints beat the Liga Uruguaya XI 8-1.[13] Nottingham Forest followed a year later, playing one match in Rosario against a combined Rosario team – and winning 5-0 – before heading to Buenos Aires. In the capital, Forest won by margins of 7-0, 13-1, 9-0 and a couple of 6-0s for good measure. One of those six-goal victories was against Alumni. In attendance that day was Arístides Langone, president of the recently formed Club Atlético Independiente. Langone suggested that the club switch from white and blue to the red of Forest.[14]

In the first decade of the new century, competition would hot up between Argentine clubs and those across the River Plate, as we will explore further in our Uruguay chapter. Both Everton and Tottenham Hotspur toured in June 1909, with only the combined Liga Uruguaya team in Montevideo giving Everton a close game. By the time Southern League

Division One side Swindon Town visited in June 1912, the gap had closed between the Argentinians and the English visitors. Swindon Town won five and drew two of its games in Argentina. It was not until Exeter City's tour of 1914 that an Argentinian team would defeat a team from England for the first time, when a select team of players drawn from the north of Argentina beat the Devonians 1-0 in Buenos Aires. It appears the press back home in Devon could not quite believe the result. *Exeter and Plymouth Gazette* reported that it had received a cable that the team had arrived safely and that, owing to the absence of punctuation marks, it was hard to interpret the cablegram. They were of 'the general opinion that Exeter City have been successful'.[15] Exeter City did indeed win all but one of its remaining seven matches in Argentina.

## Argentina takes on the world

By 1912, the Argentine FA had become the first on the South American continent to be affiliated with FIFA. In 1916 Argentina hosted the first international football tournament outside of the British Home Championship. The *Campeonato Sudamericano* (South American Championship of Nations) – now known as the *Copa América* – was timed to coincide with Argentina's independence centenary celebrations. It would include Argentina, Uruguay, Brazil and Chile in a round-robin tournament, with teams awarded two points for a win, one for a draw and none for a defeat. The tournament also saw the founding of the *Confederación Sudamericana de Fútbol* (the South American Football Confederation – CONMEBOL). The Argentine team featured players from the Buenos Aires and La Plata area, plus two from Rosario Central. The spine was based on players from Racing Club, which was in the middle of a historic run that delivered seven titles in seven years. Argentina thrashed Chile 6-1 in its opening match with two goals apiece for Racing Club stars Alberto Ohaco and Alberto Marcovecchio, and Quilmes's Juan Domingo Brown. Four days later, Argentina drew with Brazil to tee up a decider with Uruguay. The first attempt to stage the match at Gimnasia y Esgrima (of Buenos Aires) was called off after just five minutes due to dangerous overcrowding in the stands. Some fans were so incensed by the decision that they started fires in the ground. The two sides met the next day at Racing Club's ground instead and fought out a disappointing goalless draw, meaning Uruguay secured the point it needed to top the table.[16] Uruguay took home the trophy, beginning a decade and a half of footballing dominance.

Argentina would have to wait until 1921 to host the rotating tournament again, and this time the team would lift the trophy, as it would once more in 1925. Domestically, the game was on the up. Visiting team Plymouth Argyle of the English Division Three (South) lost three matches in 1924, twice to a national side and once to a Rosario select side. Boca Juniors held Argyle to a goalless draw. A month before the Argentinians were entertaining Plymouth Argyle, fierce rivals Uruguay were away at the Olympics in Paris. There, they dazzled the world with their brand of football and brought home the gold medal to a hero's reception at Montevideo docks. Argentina had not entered a side.

Uruguay's success at the 1924 Olympics spurred the Argentines to challenge their neighbours to a two-legged competition to prove who really was the better of the two sides. After a 1-1 draw in Montevideo, the first attempt at a second leg had to be abandoned after home fans once again overspilled on to the pitch and threatened the safety of the players. More than 30,000 spectators crammed into the Sportivo Barracas stadium a few days later on 1 October and after just a quarter of an hour were treated to a moment of history. Huracán's Cesáreo Onzari swung in the ball from a corner which no one touched before it crossed the line. Under new rules, this goal stood. The Uruguayans were incensed in what was already a tense match. There was a repeat of crowd trouble as stones flew through the air. Onzari's *gol olimpico* (Olympic goal) entered Argentine football folklore and lexicon for a goal scored direct from a corner. Although the Argentines won that match 2-1 and the two-match series 3-2, the challenge was to repeat it on the world stage. The following year, Boca Juniors toured Spain and Germany, finishing with a single match in Paris. The tourists would show the strength of the *Porteño* game with 15 wins, one draw and just three defeats, to Celta Vigo, Real Unión and Athletic Club de Bilbao.

The Amsterdam Olympics of 1928 presented the opportunity for Argentina to make up for missing out in 1924. The *Albiceleste* signalled their intent early on with an 11-2 demolition of the United States in round one. Boca Juniors' Domingo Tarasconi notched four goals, and team-mate Roberto Cerro claimed a hat-trick of his own. In the second round, Tarasconi bagged four for a second time in Argentina's 6-3 defeat of Belgium. In the semi-finals, he bagged another hat-trick as Argentina hit Egypt for six without reply. Argentina had strolled to the final. Uruguay awaited them in the final in front of 28,000 at the Olympic Stadium in Amsterdam. The match ended in a draw, Nacional striker Pedro Petrone giving Uruguay the lead on 23 minutes before Estudiantes's Manuel Ferreira levelled just after the break. The replay had also been tight, with Uruguay taking an early lead only for future World Cup winner with Italy, Luis Monti, to level for Argentina. The legendary Héctor Scarone netted for Uruguay, and once again the *Celeste* would head back to Montevideo with the gold medal and title of unofficial World Champions.

While Argentina's best 22 players were winning silver in Amsterdam, Scottish side Motherwell was touring South America, losing its first three games in Buenos Aires. Motherwell drew crowds of 40,000-plus but disappointed early on. Having witnessed Spurs, Exeter City, Swindon Town and now Motherwell play in Argentina, an Anglo-Argentine wrote into *Athletic News* to complain about the visitors' 'monotonous' style of play. Rather than teach the local amateurs how to play, 'it seems the other way around', despite the best Argentine and Uruguayan players being away at the Olympics.[17] The experience of Motherwell, from the homeland of Watson Hutton and the Scotch Professors, was indicative of the changing of the guard. The South Americans had taken the British game and put their own definitive stamp on it. Motherwell did win its next five before Boca Juniors sent the Scots off with a 2-0 defeat. The following year, Chelsea lost six of its 11 games in Argentina, including a 5-0 reverse to Unión Santa Fe. The English language *Buenos Aires Herald* wrote a scathing piece under the title 'Farcical Football Tours' and a reader lambasted Chelsea's 'dreary Odyssey'.[18] Chelsea was the last British club to tour. Argentina no longer needed the sport's evangelists. It was already poised to overtake the British game. By now, Argentinian players were attracted to Europe's newly professional leagues. Julio Libonatti of Newell's Old Boys was the first to go in 1925. On signing for Torino, he became the first recorded transatlantic football transfer. Independiente's Raimundo Orsi would also head to Turin in 1928, joining Juventus. Here, he would win five straight *scudetti* (Series A titles) and the World Cup as an Italy player in 1934, one of many *oriundi* – a player of Italian descent born outside Italy but selected to play in the Italian league or for its national side, the *Azzurri*.

Argentina once again won the South American Championship on its home rotation in 1929, but a bigger prize was now on offer – the first FIFA World Cup. Uruguay was awarded the right to host the tournament by FIFA, partly due to its recent successes on the Olympic stage but also to coincide with its centenary of independence. The small country of just two million inhabitants also offered to pay for passage and board for all competing teams. Seeded in Group 1 alongside Chile, France and Mexico – the only four-team group – the Argentinians faced the French first at the Estadio Parque Central in Montevideo. The future *oriundo* Luis Monti scored the only goal in an ill-tempered affair, scoring direct from a free kick 20 metres out with nine minutes remaining. The referee blew for full time with France's Marcel Langiller bearing down on goal for what might have been the equaliser. This decision sparked chaotic scenes as the Argentinian fans invaded the pitch and the French players surrounded the Brazilian referee, Almeida Rêgo. Argentina threatened to withdraw from the tournament unless the result stood. The Uruguayan team were quick into the psychological games, declaring that France deserved to win. Argentina moved on to the just-completed Estadio Centenario to thrash Mexico 6-3 in front of 42,000 spectators. The hero was Huracán striker Guillermo Stábile, who bagged a hat-trick and would go on to be the tournament's top scorer. His performance in Uruguay earned him a move to Italy with Genoa, where he scored a hat-trick on debut against Bologna. With only the group winners progressing to the semi-finals, Argentina's match with familiar neighbours Chile became a winner-takes-all match. The Chileans had beaten Mexico and

France without conceding. Stábile notched two goals in a minute before the quarter-hour mark in a match marred by brawls. Argentina eventually won 3-1 to meet the USA at the Centenario on 26 July. In front of 73,000 fans, Argentina transformed a 1-0 half-time lead – courtesy of Monti – into a final score of 6-1, with two more for Stábile.

The final created a fever across the River Plate. Thousands of Argentines hoped to sail to Montevideo and supply could not meet demand. Those lucky enough to secure a ticket on a ship enjoyed a noisy send-off from well-wishers on the Buenos Aires dockside. On arrival in the port of Montevideo, fans were checked for weapons. A crowd rumoured to be 80,000 strong got into the Centenario, despite the official attendance of 68,346.[19] Belgian referee John Langenus demanded guarantees for the safety of match officials, while each team insisted on using a ball made in their country. A compromise was struck, and a ball from each country was used in either half. Despite missing Orsi and with Monti not fully himself after receiving death threats, Argentina went into the break 2-1 up. The hosts then drew level just before the hour mark with a great run from Pedro Cea, the tournament's second-top scorer, and added two more before the end. Both teams 'won' the half in which they used their domestic-made ball. Back in Argentina, fans awaiting the final result outside the *La Crítica* newspaper offices went on the warpath, stoning Uruguayan fans and societies, and even the Uruguayan Consulate. Shots were heard, and police eventually dispersed the crowds.[20]

Esteban Bekerman is a football historian and journalist based in Buenos Aires. Bekerman tells me that the early encounters between Argentine and Uruguayan teams were critical to generating public interest in football in the first decades of the 20th century. 'Competition between

Argentina and Uruguay drove interest in the sport on both sides of the River Plate, certainly until the 1930s,' he says. 'Since the peak of the rivalry in the 1920s and early 1930s, Uruguay was eclipsed as Argentina's chief opponent by the rise of Brazil as a footballing power. Argentina versus Brazil is now the biggest international rivalry in South America.'

## The Argentine pioneers today

While Argentina may have established the first league outside of Britain or Ireland, the country would have to wait until 1931 to have an established professional league. The familiar debates around professionalism that grasped the growing game in every country raised their heads in Argentina, until a meeting on 10 May 1931 involving representatives of leading clubs paved the way for the creation of an 18-team professional championship.

Argentina's first football-playing club, the Hogg brothers' Buenos Aires Football Club, who played Argentina's first match in June 1867, folded in 1881. The stone marking the location of their first match at Palermo stands testament to their legacy, but far more fitting is that Argentina took to the game and gave the sport some of its best players and moments. Watson Hutton's Buenos Aires English High School side – later the Alumni Athletic Club – won ten national titles before folding in 1913 after Watson Hutton retired. Neighbourhood rivals Belgrano Athletic Club won three titles and delivered River Plate its worst defeat in its history – 10-1 – before migrating away from football after the First World War. Likewise, Lomas Athletic migrated to rugby, as did Flores Athletic Club before it folded in 1907. Quilmes – founded in 1887 – is the oldest club still active in senior tournaments, and at the time of writing resided in Argentina's second division, the Primera B Nacional.

While the English-speaking community may have lost influence since the Second World War, descendants of the old country still crop up from time to time; players such as Carlos Babington, *el inglés* of the Huracán club that represented Argentina at the 1974 World Cup. Or José Luis Brown – descended of Scotsman James Brown from Greenock – who headed the opening goal of the 1986 World Cup Final. Or even the red-headed Carlos MacAllister of Boca Juniors, of Irish and Scottish descent, who was capped three times at left-back for Argentina in the 1990s. Alexander Watson Hutton died aged 82 in 1936. His grave at the Chacarita cemetery in Buenos Aires often receives grateful football pilgrims.

1  https://www.historytoday.com/britain-and-argentinas-shared-history

2  https://www.afa.com.ar/es/pages/historia

3  http://www.bacrc.com/historia.php

4  Campomar, Andreas, *¡Golazo! A History of Latin American Football* (London: Quercus, 2014)

5  https://www.afa.com.ar/es/pages/historia

6  Wilson, Jonathan, *Angels with Dirty Faces: The Footballing History of Argentina* (London: W&N, 2017, p6)

7  https://www.scotsman.com/sport/argentine-football-returns-to-roots-of-its-scottish-founder-1-1146916

8  Ibid.

9  http://www.rsssf.com/tablesa/arg1891.html

10  http://quilmesaclub.org.ar/institucion/historia

11  http://www.rosariocentral.com/institucional/nuestros-origenes/

12  https://www.fifa.com/news/newell-argentinian-hotbed-1023264

13  http://www.rsssf.com/tablesb/brit-ier-tours-prewwii.html#s

14  https://www.ole.com.ar/independiente/independiente-nottingham-forest-unidos-siempre_0_BkmlCVNxs3l.html

15  *Exeter and Plymouth Gazette*, 17 June 1914 (p5)

16  Wilson, Jonathan, *Angels with Dirty Faces* (London: W&N, 2017, p16)

17  *Athletic News*, 18 June 1928 (p10)

18  *Buenos Aires Herald* referenced in *Athletic News*, 5 August 1929 (p10)

19  Wilson, Jonathan, *Angels with Dirty Faces* (London: W&N, 2017, p42)

20  *Evening Herald (Dublin)*, 31 July 1930 (p1)

# 11.

# Uruguay

GIVEN ITS tiny size on the global stage – just 3.4 million inhabitants spread over 176,000km² – the Oriental Republic of Uruguay has punched above its weight arguably more than any other country in world football. South America's second-smallest country (after Suriname) was the first FIFA World Cup host nation – and first world champion. The Estadio Centenario in Montevideo was built in 1930 especially for that tournament and also to mark the centenary of Uruguay's constitution. Immigrant labour toiled over nine months to get it ready just in time. Jules Rimet himself referred to the structure as a 'temple to football'.[1]

When I went to Montevideo at the turn of the 21st century, I got a great sense of its faded glory. With its Spanish colonial architecture in desperate need of a lick of paint, it had the feel of Havana about it. Down on the docks, huge slabs of meat are grilled on the *parrilla* and tossed by burly men, barbecue smoke drifting out on the stiff breeze. I pounded up the blocks to the Parque Batlle and the Estadio Centenario for a Copa Mercosur match in 2000. The Copa Mercosur was a short-lived tournament that ran from 1998 to 2001 before being wrapped together with the

Copa Merconorte to create the Copa Sudamericana. On this cold night, Nacional – one of Uruguay's traditional duopoly along with Peñarol – drew 1-1 with Corinthians of Brazil. I sat beneath the Centenario's imposing art deco tower, which reminded me a lot of Fiorentina's Stadio Artemio Franchi. Looking around at the sparse ground, barely a quarter full, it was hard to gauge the significance of this venue. History is made here – Copa America finals, Copa Libertadores matches and even domestic *Clásico* derbies between Nacional and Peñarol – the oldest cross-city derby outside the UK. And, of course, the very first World Cup Final.

FIFA had decided at its 1920 convention, timed to coincide with the Antwerp Olympic Games, that an international football tournament could no longer be confined to solely the Olympics. It needed its own dedicated competition, especially because teams could not send their best players who, by now, were often professional when the Olympics demanded amateurism. Uruguay had surprised everyone by winning the gold medal at Paris 1924 with some scintillating play. It successfully defended the title in Amsterdam in 1928. FIFA's Jules Rimet and Henri Delaunay would have their way – there was to be a World Cup, and Uruguay was selected to host the first tournament in 1930. The four other contenders to host the first World Cup were all European: the Netherlands, Italy, Sweden and Spain. In part due to their non-selection, and also the daunting three-week journey to the South Atlantic, the four countries refused to travel, as did the other major European powers and the British associations. Eventually, Belgium, Yugoslavia and Romania – whose team was picked by King Carol himself – made the trip from Europe, as did FIFA president Jules Rimet's home nation, France. The original World Cup trophy was, of course, named after him.

In the 1930 final, Uruguay triumphed against Argentina as it had in the Olympics two years earlier to successfully defend its 1924 gold medal. This was just the latest chapter in an international footballing rivalry that is older than any other outside Britain and Ireland. In a letter to *Athletic News* in September 1930, James Iceton, assistant auditor of the Buenos Aires and Pacific Railway, chastised England for not taking part in the World Cup and proving its assumed superiority on the pitch. Iceton laments the Football Association's reluctance to acknowledge the footballing supremacy of the River Plate countries or even play them. Iceton asks when the Home Nations will 'come down from their pedestal into the field of play and find out just where the Old Country stands amongst these lusty infants to whom she taught the game?'[2] England did not play Argentina until 1951, at Wembley, and Uruguay until 1953. England would not enter a FIFA tournament until 1950 in Brazil. The country's second match was a humiliating 1-0 defeat to the USA in Belo Horizonte, the rudest possible awakening for a team featuring Stanley Matthews, Jackie Milburn, Tom Finney, Billy Wright and Wilf Mannion. Scotland refused to travel to the 1950 World Cup, despite qualifying via the British Home Championship, as it had finished second to England. In that 1950 tournament, tiny Uruguay – perennial spoilers to this day – sent Brazil into mourning in their own World Cup Final.

In recent decades, Uruguay has acquired something of a reputation. My first introduction to Uruguay was watching *La Celeste* – the Sky Blues – take on Scotland in the Mexico 86 World Cup. Infamously, Scottish midfielder Gordon Strachan was floored in the first minute by José Batista, who was red-carded after just 56 seconds – a World Cup record. Uruguay continued to play dirty, held on for a goalless draw and went through, while Scotland went home. Fast-forward to South Africa in 2010, when Luis Suárez handled on the line to deny Ghana a well-earned place in the World Cup semi-final. Ghana would have been the first African side to have achieved a semi-final berth, and on African soil too. Uruguay finds a way to win. The Uruguayans call this spirit *la garra charrúa* (the Charrúa claw), named after the indigenous tribes who were massacred by European colonisers in the 19th century. It is meant to symbolise a fighting spirit inside every Uruguayan who never knows when they are beaten, to overcome odds by any means necessary. It helps explain why this tiny country has achieved so much on the international football stage.

## The birth of Uruguayan football

As was so often the case, it was British financial interests that brought an expat community firstly, followed swiftly by its sporting establishments. Uruguay was a small but attractive investment proposition, especially for farming produce. By 1914, when the First World War broke out, Britain had more than £46 million invested in Uruguay. Almost all the country's foreign debt was held in London and British companies owned and operated the entire railway system. British companies also ran utilities in Montevideo and dominated imports.[3]

Montevideo Cricket Club was founded in 1861, becoming a multisport club. The Twickenham Museum of Rugby recognises Montevideo Cricket Club as the world's eighth-oldest rugby club.[4] The first Association rules football match recorded was contested in 1881 between the Montevideo Cricket Club and Montevideo Rowing Club, which had been founded in 1874.

But the first club established with sole intention of playing football was the Albion Football Club, set up in the

May of 1891 by Henry Lichtenberger and fellow students at the English High School in Montevideo. It was originally called 'Football Association' and played its first match against Montevideo Cricket Club on 2 August 1891, losing 3-1.[5] Football Association soon became Albion FC and adopted red, white and blue in tribute to the mother country of many of the players. *Albion* is the Greek-Latin word for England or Britain. One Albion FC player in particular, William Leslie Poole, a British teacher at the English High School, is considered the 'father of Uruguayan football'. Poole, a former student at the University of Cambridge, is credited with opening the game up outside the Anglo-Uruguayan community into the wider population. Something of a footballing polymath, Poole was a player, organiser and referee. He was influential in establishing the Uruguayan Association Football League on 30 March 1900, now Uruguayan football's governing body, the *Asociación Uruguaya de Fútbol* (AUF). Poole has a public space dedicated to his honour at a major junction in Montevideo, near the AUF headquarters. It is a humble cordoned-off tree with benches in the middle of a busy thoroughfare, but it recognises his contribution to the adoption and growth of Uruguay's national game.

Juan Carlos Luzuriaga is a Uruguayan historian. For him, it was Lichtenberger who was the more influential of the two football pioneers and was instrumental in the foundation of the Uruguayan league. 'It was he who had the dream of a club dedicated principally to football, and he made it happen on 1 June 1891 with Albion,' he tells me. 'Let's remember that the previous clubs were dedicated to other sports.' Along with Albion FC, the founder member clubs of the Uruguayan Association Football League included Deutscher Fussball Klub, Uruguay Athletic Club and the Central Uruguay Railway Cricket Club (CURCC). It was CURCC's Percy Davidson Chater – originally from Beckenham, in Kent, England – who was the Uruguayan Association Football League's first president. Poole would later succeed him. CURCC was formed on 28 September 1891 in the northern Montevideo suburb of Peñarol. Its 118 founding members included 45 local-born *criollos*, 72 Britons and one German.[6] Within a year of its foundation, CURCC had added Association football to its repertoire of cricket and rugby at the instigation of the engineer John Woosey. As a nod to railway heritage, the club opted for black and yellow as its colours to replicate Stephenson's Rocket, the steam locomotive, and the wider railway guild. Early shirts included black and yellow quarters, then halves, before settling on stripes from 1910 onwards.

CURCC's first Association football match was against a team from the English High School, with the railwaymen winning 2-0. An inclusive club from the off, by 1895 CURCC had a Uruguayan captain in Julio Negrón. The railway team kicked off the first Uruguayan league with a 2-1 win over Albion FC, and went on to win that title, defending it in 1901, then winning again in 1905 and 1907. By 1914 the football section had broken away completely from the CURCC and took its place in the Uruguayan Football League under the name Club Atlético Peñarol. It is now one of South America's most successful clubs, with five Copa Libertadores and three Intercontinental Cups.

Much like its neighbour Argentina across the River Plate, Uruguay had been attracting large numbers of economic migrants from Spain and Italy during the 19th century, which far outnumbered the British and German industrial classes. While the founding four members of the Uruguayan Association Football League were all formed by foreign-born or second-generation British and German immigrants to Uruguay, on 14 May 1899, the first *criollo*-founded club in Latin America was founded at the home of Dr Ernesto Caprario. Members and players were drawn from the Uruguay Athletic Club and Montevideo Football Club to create Club Nacional de Football. It is the third-oldest club still in existence in Uruguay after Albion FC and Peñarol. As with other rivalries in world football, one side is perceived as authentically local and the other as an immigrant club. In Uruguay, Nacional fans see themselves as the Uruguayan side and Peñarol as the outsider club. Nacional even produced the world's first superfan – Miguel Prudencio Reyes Viola. Reyes was a leather worker whose job at Nacional in 1900 was to inflate the English-made match balls. He was known as *el hinchador* – the puffer. In the austere, polite, British-run league, Reyes broke the silence with his enthusiastic cries of *¡Arriba Nacional!*.[7] As 'the puffer', he earned the nickname *hincha*, which is now the common term for football fans in the Spanish language.

By now it was clear that – as across the River Plate in Argentina – *criollo* Uruguayans were taking the game to their hearts and creating their own unique style of play. How did the *criollo* population get into football? Why wasn't it viewed like many of the other 'exclusive' British sports, like rugby, cricket and rowing? According to Luzuriaga, interest among the *criollo* population and new immigrants to Uruguay – mostly from Spain and Italy – really picked up after 1895. 'Uruguay, like Argentina and other Latin American countries at this time, was looking to affirm its national identity,' Luzuriaga explains. 'They were nationalists as there were in other contemporary European countries, like in the 1870 unification of Germany or Italy, for example.' This affirmation of nationhood needed to include immigrants and their children, which in 1880 was particularly strong. The *criollos* started to show a keen interest in football and began to participate in the mid-to-late 1890s. This movement naturally included the young Italians and Spaniards, who Luzuriaga says for cultural reasons were much more closely aligned to the *criollo* population than the British. 'At first, the *criollos* looked with curiosity upon the *ingleses locos* (crazy English), but later went on to understand the game and participate,' Luzuriaga says. 'They admired clubs like Albion and CURCC, but by 1898/99 the criollos had created tens of clubs and teams following the example of the British that they admired.' Some of these clubs even had English names, like London or Britannia, Luzuriaga told me. But there were other *criollos* who went the other way to confront the *maestros* and the Anglo-Saxon culture. By 1899, all clubs – including CURCC – contained players with Italian or Spanish names. The game was now embedded in the *criollo* culture, culminating in the formation of not only Nacional.

Between 1896 and 1899, Albion was the key player in Uruguay's fledgling league and association. Notes exist of regulations that were 'supervised by Albion FC'. In 1896, Albion tested its mettle against Argentine opposition with a tour of Buenos Aires, winning against Retiro 4-1 and beating a strong Belgrano side 5-3, becoming the first Uruguayan team to win abroad. In 1899, Albion was the first club in Uruguay to build a stadium purely to host football matches, in the suburb of Prado de Montevideo. This ground could hold 1,000 spectators. By the turn of the century, however, with increased competition, Albion found it harder to retain players. Those who couldn't find first-team opportunities took their boots elsewhere and even formed other clubs. A lack of opportunity at Albion was the driver for Ernest Caprario, Carlos Carve Urioste and Domingo Prat to found

Uruguay Athletic, later part of Nacional, in 1898, and others who left to found Montevideo Wanderers in 1902.

The game continued to grow in strength. CURCC won the first two editions of the national championship, launched in 1900. Nacional, Montevideo Wanderers and River Plate FC – not to be confused with its Argentinian namesake – also won titles in the first decade. A useful test as to the level of the Uruguay standard came in July 1904 when Southampton FC docked after a victorious five-match winning streak in Buenos Aires. The Saints dispatched a Liga Uruguaya XI 8-1. In 1909, Albion's directors withdrew the club from the football league that Lichtenberger himself had founded and – until the 1960s – played in the University League. Across town, Club Atlético Peñarol moved into a new stadium at Las Acacias in 1914. Football was already huge among the local population before 5 March 1918, when 25-year-old Nacional player Abdón Porte – apparently distraught at his loss in form and subsequent dropping from the team – took a tram to the club's ground at the Estadio Gran Parque Central and shot himself dead in the centre circle. The event has taken on mythical status in Uruguay where, by 1918, the country had already picked up plenty of international silverware.

## The River Plate rivalry

As both Uruguay and Argentina were among the early adopters of football at a domestic level, it's only natural that they became the oldest international rivals outside of the British Home Championship competition, which featured England, Scotland, Wales and – at this time – the whole of Ireland. By 1901 an Argentine team, made up predominantly from players of the Lomas and Alumni clubs, travelled to Montevideo and beat the Uruguayan team 3-2, with

Uruguay returning the compliment by the same scoreline a year later in Buenos Aires.

So popular was the fixture that by 1905 the tea merchant Sir Thomas Lipton had donated a trophy for the two nations to contest. The *Copa de Caridad Lipton* (the Lipton Charity Cup) was reminiscent of the current FIFA World Cup trophy. Three long-shorted footballers stand on a plinth bearing the arms of both countries and hold a large ball above their heads. Atop the ball, an angel stands, arms aloft, holding a wreath. The cup was crafted by Messrs Elkington and Co. of Regent Street, London. It was to be contested annually by sides representing Argentina and Uruguay, with the proceeds going to charity. Thomas Johnstone Lipton was a self-made man, born in a Glasgow tenement in 1848 not far from Argentina's football pioneer, Alexander Watson Hutton. Lipton's parents had fled Ireland at the height of the famine in 1845. Lipton donated the trophy on the condition that teams were made of River Plate-born players. The *Copa de Caridad Lipton* is the oldest existing trophy in international football and is exhibited at the AFA headquarters in Buenos Aires. Sports enthusiast Lipton also established a trophy for yachting, and played a significant role in developing Italian football. Other tournaments in the opening decades of the 20th century between the two River Plate countries included the *Copa Newton*, *Copa Tie* and *Copa de Honor Cousenier*.

The *Copa Newton* team line-ups from 1911 in Montevideo makes interesting reading and contrasts the differences in the game's development either side of the River Plate. The visiting team is predominantly Anglo-Argentine – Wilson, Yates, Dickinson, Hayes and four members of the Brown family, while Uruguay is entirely made up of Italian and Iberian names. The cross-River

Plate tournaments spurred interest from Uruguay and Argentina's neighbours, Brazil and Chile, where the game had already caught on, to create an expanded tournament. The tournament that would later become the *Copa América* was born. There had been international tournaments before the 1916 *Campeonato Sudamericano de Football*. To commemorate the centenary of the May Revolution, Argentina had hosted a tri-nations series with Uruguay and Chile in 1910. But it's the 1916 edition, held between 2 and 17 July in Buenos Aires, that is the first truly continental football championship. The South American Football Confederation – CONMEBOL – was also founded during the championship at the behest of AUF board member, Héctor Rivadavia. The tournament featured a round-robin format, with Uruguay topping the table after trouncing Chile 4-0 in the opening match. In another pioneering first from Uruguay, two of its players in the match were black, making Uruguay the only national side in South America at that time to field black players. Isabelino Gradín and Juan Delgado were both descendants of African slaves forcibly brought to South America. Gradín had scored two of *La Celeste*'s goals that day, prompting the Chilean delegation to insist that the game be scratched because Uruguay had two 'Africans' in its line-up.[8] Gradín would go ahead and score in Uruguay's next match, versus Brazil, a country also resistant to promoting its own black players at the time. The 2-1 victory, together with Argentina dropping points in a draw with the Brazilians, meant *La Celeste* just needed to draw against Argentina to win the inaugural tournament. The match, played at Racing Club's Avellaneda ground, ended goalless and Uruguay began a decade and a half of dominance over its larger southern neighbour.

While the First World War had put a stop to football in Europe, in South America, it was flourishing. Uruguay would host and win the 1917 edition of the new continental championship. Despite a break for the Spanish flu outbreak in 1918, Brazil hosted and won the 1919 tournament – the first of plenty of silverware heading its way in future years. By 1921, the Paraguayans had joined. Paraguay's first club, Club Olimpia from the capital Asunción, was founded by Dutch immigrant William Paats in 1902. The club's white shirt with distinctive single black band was inspired by the founder's breakfast bowl as a child.

The build-up to the Paris Olympics in 1924 was dominated by a debate around professionalism in the Uruguayan game. In 1922, Peñarol broke away from the governing body to form the *Federación Uruguaya de Football* (FUF) – the Uruguayan Football Federation. The argument was not resolved until 1925 with the intervention of Uruguayan president, José Serrato. No Peñarol players sailed with the Uruguay Olympic team to Vigo, Spain, where the ensemble enjoyed a successful tour of Spain before pushing on to Paris.

The Uruguayans swept all before them at the 1924 Olympics in Paris. In the opening round, Yugoslavia found itself on the receiving end of a 7-0 drubbing. The USA were brushed aside 3-0 in the second round, with Pedro Petrone of the Charley Football Club notching his second brace of the tournament. Petrone bagged a third successive brace in the quarter-finals as *La Celeste* dumped out the hosts, France, 5-1 at the Stade de Colombes. A late Scarone penalty sealed a 2-1 semi-final victory over the Dutch before the Uruguayans sealed gold with a 3-0 win over the Swiss in the final. 'The winners are a sound all-round side, with a fast, clever forward line which combines like clockwork,' the British press enthused.[9]

Half the team that sailed to the Netherlands to defend its Olympic crown in 1928 was made up of either Nacional or Peñarol players. The attack was fronted by the deadly Nacional trio of Pedro Petrone, José Pedro Cea and Héctor Scarone. Again, Uruguay dispatched the hosts, beating the Netherlands 2-0 in the opening round, before a feisty win against Germany and then Italy put them in the final against neighbours, Argentina. It would take a replay to separate the two sides. In the replay, Montevideo Wanderers forward Roberto Figueroa fired home the opener for Uruguay on 17 minutes before Luis Monti levelled for Argentina. Scarone hit home with a quarter of an hour remaining after a head-down from René Borjas. Borjas's shout *¡Tuya, Hectór!* (Yours, Hector!) as he nodded down to Scarone to volley the winner is folklore in Uruguayan football. Vadim Furmanov has written extensively on *Rioplatense* football. He tells me that a heavy thunderstorm passed over Montevideo as the final was played in Amsterdam. 'Tens of thousands of people packed the squares in Buenos Aires and Montevideo to hear the updates sent across the ocean by telegraph,' Furmanov informs me. 'In Montevideo, the horn that announced the goal was obscured by thunder, so it took a few seconds for the news to register. Once it did, the crowd erupted!'

Uruguay had retained the unofficial 'world champion' title. Now, for the World Cup.

## Uruguay rules the world

FIFA awarded Uruguay the chance to prove its global supremacy by hosting the first World Cup tournament in 1930. It was branded 'the world title no one wants'[10] by sections of the British media after, one by one, European nations declined to take part. Uruguay, with home advantage and its already proven world-beating team, were overwhelming favourites. Had England, Scotland or Austria's *Wunderteam* of the time also travelled, we may have a fair assessment of who was the best team in the world in 1930. With the Estadio Centenario still unfinished, early tournament matches were split between Nacional's Estadio Gran Parque Central and Peñarol's Estadio Pocitos. The centrepiece stadium was ready, however, for Uruguay's opening pool match on 18 July against Peru. Nacional's Héctor Castro scored the first-ever goal at the new home of Uruguayan football in the 65th minute. The hosts were off to a winning start to the joy of nearly 60,000 inside the new Centenario. There would be 10,000 more in the ground to see *La Celeste* blow Romania away 4-0 three days later, with all goals scored within the first 35 minutes. And the goals kept on coming, with Yugoslavia falling to a tennis score – 6-1 – in the semi-final, despite having taken a shock lead after just four minutes. Cea bagged a hat-trick.

Once again, Argentina would be the team to beat in the final. Each team insisted on using a ball made in their own country for the final, so a compromise was struck; an Argentine ball would be used in the first half, and a Uruguayan ball in the second. Tensions were high with boatloads of Argentinians sailing in for the event. Fans were checked for revolvers, and the army had bayonets fixed at the Estadio Centenario. Argentina's star, Monti, apparently fearing death threats, was not his usual self. Pablo Dorado of Bella Vista became the first player to score in a World Cup Final, after 12 minutes, beating Argentina's goalkeeper Juan Botasso at his near post with a low shot. The Argentines levelled through Peucelle eight minutes later, then, minutes before the break, Stábile made it 2-1 to the *Albiceleste*. Would the Argentinians finally get revenge for Olympic defeat? No. In the second half – and with their own ball – the

Uruguayans ran in three lovely goals, sending the crowd into ecstasy. The Jules Rimet Trophy – 35cm high, nearly 4kg in weight made of gold and lapis lazuli, and made at the cost of 60,000 Swiss Francs – had been locked in the treasury at the Banco República since its arrival. It now belonged to Uruguay. Although it wasn't the same trophy that captain José Nasazzi and his team paraded around the Centenario at the end of the game, having been given an alternative for safety reasons, history was made.[11]

Uruguay did not defend its title in Italy in 1934 in protest at its treatment by most European countries four years previously. It would be the only time a defending champion would not be present at a World Cup. Likewise, in 1938, in protest at Europe being chosen to host successive tournaments, Uruguay did not enter. The next time it did – in 1950 in neighbouring Brazil – Uruguay would again be crowned world champions.

## Albion FC today

Many of Uruguay's football pioneers are laid to rest in the British Cemetery in Montevideo. William Leslie Poole, the 'father of Uruguayan football', born in Bromley, Kent, England, is among them, as is Percy Chater from down the road in Beckenham, the CURCC player and the first AUF president. Fellow CURCC players, Scotsman John Harley, and Francis Jackson, who lifted the first Uruguayan championship trophy, are also buried there, as is the founder of Montevideo Wanderers, Jorge Sardeson. Albion's British roots are still evident in its contemporary badge, a white lion is rampant against a blue and red background. So, does the Uruguayan football public know that Albion is the country's pioneer football club? 'It's little known,' Luzuriaga concludes. 'Albion is a club that has historically had a low profile. Albion disappeared from the First Division in 1908 and has been in the lower divisions.' There are green shoots of recovery – in 2018, the club gained promotion to the Second Division.

1  http://www.fifa.com/fifa-tournaments/classic-stadiums/stadium=34866/index.html
2  *Athletic News*, Monday, 1 September 1930 (p16)
3  Finch, M.H.J., *The Political Economy of Uruguay since 1870* (London: Palgrave Macmillan, 1981, p192)
4  http://www.mvcc.com.uy/
5  https://www.ovaciondigital.com.uy/futbol/albion-puntapie-inicial.html
6  http://www.padreydecano.com/cms/fundacion/
7  https://www.pasiontricolor.com.uy/noticias/el-primer-hincha-de-la-historia/
8  https://thesefootballtimes.co/2019/02/13/isabelino-gradin-the-first-black-icon-of-uruguayan-football/
9  *Belfast Newsletter*, 10 June 1924 (p3)
10  *Sunderland Daily Echo and Shipping Gazette*, 2 November 1929 (p9)
11  https://www.elobservador.com.uy/nota/el-misterio-de-la-copa-del-mundial-de-1930-que-gano-uruguay-y-que-nunca-recibio-2019102320651

# 12.

# Brazil

IN THE São Paulo suburb of Pacaembu stands the impressive art deco hulk of the Estádio Municipal Paulo Machado de Carvalho. It was opened in 1940 and is named after the delegation chief of Brazil's first World Cup victory in Sweden in 1958. In that final, Brazil fielded a 17-year-old Pelé on the way to the first of its five world titles. Fast-forward 50 years and Pelé is back at Pacaembu opening Brazil's *Museu do Futebol* (Museum of Football), housed within the stadium's grounds. Right outside the stadium is the Praça Charles Miller, a square named after the man who stepped off the boat from Southampton in 1894 with two balls, a pump and a rule book and changed Brazil forever. Charles William Miller had been born in São Paulo on 24 November 1874 to a Scottish railway engineer father and an Anglo-Brazilian mother. Aged nine, he was sent to Southampton, England, to school, becoming an accomplished player in his own right with the St Mary's Church of England Young Men's Association – now better known as Southampton FC. He also turned out for prestigious amateur side Corinthian FC, whose legacy looms large over Brazilian football. Miller wanted to continue playing when he returned to Brazil. The story of the birth of Brazilian football is a familiar one: a British community nestled in a port city with its own exclusive societies and pursuits inadvertently finds it has spawned huge local interest that would snowball quickly into a national obsession.

## The father of Brazilian football

Like its neighbours to the south in Uruguay and Argentina, Brazil was never part of the British Empire. Still, it was part of its economic sphere of influence in the 19th century. Britain was Brazil's most important trading partner until the First World War. For the Brits, Brazil held attraction in its minerals, agriculture and the railway infrastructure that was required to support these industries. It was the railways that had brought both sides of Miller's family to Brazil. His father, John, was born in Largs, west of Glasgow, into a shipping family that ran coal, coffee and other produce between Brazil and the Scottish port of Greenock. His maternal side, Fox, had designed and built the São Paulo Railway in the 1860s that had been completed ten months ahead of schedule and deployed a number of innovative incline systems to handle the challenging terrain. São Paulo today is a sprawling metropolis of 12 million people and Brazil's largest city. Back in the 1880s, it was a town on an intersection of railways with just over 30,000 inhabitants. Coffee was its key produce and, thanks to the close historical ties between England and Portugal, this former Portuguese colony enjoyed friendly relations with Britain. Its proximity to the port of Santos also proved to be São Paulo's route to wealth.

The British expatriate community in São Paulo was small but influential – just over 2,000 in the 1880s, the same decade in which Brazil finally abolished slavery, partly due to British pressure. In the absence of a strong British school system, such as that in Buenos Aires, those who could afford to would send their children back to Britain for schooling. São Paulo would not have its own British school until the 1900s. Nine-year-old Miller sailed on the merchant ship *Elbe* in 1884 for the three-week voyage to Southampton. He attended the small Banister Court public school in the city where he excelled at cricket, a sport he would have been aware of within the British community in São Paulo. Banister Court instilled Miller and its other pupils with the Victorian values of its time at the peak of the British Empire. It is also where Miller first encountered the Association game in 1884. The game was already well established in England; it was just one year until the FA would accept professionalism (1885) and just four years before the establishment of the Football League (1888). By 1892, when Miller was 17, his sterling performances for Banister Court gained him a recommendation to join Corinthian FC, who were in Southampton to play Hampshire and were short of a forward.

At the cusp of professionalism in the mid-1880s, nine Corinthians featured in the England team. The team that Charlie Miller joined included the legendary all-rounder, Charles Burgess (C.B.) Fry, who was the same age.

Of Charles Miller's Southampton days, Miller's biographer, Josh Lacey, describes him as a man caught between two worlds. In a team photograph – he is the only one sans moustache – Miller looks, Lacey writes, out of place, potentially feeling foreign in both countries.[1] To be fair to Miller, he was the junior member of the team, but his time with the Saints – which included games against international quality in the FA Cup – was short and, aged 19, he was on a ship called *Magdalena* sailing home to

Brazil. Miller's own account of his disembarkation back in Santos with a football in each hand is the stuff of legend.[2] By the time Miller returned to São Paulo in 1894, a decade after he had first left for schooling in England, Brazil had changed. Slavery had finally been abolished, the country was a republic, and the population had increased fourfold, fuelled by Brazil's coffee growth.

Miller arranged what is thought to be the first football match ever played in Brazil, with São Paulo Railway staff taking on employees of the Gas Company on 14 April 1895.[3] Critically for Miller, in 1888, the British community had founded the São Paulo Athletic Club (SPAC), which counted Miller's cousin William Fox Rule and two uncles as members. SPAC had already played other British cricket teams from elsewhere in Brazil.

By 1901, there were enough teams in the São Paulo area for Miller to found the *Liga Paulista de Foot-ball* (Paulista Football League – LPF). This would feature Miller's SPAC, Sport Club Internacional, Mackenzie College, Sport Club Germânia and Paulistano. SPAC won the first three titles, with Miller top scorer in the first season. Within two years, English papers reported 'tremendous enthusiasm' for football in Brazil, with around 60 clubs now active in São Paulo.[4] In 1906, Miller welcomed a South African team off the boat at the port of Santos and brought them into São Paulo on a special train. The visitors – all made up of white players due to racial segregation in South Africa – were inspired by two prior Corinthians tours of the Cape and were clearly far advanced of the Brazilians, winning 6-0 in front of 6,000 people at the Velódromo, home of Paulistano. The following year, Paulistano brought Fulham's Scottish international John Hamilton across to coach during the English close season, the first such example of a foreign coach coming to

Brazil. He only stayed three months but must have made an impression as in 1908 Paulistano won its second title.

## Brazil's other Scot

While Charles Miller is widely accepted across the country as the father of Brazilian football, as is often the case, there is a rival claim. Once again, the story features a Scotsman. Thomas Donohoe was born in Busby, Renfrewshire, in 1863 and worked as a dyer in the Busby Printworks. He moved to Brazil in 1892 to take up work at a new factory in Bangu, west of Rio de Janeiro. Missing the game he had been used to playing in Scotland, Donohoe had to import footballs and boots from Britain and in April 1894 organised a five-a-side match a full six months before Charles Miller's first game. In July 2014, ahead of Brazil's World Cup, a 4.5m-high statue of Donohoe was unveiled outside a Bangu shopping mall that stands on the site of the factory where Donohoe had worked as a calico dyer. Donohue is immortalised in fibreglass cast in long shorts standing atop a globe. He cradles a ball in his left hand while his right arm is aloft, his index finger pointing to the sky as if to say 'I was first'. It was the Bangu Athletic Club, founded by British factory managers ten years later in 1904, that helped break down the racial divide by allowing non-white players to play in the team, becoming the first team in Rio de Janeiro to do so.

## The growth of the game in Brazil

The football scene in Rio de Janeiro would grow up as a keen rival to São Paulo. In September 1901, the Anglo-Brazilian Oscar Cox, who had first played football while a student in Lausanne, Switzerland, had arranged the first formal match in the state of Rio de Janeiro. The following month, Cox travelled to São Paulo with a *Carioca* team to

take on a *Paulista* XI in São Paulo that featured Charles
Miller. The first match ended 1-1 and the second 2-2,
but crowds were large. Seeing the potential of football's
popularity, Cox founded Fluminense Football Club a year
later, becoming the first Brazilian club to carry the word
'Football' in its title.[5] In the early 1900s, several clubs
emerged in Rio de Janeiro, including America Football
Club, Botafogo Football Club and Paissandu Atlético
Clube. Famous *Carioca* clubs Flamengo and Vasco da
Gama's footballing branches would not arrive until the
following decade. The *Campeonato Carioca* (Rio State
Championship) kicked off in 1906, just a few years after
Miller's *Paulista* tournament, with Cox's Fluminense
winning the inaugural six-club competition. In 1911, Cox
brought over English coach Charles Williams, who had
led Denmark to Olympic silver in London three years
earlier. He would go on to lead Fluminense to the Rio
Championship in his first season. Much as it still is today,
Brazil was a deeply divided country socially, economically
and demographically. But the local population fell for this
expat game straight away, mostly because of its simplicity.
Football quickly became the country's number one sport.

Middling Southern League side Exeter City travelled
down to tour Brazil and Argentina in 1914. The entire
team had been arrested in Santos on the outward journey
for training on a beach where bathing was banned. The
players were later released. Exeter City won six of its eight
games in Buenos Aires, Avellaneda and Rosario before
stopping off in Rio de Janeiro on the way back, beating
a select Rio-based British XI 3-0 and a combined Rio de
Janeiro 5-3 the following day. But it is Exeter City's third
match in Rio de Janeiro that is the standout in Brazilian
football history. Combining the best players of both Brazil's

nascent football capitals, Rio de Janeiro and São Paulo put together what was the first Brazilian national side. The game took place at Fluminense's Estádio das Laranjeiras with an estimated 10,000 spectators crammed into the ground.[6] Oswaldo Gomes on his home ground and Osman bagged Brazil's goals in á 2-0 win. Exeter's players had apparently turned nasty after going a goal down, with Brazil's first dual-heritage international, Artur Friedenreich, son of a German businessman and a Brazilian mother, reputedly losing two teeth in a charge from an Exeter City player. The national press went wild at the victory and football was well on its way to becoming a core part of the Brazilian national psyche.

## International stirrings

I went to three group stage matches at the Maracanã in Rio de Janeiro at the 2014 World Cup hosted in Brazil. The first game featured Argentina, Brazil's biggest rivals. Whenever pockets of sky blue and white-shirted Argentines popped up around the immense Maracanã bowl to jump, wave and chant, a chorus of boos would follow shortly from the home fans, who were clearly backing Bosnia-Herzegovina in this tie. The Brazilian fans, clad in their canary yellow national shirts, or those of their favourite Rio club – the black and red hoops of Flamengo, the white shirt and black sash of Vasco, the green and red of Fluminense or the white five-pointed star of Botafogo – would often jump up and show their palms and five fingers to their southern neighbours. *Penta campeão! Penta campeão!* went the cry (Five-time champions). Brazil is the most successful country in World Cup history. After the country produced what many consider the pinnacle of the beautiful game in 1970, the country was given the Jules Rimet Trophy to keep by FIFA, who replaced it with the current World Cup Trophy, first handed to West

Germany in 1974. The Jules Rimet Trophy was stolen from the Brazilian Football Confederation headquarters in 1983 and never recovered. The rumour is it was melted down into gold bars, but experts say it would have been worth more left as it was.

Back on the pitch, Brazilian footballing dominance was not always guaranteed. The current and iconic canary yellow shirt, sky blue shorts and white socks only came about after the calamity of Brazil's losing the final match of its home World Cup in 1950. Until then, Brazil had worn white. Brazil's football association had been formed on 8 June 1914, coming under the auspices of the *Confederação Brasileira de Desportos* (Brazilian Sports Confederation – CBD) two years later in 1916. That year, a Brazilian team sailed to Buenos Aires for the inaugural South American Championship – now known as the *Copa América*. The squad names indicate that this Brazilian team was indeed made up of Brazilians and not Anglo or German expatriates. However, the Brazilian game was still very much a white man's game, something that would take decades to change. On 8 July 1916 at Gimnasia y Esgrima's ground in Buenos Aires, the Palmeiras forward Demósthenes scored Brazil's first competitive goal as Brazil took the lead against Chile, only to be pegged back with five minutes to go. Brazil's first match in international competition ended 1-1. Two days later at the same ground, Brazil played its first match against Argentina, again drawing 1-1. In its final match, Friedenreich put Brazil ahead after just eight minutes against eventual tournament winners Uruguay. Brazil held the lead for 50 minutes of play before fading to a 2-1 defeat.

Brazil had competed respectably against countries with longer footballing traditions. When Brazil hosted the third South American Championships at home in 1919, it made the most of home advantage, winning its first piece of international silverware. The venue would be the newly expanded Estádio das Laranjeiras, which could now hold 20,000 five years after its first 'international' against Exeter City. Brazil got off to a flyer with a 6-0 drubbing of Chile, Friedenreich bagging a hat-trick. Brazil then beat Argentina 3-1 the following week before pulling back a 2-0 deficit to draw with Uruguay in the final match. As it was a league system with both Brazil and Uruguay tied on five points, a final match was arranged for three days later back at Laranjeiras. Goalless after normal time, the game was 122 minutes old when Friedenreich struck to deliver Brazil's first of many titles. Uruguayan writer Eduardo Galeano credits Friedenreich with inventing the style of football we have come to associate with Brazil.[7] The CBD joined FIFA in 1923. The *Confederação Brasileira de Futebol* (Brazilian Football Confederation – CBF) was created as an independent body in 1979 to govern the country's football and national team.

## The Corinthian legacy in Brazil

Sport Club Corinthians Paulista was founded in September 1910 and notably it was not formed by wealthy patrons as a recreation for other upper-class Brazilians, but by workers of the São Paulo Railway. If the club's name sounds familiar, it should; the founders named their club after the English amateur football evangelists who dazzled them. The visiting English Club Corinthians' FC's 1910 tour started with a 10-1 demolition of Oscar Cox's Fluminense on 24 August, followed by an 8-1 thrashing of a Rio de Janeiro XI two days later. Corinthians managed to fit in a cricket match in Rio before a specially selected local XI were next to fall 5-2. Corinthians moved on to São Paulo, dispatching Palmeiras

2-0. Club Atlético Paulistano were next up, with Corinthians winning 5-0 before the tour wrapped up on 4 September with an 8-2 win against Miller's SPAC.

Attending the Palmeiras match on 31 August at the velodrome were railwaymen Joaquim Ambrósio, Antônio Pereira, Rafael Perrone, Carlos Silva and Anselmo Correia. So inspired were these five that within 24 hours they had created their own football club in the Bom Retiro district. It was just a gathering held in a public space to play a game with other residents of their neighbourhood, but it was the genesis of something big. Four days later on 5 September 1910, the name of Sport Club Corinthians Paulista was officially adopted and the news was announced by new club president, Miguel Bataglia. Money was raised from members to buy a ball and equipment, and a week later, the new Corinthians were ready for their first match against another established club, União da Lapa. SC Corinthians Paulista only lost by one goal to nil, which surprised many. They won their next game against British team Lapa Athletic Association 5-0. Corinthians had arrived! Up until this point, they had only played in the white shirts that they went to work in, so they bought cream shirts that eventually washed white and black shorts. The colours – which looked similar to the English Corinthians – stuck, but the club was still confined to playing on a floodplain. In 1913, SC Corinthians Paulista qualified for the São Paulo regional league and won the title only a year later.

The English Corinthians returned to Brazil in August that same year, going down 2-1 to a combined Rio de Janeiro XI in their first match, but won the next four before Palmeiras held an injury-hampered Corinthians to a draw. Corinthians were scheduled to revisit Brazil in 1914, but instead answered their country's call while en route. The team returned to England to sign up to fight in the First World War, narrowly avoiding a German gunboat as they did so. Just one of the 14 Corinthians aboard the ship on the aborted 1914 tour would play for the club again. In total, 22 Corinthians would die on active service during the First World War.

In 2015, the modern-day Corinthian-Casuals of England's Isthmian League Premier Division, the seventh tier of English football, went back to São Paulo to play SC Corinthians Paulista. The journey was chronicled by Corinthian-Casuals' player and press officer Chris Watney in his film *Brothers in Football*. The English non-leaguers were swamped by thousands of fans at the airport on arrival, feted throughout and even played in front of 26,000 fans at the World Cup venue Arena Corinthians, losing 3-0 to SC Corinthians Paulista. Corinthian-Casuals' King George's Field ground in Tolworth, south-west London, has become something of a pilgrimage site for SC Corinthians Paulista fans.

## Brazilian football in the 1920s

The 1910s had seen wide democratisation of football throughout Brazil. No longer was it a pastime just for the rich in the big conurbations. When the crew of the British ship SS *Corinth* stopped off in Santos in June 1914, it played the Africa Football Club. The crew won 3-1, but it is evidence that football was becoming popular among the black population of Brazil. 'Association football has made a wide conquest. Every town in Brazil has its ground and even away in the far interior the game is played,' reports the *Edinburgh Evening News* in 1915, highlighting the large crowds that gathered for interstate matches and the use of English terms.[8] Brazilians still use English terms. *'Time'* (pronounced 'chee-may') comes from 'team', and 'crack' is used to describe a striker or key player.

In 1922, the South American Championships returned to Laranjeiras. Brazil scored within nine minutes in its first match against the Chileans, only to be held to 1-1. The hosts' poor form continued in the second game as they again took the lead against Paraguay only to squander it late on, before a third successive draw followed, 0-0 versus Uruguay. Brazil won its final crunch match with Argentina to set up a final play-off victory against the Paraguayans. Brazil went on to win its second title but would now enter a barren period as Uruguay and Argentina dominated affairs in the coming decade.

Elitism and racism were still rife in Brazilian football, much as they were in wider society. In 1923, *Carioca* club Vasco da Gama – a club that prided itself on fielding black and working-class players – won the *Campeonato Carioca*, run by the *Liga Metropolitan de Desportos Terrestres* (LMDT – Metropolitan Field Sports League – ) with its diverse team. A year later, the club faced pressure from the league's major clubs to exclude 12 of its players deemed unsuitable for a new elitist league on account of their background. Vasco refused. So, the other 'aristocratic' clubs broke away to create their own association, the *Associação Metropolitan de Esportes Athleticos* (Metropolitan Athletic Sports Association – AMEA). They then barred Vasco from joining unless the club fulfilled their criteria. Vasco's Portuguese president, Dr José Augusto Prestes, issued his 'historical response' in reaction, in which he expresses his unwillingness to 'sacrifice' the 12 players that helped Vasco win the championship. Vasco's exclusion meant it had to play against Rio's smaller teams left in the LMDT for a year, such as Bonsucesso and Villa Isabel, who also failed to meet the demands of Rio's elite clubs. Vasco later reached an agreement with the new association to compete again with the elite. The gesture was a watershed moment in Brazilian football history and opened the door a little wider for black players, such as Leônidas da Silva. Leônidas would be credited with inventing the bicycle kick and appeared for Brazil at the 1934 and 1938 World Cups. Whereas Uruguay had embraced and promoted its black players right from the start, in Brazil it took decades. Pioneer dual-heritage players felt they needed to hide their origins. Artur Friedenreich parted his hair while Fluminense's Carlos Alberto dowsed his face in rice powder to hide his dark skin, risking the abuse of opposition players when the powder sweated out.

In the 1920s, both the Rio de Janeiro and São Paulo championships were shared out among teams from across the respective cities. Corinthians, Paulistano, São Bento, Internacional and Palestra Italia – renamed Palmeiras during the Second World War – all won *Paulista* titles, while in Rio de Janeiro the *Fla-Flu* rivalry between Flamengo and Fluminense picked up pace. The 1920s also saw the advent of floodlights in Brazil. One British visiting side to play under the lights was Motherwell FC of Scotland in its 1-1 draw with a select Rio de Janeiro XI in June 1928. Motherwell's next match was against a combined Brazil side, the first time the national side had played European opponents since Exeter City 14 years previously. Brazil would once again be the victor, this time by a margin of 5-0. To be fair to the Motherwell players, they were on the tail end of an intensive tour that had included 11 games in Uruguay and Argentina. *Athletic News* praised the Brazilians' 'speed, aggressiveness and enthusiasm', in contrast to the lacklustre Scots visitors, reckoning them to not be far off Uruguay and Argentina in their development, and fearful of Britain's place at the top of world football.[9] In 1928, Brazil did not take the opportunity to prove the *Athletics News* right. Due to a lack of financial support from the government, Brazil was playing Motherwell at home rather than joining fellow Latin American sides Argentina, Chile, Mexico and Uruguay at the Amsterdam Olympics.

Brazil's first tournament on the world stage came two years later at the first World Cup in Uruguay. The squad was picked up in Rio de Janeiro on the SS *Conte Verde*, the same boat that carried the French, Belgian and Romanian teams, as well as Jules Rimet and his trophy en route to Montevideo. Brazil's young squad was made up entirely of Rio de Janeiro-based players and were managed by former Fluminense and Flamengo player Píndaro de Carvalho Rodrigues. Brazil lost its opening match 2-1 to Yugoslavia at the Estadio Gran Parque Central. By the time Brazil played Bolivia at the Estadio Centenario on 20 July, the team had already been eliminated due to Yugoslavia's 4-0 thrashing of Bolivia three days earlier. Brazil dished out another 4-0 defeat for the Bolivians, with Flamengo's Moderato and Fluminense's Preguinho chipping in with a brace each. Brazil is the only country to have appeared in every single FIFA World Cup tournament.

### Where are the Brazilian pioneers now?

Three years after the first World Cup, Brazil followed its River Plate neighbours into professionalism, with Bangu winning the first professional *Carioca* championship and Palestra Italia (Palmeiras) achieving the equivalent in São Paulo. Miller's São Paulo Athletic Club has long since de-anglicised its name to the Clube Atlético São Paulo and, while the club no longer plays cricket or league football, it does have a rugby team. SPAC stopped playing competitive football in 1912 after winning four *Campeonato Paulista* titles. Of the other founding Liga Paulista de Football clubs, Sport Club Internacional (not to be confused with the Porto Alegre club) dissolved in 1933, five years after winning its second title. Mackenzie College competed until 1923; SC Germânia, founded by the German Hans Nobiling, abandoned football when it turned professional in the early 1930s, and is now a multisport club known as Esporte Clubs Pinheiros. Paulistano also ditched football when it professionalised and became a multisport club, although former members of Paulistano went on to form São Paulo da Floresta – now São Paulo Futebol Clube. Charles Miller died in 1953 and is buried in the Protestant Cemetery in São Paulo.

1   Lacey, Josh, *God is Brazilian: Charles Miller, The Man Who Brought Football to Brazil* (Stroud: Tempus Publishing, 2005, p75)
2   https://bleacherreport.com/articles/11611-charles-miller-scotlands-gift-to-brazil
3   https://www.bbc.co.uk/sport/football/24537173
4   *Portsmouth Evening News*, Tuesday, 19 May 1903
5   http://www.fluminense.com.br/sobre/english
6   https://www.theguardian.com/football/2004/may/31/sport.comment1
7   Galeano, Eduardo, *Soccer in Sun and Shadow* (New York: Nation Books, 2013, p47)
8   *Edinburgh Evening News*, 19 February 1915 (p7)
9   *Athletic News*, 23 July 1928 (p2)

# 13.

# North America

'LET'S BE honest. If David Beckham doesn't come over, the League's gone.' I'm on Skype discussing Major League Soccer (MLS) with football writer and podcaster Stephen C. Brandt, who covers football in the US and beyond. According to Brandt, David Beckham's pulling power was key to providing new momentum to the MLS as he was able to attract new fans to the game. Major League Soccer is the latest attempt to launch Association football as a successful commercial concern in the United States. The 1994 World Cup was designed to provide the catalyst for the game at the end of the 20th century. The North American Soccer League (NASL), which ran for 16 years between 1968 and 1984, certainly attracted the stars – Pelé, Beckenbauer, Moore, Cruyff, Best – but ultimately proved unsustainable.

Yet these relatively recent attempts to kick-start Association football in the United States do much to feed the perception that the US is new to soccer. It's not, far from it. 'Football' may mean the 'Gridiron' game in the States, but the Association game has been present in the US almost as long as in England. Soccer has flourished at various stages, especially during the 1920s. The USA even finished third at the first World Cup in 1930. The Association game was professionalised in the US in 1894, making it the first country outside Britain or Ireland to legalise the payment of players. Yet the round-ball game lost out in the public consciousness over the long term to the domestic college game – at least in the men's format. At women's soccer, the United States has excelled, with four World Cup triumphs and four Olympic gold medals. Soccer's struggle to establish a foothold among men's elite sports in the US goes back to its roots.

## The genesis of soccer in the US

Historically, people living in what is now the United States of America already had their own kicking games long before European colonisers arrived in the 16th and 17th centuries. After European settlement and in common with other countries, there was a long tradition of different types of football existing in the US before the Football Association rule book was first published in the country in 1866, and there may have been a game played under these rules in the state of Wisconsin that year. In 1862, during the American Civil War, the Oneida Football Club in Boston was formed by Gerritt Miller. The club was the first football club of any code in the US, played 'Boston rules' on Boston Common, and a small monument was erected there in 1925 to mark the significance.

Brian D. Bunk, a US soccer historian, told me that it is difficult to pin down the first men's game using Association rules. The Rutgers and Princeton schools met in 1869. This match is often cited as the first soccer game in the US, but that was using a set of college rules that had been negotiated between the two sides. A match took place on 6 December 1873 between alumni of the English school

Eton and American college Yale at Hamilton Park, New Haven, Connecticut. It may well be the first time that a football match of any code was contested between a British team and that of another country outside of Britain and Ireland. The four-page matchday programme, also one of the earliest recorded, sold at auction for £15,000 in 2016. The match was 11-a-side, but most likely a hybrid of football rules agreed between four leading US schools – Yale of New Haven, Columbia from New York, and New Jersey-based Princeton and Rutgers.[1] The location of these universities in the north-eastern seaboard of the United States probably had some bearing on the game taking off most prolifically in this area – especially Fall River, Massachusetts, and Pawtucket and Providence, Rhode Island. Other teams emerged all across the US from San Francisco to St Louis, Chicago and Philadelphia. 'It was a game that by the 1880s and 1890s was predominantly played by immigrants. I've discovered more recently in the course of my research that it was really Scottish immigrants in many of these communities that formed the main clubs and ran the organisations,' Bunk tells me. 'There were also English immigrants and people from other nationalities as well, but the Scots really seem to be pretty key in developing these communities.'

In 1884, the American Football Association (AFA) was founded in Newark, New Jersey, with a sum of $500 raised from local businesses, in particular the Clark Thread Company. As in Britain, the link between soccer and industry was strong. Of the 13 inaugural members, eight came from New Jersey, two from New York City, one from Connecticut and two from Fall River, Massachusetts. All entered the inaugural AFA Challenge Cup that year, which was open to any club in the north-east, regardless of which league they played in. Clark met New York FC in the first final and won that year and the following two editions, touring Canada in the interim. This was to lead to an AFA XI playing a Canadian XI at Galt in 1885, with the Canadians winning 3-2. The return match, held at Clark's East Newark ground the following year, resulted in a resounding 5-1 win for the US.

For a seven-year period between 1888 and 1895, the AFA Challenge Cup would be dominated by 'Down East' clubs from Fall River and Pawtucket, until a Scottish immigrant club from East Newark, Caledonia Football Club, brought the trophy back to New Jersey. In this period the first women's match took place in 1893. In 1894, the National League, which managed baseball in the US, created a professional Association football league – the first professional league outside Britain and Ireland and three decades before Continental Europe's first professional league. The American League of Professional Football (ALPF) was designed to make use of baseball stadiums during the winter months, comprised six clubs and ran from October to January. Association football was chosen because the organisers did not believe that players of the more popular American college football game would want to turn professional. The six clubs involved were Brooklyn Bridegrooms, Baltimore Orioles, Boston Beaneaters, New York Giants, Philadelphia Phillies and Washington Senators. The AFA banned its member players from engaging in the ALPF and the season folded after one edition. A letter writer based in Pawtucket, Rhode Island, wrote to the *Scottish Referee* newspaper in April 1894 to report that the standard of play among the leading teams was equal to that of the Second Division back in Scotland and that big games could attract crowds of around 2,000 spectators.[2] Prophetically, the writer warns that Scottish clubs will soon have to be wary of American scouts hunting for Scottish talent.

## Toronto: Canada's football heartland

North of the border in Canada, part of the British Empire, the summers were dominated by the small ball, with cricket, baseball and local sport lacrosse taking centre stage. It was in this backdrop that in 1876 the very first Association football match in Canada was played on Parliament Street, Toronto, between the Carlton Cricket Club and Toronto Lacrosse.[3] A year later, the very first football association outside Britain and Ireland was formed – the Dominion Football Association. It disappeared within four years but in Berlin – modern-day Kitchener – 100km west of Toronto, a Scottish-born science teacher called David Forsyth was busy teaching his students the round-ball game. Forsyth, whose family moved to Canada when he was just one year old, is considered the 'father of Canadian soccer' and was instrumental in founding the Western Football Association in 1880. Forsyth captained a Canadian team in a series of matches in East Newark, New Jersey, in November 1885. For one of the matches against a US team, a crowd of 2,000 people – including around 60 women – witnessed a rough encounter that often descended into fist fights but finished with a 1-0 victory for the visitors.

Soccer flourished in the schools west of Toronto, such as Cambridge, Seaforth and Aylmer, which was to host the first home international match between Canada and the US in 1888. Ontario's football community was made up largely of Canadian-born players rather than expats. They included professors, dentists, journalists and surgeons. Forsyth believed the Canadians to be good enough to take on the British and Irish teams in their own backyard, and, in the autumn of 1888, Ontario's finest sailed off to test themselves against the best. The Canadians, dressed in dark blue and in peak physical condition, immediately surprised a Country Antrim side at Shaftesbury Grounds in Belfast.[4] A local match report praises the Canadians' combination play in a game contested on a terrible pitch in windy conditions. The team, comprised of men from Toronto, Galt and Berlin, ran out 6-2 winners. Perthshire-born Forsyth was the only foreign-born member of the Canadian team. The Canadians then defeated both Distillery and Clarence by 3-2 scorelines before drawing 1-1 with the YMCA, with Forsyth on the scoresheet. The team moved on to Scotland, where they beat Heart of Midlothian and drew with Glasgow Rangers, but lost to Queen's Park, Ayr and an All Scotland XI. In England, the Canadians worked their way south with wins at Sunderland, Middlesbrough, Lincoln City and Newton Heath – the future Manchester United – and drew at Sheffield FC but lost at Notts County and Blackburn Rovers. In all, the team won nine, drew five and lost nine, surprising the British sportswriters of the day.

In 1901, Forsyth was again key to the foundation of the Ontario Association Football League (OAFL), which produced the great Galt Football Club side that won the Ontario Cup three years in a row. The team went on to represent Canada – and triumph – at the St Louis Olympic Games in 1904. The Association game was moving west from Toronto, with a healthy scene emerging in Manitoba and Saskatchewan. Corinthians stopped by on their 1911 tour, being run close in Winnipeg and Calgary, and drawing 2-2 with Ladysmith before thrashing west-coast side Vancouver 4-1. Regional associations had been springing up since the 1890s and in Winnipeg in July 1912, the Dominion of Canada Football Association – now the

Canadian Soccer Association – was formed to bring them together. By the close of the year, the body was a member of FIFA. To celebrate this unity, the Governor General of Canada, the Duke of Connaught, presented the Association with a trophy to be contested nationwide. The Connaught Cup became a national championship, and Winnipeg side Norwood Wanderers won the first edition in 1913.

## The fight for code supremacy

In the US, soccer entered a period of decline at the end of the 1890s, as several clubs folded during a deep recession and the onset of the Spanish–American War of 1899. The AFA Challenge Cup was suspended between 1899 and 1906. In 1904, one of the US's top soccer hotbeds, St Louis, hosted the third modern Olympiad. Due to the distances required to ship to the US then catch the train to the middle of the country, and in November, halfway through most football seasons, only two nations – the hosts USA and neighbours Canada – entered teams for the football tournament. As an amateur competition, the round-robin would take place between three teams – Canada's representative, Galt Football Club of Ontario, and two American teams – Christian Brothers' College and St Rose Parish. Galt dispatched Christian Brothers' College 7-0 with a hat-trick from Alexander Hall and then trounced St Rose 4-0 to take gold at Francis Field.

In the absence of teams from outside North America, the feeling was that Galt FC was not – as it appeared – de facto world champions, so the following year, Galt FC was invited to take on a team of touring English amateurs. Pilgrims FC was a selection of invited amateurs who made two tours to North America, in 1905 and 1909. The 1905 team featured players from Sheffield United, Nottingham

Forest, Blackburn Rovers, Spurs and others. The tour was financed by US businessman C.H. Murray to promote the Association rules game in North America. Bunk told me that there was still a close connection for these Scottish and English migrants towards the motherland, so whenever a British team visited, it became a big occasion. Pilgrims played 17 matches over September and November 1905, winning 14 – two by a ten-goal margin – losing two and drawing one, 3-3 against Olympic champions Galt at Dickson Park. Pilgrims' game was slightly impaired in Canada, where at least some matches appear to have had elements of 'Canadian Rules'. These permitted more violent play – such as hacking at players' legs and even jumping on the back of players in possession of the ball – exactly the issues that led to the divisions at the creation of the Association rules. The tour had been well attended. In Pilgrims' two St Louis matches, crowds of 17,000 and 23,000 respectively were recorded. Sheffield United's F.H. Milnes, who captained the Pilgrims side, commented after the tour that he was confident that with a little help the English game could take the place of the American code.[5]

The American game – college football – was indeed causing great concern. The Pilgrims players attended one match between Pennsylvania University and Gettysburg during the tour, during which seven players were injured, one with a broken leg. The college game had gained enough popularity in the last few decades of the 19th century that, by 1900, the public was flocking in their tens of thousands. But by 1905, the game was in crisis due to the sheer number of casualties the full-contact sport was creating. In 1905 alone, 18 players were killed during play – including two during the eight-week Pilgrims tour – bringing to 45 the number of college football deaths since the turn of the century. Most came from concussion, broken necks, internal injuries or broken backs.[6] The startling numbers drove football fan President Theodore Roosevelt – whose son was injured while playing at Harvard – to summon representatives from Harvard, Yale and Princeton to the White House to address the problem. Rule changes the following season enabled forward passing of the ball and stoppages when players fell on the ball to eliminate heaps, although wearing a helmet did not become mandatory until 1939.

The further introduction of soccer into North America that Milnes craved came just a year after his Pilgrims tour when, in 1906, Corinthian FC visited Canada and the US. A crowd of 3,000 turned up to Corinthians' first match at Montreal, waiting 90 minutes for the team to arrive as their train was delayed. The tourists won their first match before Canadian champions Seaforth Hurons held Corinthians to a 1-1 draw in front of 7,000 people. The tour was becoming a one-sided affair as Corinthians racked up a 19-0 win in Cincinnati, a 12-0 win against All Philadelphia, followed by an 18-0 win versus All New York. But on 13 September, the Corinthians endured only its second defeat on overseas tours to date, with a 3-0 reverse in Fall River, which surprised many. Pilgrims returned in 1909 at the invitation of the American International Soccer Football Association. The tourists won 16 of their 22 games, losing at Haverford in Philadelphia and against Fall River Rovers. Corinthians also returned to tour Canada and the US in 1911, winning 19 and losing just once to Winnipeg.

Yet the organisational challenges of arranging matches in such a geographically large and diverse country was causing discontent. The American Amateur Football Association (AAFA) was formed as a counter to the AFA's New England power base,[7] which in turn launched its own competitions. The two organisations asked FIFA to arbitrate, with AAFA founder member Thomas W. Cahill travelling to FIFA's 1912 congress in Stockholm to make his case. The federation came down on the side of the AAFA, which enjoyed wider membership. A year later, the AAFA rebranded as the United States Football Association (USFA) with a nationwide remit and would later become the United States Soccer Federation (USSF). In 1916, the USA fielded its first official international team and beat Sweden 3-2 in Stockholm. Meanwhile, the AFA and its competitions went into decline.

## Foundation of the American Soccer League

The United States remained neutral for much of the First World War, entering in 1917 after escalated German U-boat attacks on US merchant vessels and attempts by the German government to encourage Mexico to enter the fray. During the US's involvement, more than 1.3 million American men and 20,000 women mobilised. Throughout this period, Americans met with soccer-playing working-class men from Britain and France or played the game in military training camps in the US, which led to something of a post-war boom, according to Brian D. Bunk. 'A lot of people, maybe for the first time, had the opportunity to either play the sport or see it, and the government was really interested in promoting it because they felt it was a simpler game to play and to watch and appreciate than other sports,' he tells me. Soccer gave Americans a chance to interact with the Allies during the course of the war. At home, momentum had already been growing towards a new attempt at an American league. It was Cahill as USFA president who made it happen in 1921 in a meeting at the Hotel Astor in Manhattan. The American Soccer League (ASL) would bring together teams from the National Association Soccer League and Southern New England Soccer League.

In the summer of 1921, before the first ASL season kicked off, Third Lanark of Glasgow became the first Scottish club to tour North America with 25 matches over two months. In tandem with touring teams before them, the Glaswegians won all their games until they arrived in Fall River, where they drew. Eight teams competed in the inaugural ASL season 1921/22. There was a high turnover of clubs, including a dropout in the first season. The league centred in the north-east, with Philadelphia FC pipping New York FC to the first title, while J&P Coats FC of Pawtucket, Rhode Island, won the second title. Fall River Marksmen went on to win seven titles in the first decade, including a league and National Cup double in the 1923/24 season, beating Vesper Buick in St Louis in the final. Grainy, silent footage of the final is possibly the oldest surviving film of soccer in the United States. It depicts a band marching across the pitch prematch, and the Vesper Buick team lined up with the distinctive 'Buick' logo emblazoned on their shirts. In contrast, the Marksmen simply have the letters 'FR' on theirs. The 15,000-strong crowd looks like any British audience of that day – numerous, almost exclusively male and white, and everyone to a man is wearing a cloth cap. Bethlehem Steel of Pennsylvania was another key competitor, winning one title and finishing second in three consecutive years. Some of the other names to appear during the ASL's decade are truly wonderful: Bohemian Queens, Hakoah All-Stars, Indiana Flooring Co., Providence Gold Bugs, Falco FC and Todd Shipyards. In 1924, Corinthians came for a third tour but only played one major US club – Brooklyn – spending most of their time in Canada, where, short of players and a specialist goalkeeper, the team endured an uncharacteristic eight defeats during the six-week tour. It was no real acid test of the quality of the ASL against the top English amateur side. The Olympic Games that year in Paris ended with a second-round exit for the USA to eventual champions, Uruguay.

While it is not known how many of the ASL players came from overseas, many were likely to be British, including estimates of 50 European international players.[8] The Derby-born former Chelsea striker Harold Brittan was top scorer in the first season for Philadelphia Field Club, while Glasgow-born Archie Stark was key to Fall River Marksmen's early success. Articles appear in both Scotland and England throughout the 1920s reporting that American football agents were talent spotting to lure players to the lucrative ASL. One of those foreign players tempted over to the US was future Benfica coach Béla Guttmann. The Hungarian had toured the US with the Viennese Jewish club, Hakoah Wien, and spent half a decade in the US for various New York-based clubs. Hakoah Wien's visit in 1926 had been arranged by ASL club Brooklyn Wanderers' owner, Nat Agar. One of its matches drew 46,000 spectators, then a record for US soccer. Meanwhile, in Canada, after two years of debate, a professional league was founded in 1926. Following the First World War, which had claimed 61,000 Canadian lives and wounded 172,000, the Canadian game became the domain of new migrants from Britain. This fuelled the perception of soccer as the game of the 'Old Country'.

While British players had also formed the majority of the overseas contingent at the outset in the ASL, Central Europeans filtered through around the middle of the 1920s. On the amateur scene, immigrant clubs often reflect their ethnic origins. Irishmen formed the New York Bohemians and in the 1920s even welcomed their Dublin namesakes to visit, while Spanish immigrants formed Galicia FC and even held Real Madrid 1-1 in front of 5,000 fans on the Castilian team's first US tour in September 1927. Again, it was Agar that had arranged this tour, as he also did for Nacional of Uruguay and Maccabi FC of Tel Aviv. Fall River Marksmen even toured Central Europe in 1930, playing in Vienna, Budapest, Prague and Bratislava. Towards the end of the decade, American-born players started coming to prominence. Billy Gonsalves, son of Portuguese immigrants, and Bert Patenaude are regarded as two of the biggest stars in early US soccer and would form part of the US team that went to the first World Cup in Uruguay in 1930.

Following a disappointing Olympics in 1928, where US amateurs had crashed out 11-2 to Argentina, the first FIFA World Cup in 1930 offered the professionals a chance to shine. Sailing to Uruguay, there was a distinctly British feel to the US national side. Team manager Robert Millar and five members of the team came originally from Scotland, plus one Englishman, George Moorhouse. The US team focused on fitness on the boat down, barely touching a ball. Stamina would play a key role in the team's success. The US defeated Belgium 3-0 in its first group match with Patenaude bagging the third at Nacional's Gran Parque Central as the US secured the first clean sheet in World Cup history. Patenaude then scored a hat-trick – the first at a World Cup – in the second group match as the US defeated Paraguay 3-0. Patenaude's hat-trick was only recognised by FIFA in 2006 – 32 years after Patenaude's death – thanks to research from soccer historian, Colin Jose. FIFA had credited Argentina's Guillermo Stábile as the scorer of the first hat-trick, against Mexico two days after Patenaude. Confusion had emerged because players did not wear numbers or names at that point and there had been a lack of clarity over who had scored against Paraguay. Sparked by a conversation with one of Patenaude's team-mates, Jose found evidence of the Fall River man's hat-trick.[9] In a small tournament deeply affected by the lack of all but four European nations, topping the group meant the US had made the semi-finals, where some pundits even made them favourites. As it was, the American team was trounced 6-1 by Argentina. Patenaude's four goals put him third in the top scorer list for the inaugural World Cup, and third place remains the US men's team's highest finish.

James Brown is the vice-president of the Society for American Soccer History (SASH), the grandson of the US team's Scottish-born forward and National Soccer Hall of Famer, Jim Brown, and son of Hall of Famer and US Men's National Soccer Team (USMNT) forward, George Brown. 'After their two clean sheets in the group stage, the US were considered real contenders for the title,' he tells me. 'But they came up against powerful Argentina and it was an extremely tough match. The US held their own in the first half, being down 1-0 at the break, despite having the misfortune of essentially losing their goalkeeper, Jimmy Douglas, who had his knee quite badly wrenched early on and was basically one-legged throughout the match, so the second half was a whole different ball game.' USMNT player Ralph Tracy almost had his knee broken much like Douglas. Andy Auld lost four front teeth and played with a towel in the mouth, and Brown reported having dirt thrown in his face. After the tournament, the players returned to their leagues. Patenaude and Gonsalves moved to St Louis while Brown headed to Manchester United and Spurs in 1932. Alex Wood also went across the pond as Brown had done and landed with Leicester City for a number of years.

Captain Florie and Moorhouse went to the 1934 World Cup in Italy, with Moorhouse as captain.

## Domestic decline ... and revival?

Meanwhile, back in the US, the ASL was under pressure. Sam Mark, owner of the Fall River Marksmen, had moved the club to New York and renamed it New York Yankees, before merging the club with two others and moving the team again to New Bedford under the name New Bedford Whalers. The team would win the final edition of the ASL in 1932. So why did this promising league that was attracting international talent and attention, and developing a solid national side, implode so rapidly? 'Throughout the ASL there was a disagreement between the ASL club teams and the Federation about playing in cup competitions,' Bunk explains. 'The ASL teams felt like they were the biggest draw and they made the most money and attracted the most fans. They were the best clubs in the country, certainly outside of St Louis, and they felt like they deserved more of the gate receipts.' There was a constant ongoing negotiation about how many games ASL teams would play in early rounds and how gate receipts were divided between the ASL and the USFA. It all blew up in the 1928/29 season, when the ASL instructed its members not to join the Challenge Cup competitions. A few did anyway – including Bethlehem Steel – and they were suspended by the ASL. The USFA went and formed its own league, the Eastern Professional Soccer League (ESL), including Agar's Brooklyn Wanderers. The two leagues then merged in 1930 as the Great Depression started to bite to create the Atlantic Coast League, which was eventually rebranded as the ASL again.

But it all came to an end in 1933. Many American sports fans perceived the FIFA-backed USFA as having too much foreign influence, so soccer never quite grew its local base. The ghosts of the ASL can still be found. The Fall River Marksmen's old ground at Mark's Stadium in Tiverton, Rhode Island, can still be visited. It's empty grassland now with a factory in the background, but this was once the most successful field in American soccer's golden age. The decade and a half of upheaval under the Great Depression and the Second World War also spelled the end of Canada's promising rise to soccer prominence. The women's game succeeded from its outset in 1893 because it became a popular sport to play in universities and colleges throughout the 1920s and 30s, and with equality law progress in the 1970s, more opportunities arose for women to play at a high level, fuelling national success.

The legacy of the ASL is being rekindled in Massachusetts, with local enthusiasts reviving both Fall River Marksmen and Fall River FC. 'We draw inspiration from the past, and the city of Fall River was once a powerhouse for soccer in the 1920s, 1930s, and so on,' Fall River FC president, Ryan Moniz, tells me. The new amateur Fall River FC plays in the Bay State Soccer League. Down the road, Fall River Marksmen's president, André Ruette, explains that the revival of the club came while he was researching forming a lower-league club. 'I was rather shocked to see that the Marksmen name wasn't owned by anyone, nor was it being used in any formal manner, so it was a rather obvious choice for me to revive the Marksmen,' he explains. 'Their history and influence on the American game and even the global game at that time is full of impressive feats that still stand the test of time. It's my hope to not only regain the Marksmen's synonymous status of success but also help ensure that the feats of yesteryear still remain told and respected.'

The city of Fall River has a large Portuguese community, with 37 per cent of the population claiming Portuguese ancestry. Fall River FC and Fall River Marksmen compete for the two-legged *Taça de Fall River* (Fall River Cup), named by their supporters. 'The soccer community in Fall River and the surrounding South Coast area is comprised of a rather savvy group of soccer fans,' Ruette continues. 'Soccer is in general a secondary sport in the area thanks in part to the success of its other professional sports teams like the Boston Red Sox [baseball], New England Patriots [NFL] and Boston Bruins [NHL]; however the South Coast community does have a thriving immigrant population primarily made up of Portuguese, Irish and French Canadians, and many openly embrace and support the game of soccer.' The story of North American men's soccer is one of promise that was never quite fulfilled. Can the MLS achieve what the ASL and NASL failed to and turn US men's soccer into a top global league?

1   http://www.scottishsporthistory.com/sports-history-news-and-blog/a-transatlantic-football-game-in-1873

2   *Scottish Referee*, 9 April 1894 (p7)

3   http://www.canadiansoccerhistory.com/Ontario/Ontario-%20The%20 Early%20Years.html

4   *Belfast Newsletter*, 3 September 1888 (p3)

5   *London Daily News*, 3 November 1905 (p7)

6   https://www.washingtonpost.com/news/the-fix/wp/2014/05/29/ teddy-roosevelt-helped-save-football-with-a-white-house-meeting-in-1905/?noredirect=on&utm_term=.44a3d9d201c0

7   https://thesefootballtimes.co/2016/07/30/american-soccers-missed-opportunity-the-first-golden-age/

8   https://slate.com/culture/2010/06/how-soccer-almost-became-a-major-american-sport-in-the-1920s.html

9   https://www.theguardian.com/football/2015/jul/18/bert-patenaude-usa-world-cup-hat-trick

# 14.

# Germany

ON 13 July 2014 Germany and Argentina fought out a disappointing World Cup Final. Was this the same Germany that had dispatched tournament hosts Brazil 7-1 just days earlier? Mario Götze popped up to score in injury time. *Deutschland ist Weltmeister*! When Philipp Lahm lifted the trophy at the Maracanã in Rio de Janeiro that night, it signified Germany's fourth World Cup title to add to its four European Championships.

In the 21st century – since the nadir of the *Mannschaft's* disorderly group-stage exit at Euro 2000 – the way that the German team has performed and the attractiveness of the Bundesliga to overseas visitors has been a spectacular PR success. The Bundesliga was only launched in 1963 after previous regional and national leagues had been disputed, but many now view it as a beacon of how football should be. Club members benefit from a 50+1 rule, meaning they have far more say over what happens at their club than owner-led clubs in England, Spain, Italy and elsewhere. It's hard not to love the Bundesliga. The crowds are among the biggest in the world, the ultras in the *tribune* either end provide non-stop choreographed atmosphere from prematch to the final whistle, and – wait for it – you can buy beer in your seat! But where did it all begin for German football?

## Germany's oldest football club

In February 2017, the UK's *Guardian* newspaper ran a feature titled: 'Which football club champions have suffered the biggest fall from grace?'[1] One reader suggested Germany's oldest still-active Association rules football club, BFC Germania 1888. The Berlin team won the first unofficial championship in Germany, which was known as the *Bund Deutscher Fußballspieler* (BDF – German Football Players' Association). This league only included clubs from the Berlin area but was technically the first organised football championship held in the country. At the time of writing, BFC Germania plays in Berlin's Kreisliga B league, which is the tenth tier of German football, long since eclipsed by its city neighbours Hertha Berlin, 1. FC Union Berlin, Tennis Borussia, BFC Dynamo and another of Germany's oldest clubs, FC Viktoria 1889 Berlin.

BFC Germania still plays its football in the area it all began, the Tempelhofer Feld in the south of the city. An airport was built on much of the Tempelhofer Feld, which became famous as the scene of the Berlin Airlift of 1948/49. In one of the first major crises of the emerging Cold War, Stalin ordered the blockade of the Allies' access to their western sectors of the divided city. The Soviets blocked road, rail and waterway access to West Berlin. In response, the Allies simply went – quite literally – above the Soviets' heads in order to feed the population of West Berlin, by running a non-stop relay of aerial deliveries until the Soviets relented. The Tempelhofer Feld is now a rather surreal public park. Visitors can cycle or walk around the runways, or picnic on the grassy verges where vintage planes sit in situ. Today, the immense curved edifice of the terminal building – the first in the world to be connected to its city by an underground rail network – also acts as an emergency refugee centre. BFC Germania 1888 plays at the nearby Sportplatz an der Götzstraße. It was not the first club in Germany, but it is the oldest still in business.

In the north, SC Germania of Hamburg was formed in 1887.[2] On 2 June 1919, SC Germania later merged with FC Falke Eppendorf and Hamburger FC to create Hamburger SV. This famous club, whose shirt has been donned by Felix Magath and Kevin Keegan, has – at the time of writing – won one European Cup, one UEFA Cup Winners' Cup and six Bundesliga titles. It was the only club never to have been relegated from the Bundesliga since its formation until its descent into the 2. Bundesliga in 2018. Hamburger SV draws a link back to 1887 as the year of its foundation, but BFC Germania is the oldest still operating in its original guise.

## How football took hold in Germany

Germany's key sporting passion in the mid-to-late-19th century was *Turnen* – gymnastics. Much like the English public-school ethos of building 'Muscular Christianity', so the Germans believed in the character-building qualities of *Turnen*. The German Association of Gymnastics – *Turnverein* – was founded by teacher Friedrich Ludwig Jahn in 1811. Jahn now has an athletics stadium named after him in Berlin. One of the football clubs that has used the ground is Berliner FC Dynamo, which – as Dynamo Berlin – was the preferred club of the East German secret police (*Stasi*) during the Cold War.

Germany's footballing story probably begins in April 1874 in the eastern city of Dresden, in a field near the city's famous Großer Garten. The Dresden English Football Club, presided by a 'Reverend Bowden', disappeared in the 1890s despite often having enjoyed hundreds of spectators attend its matches. Meanwhile, over in Braunschweig, right in the heart of the country, in the autumn of 1874, physical education teacher August Hermann introduced a ball to his students that he had ordered from London.[3] His sister was often in England as part of her role as a director of a boarding school for British and German students. The following year, Oxford University toured Germany with their round ball, so must have had opponents. In this period of history, the ties between England and Germany were strong. Prince Albert of Saxe-Coburg and Gotha had been married to Queen Victoria of England from 1840 until his death in 1861. Germany itself was a collection of disparate states until its unification under the 'Iron Chancellor', Otto von Bismarck, in 1871. From here on, the nation would become wealthier and more powerful over the next four decades. 'There's a cultural exchange between Germany and England,' German football historian Dr Christoph Wagner explains. 'In the 19th century, when modern football emerged in England, Germany and England were on very good terms, had very good relationships.' According to Wagner, tradesmen that were educated at public schools in England came to Germany and they had seen the game – either rugby or Association football – and also British expats coming to Germany brought their games with them.

It is likely that a kicking game was played at these schools before the rift between the Rugby and Association code-playing clubs in 1863. As early as 1872, the Heidelberger rowing club had a football department. The German Football Club of Hannover was founded in 1878, although it appears it played by the Rugby rules. The earliest clubs were often set up by those attracted to the Association game by its simplicity who wanted to continue playing after their school days. One of these was Konrad Koch, a colleague of August Hermann, who formed a student association in 1875 to play the game at the Martino-Katherineum school in Braunschweig. Little is recorded of Koch's early introduction of a football, although one player reported handling an egg-shaped leather ball. Wagner tells me that Koch had two teams of students line up to play a game of football, but it was probably rugby due to the shape of the ball. 'The major fame for introducing football to Germany goes to Konrad Koch, but it's not 100 per cent clear whether it was he alone or if he had one or two assistants,' Wagner adds. People like Hermann – who ordered balls in London in the first place – or Koch's father-in-law, the military doctor Freidrich Reck, who was based in England and knew about English sports. Hermann would later introduce basketball to Germany. 'These three probably have to be seen as the men who introduced football [to Germany] on an official basis,' Wagner continues. 'Konrad Koch at the end was the one who translated the football rules and printed them in German [in 1874], so Konrad Koch gets the fame for having introduced the game to Germany.'

As many places in its early days, football in Germany was the reserve of the wealthy. Even then, it was often sneered upon, even labelled an 'English disease', and in 1898 gym teacher Karl Planck compared the movement footballers made to that of monkeys.[4] And it's these gymnastic clubs that also present us with a puzzle when it comes to identifying the pioneers of German football. Many of Germany's football clubs spun out of existing multisports clubs. Typically, these would be the *Turnen*-practising gymnastic societies. The Bavarian club Munich 1860 was not playing football in that year – it would be as old as Hallam FC if it were – 1860 was the year of the gymnastic club's formation; Munich 1860 wasn't to play football until the turn of the 20th century. Meanwhile, in Braunschweig, Koch did not want to undermine the gymnastic movement, but he did want to keep students active and healthy. Koch observed that students spent too much time indoors or in pubs, and he wanted to encourage more outside activity. Koch's journey introducing football into Germany was turned into a film in 2011. *Der ganz große Traum* (*Lessons of a Dream*) is nearly two hours long and dramatises the conflict Koch would have faced introducing a new idea to the stern German education system.

## Back in Berlin ...

Berlin in the 1880s was a city on the move. Despite already being nearly 700 years old at the time, it was only really coming into its own as the capital of an increasingly powerful and confident country. In 1892, American writer Mark Twain, who had lived in Berlin for half a year, described it as the newest city he had ever seen and compared it to Chicago, which was seen as the most modern city at the time. It was among this backdrop of modernity that football started to gain a foothold. BFC Germania of Berlin was founded on 15 April 1888 by 17-year-old Paul Jestram. He, his three brothers and his friends from the Ashkanischen Gymnasium marked out their own goals on Tempelhof Feld as there were no private sports fields at this time. The current club FC Viktoria 1889 Berlin was founded in 2013 as a merger between Lichterfelder FC – the district where the current club plays – and Berliner Fußball-Club Viktoria 1889. When it was established on 6 June 1889 – also at Tempelhof – the club was known as Berliner Thorball und Fußballclub Viktoria 1889 (BTuFC Viktoria 89). In 1890,

Germania BFC joined the new German Footballers' Union (*Bund Deutscher Fußballspieler* – BDF). A cup competition was held that year featuring Berlin teams, which *Spiel und Sport* – Game and Sport, the only German sports paper at the time – reported as a cup competition. BFC Germania emerged victorious, thus becoming the first winners of a football championship in Germany, albeit an unofficial one.

Since its inception, the BDF was at odds as to whether foreign players – mainly British – should play in competitive matches and be involved in administration. This discord led to the 'rebel' establishment in 1891 in Berlin of the *Deutscher Fussball und Cricket Bund* (German Football and Cricket Federation – DFuCB), which rejected the closed shop of the BDF and was open to non-German teams and players. These included the English Football Club 1890 and Berlin Cricket Club 1883. The breakaway league ran its first championship in 1891/92, with eight clubs taking part. Again, the venue for most clubs was the Tempelhofer Feld, but matches did take place at the park that now holds the Friedrich-Ludwig-Jahn-Sportspark. Viktoria Berlin 89 won the first two titles. This team now plays in the fourth tier *Regionalliga Nordost*.

In April 1892, a match took place between the English Football Club of Berlin and Dresden English Football Club. It may have been a fixture of some stature as Dr Kuegler of Germany's Ministry of Public Instruction and the British ambassador to Germany, Sir Edward Malet, both attended. While the Dresden team was made up entirely of Englishmen, in contrast, the 'English' club from Berlin contained German, Dutch, Danish and even Australian players, in addition to the eponymous English. The visitors proved too strong for the Berliners, running out 6-0 winners. Just three months after that match, on 25 July 1892, Hertha Berliner Sport-Club was founded. Hertha

BSC is now Berlin's premier club, playing in the historic Olympiastadion since the Bundesliga was formed in 1963. It was very different in the beginning, as Hertha was a very small club in a highly competitive field. By now, there were at least 13 clubs in Germany. All of them faced multiple challenges, such as playing fields and equipment. They also faced the abuse of a German public unaccustomed to this foreign sport.

In the coming years, there was a major growth spurt in German clubs, so much so that by the middle of the decade a team made up of players from various clubs mostly drawn from north-west Germany set off from Duisburg to England. On the morning of Tuesday, 1 September 1896, the team landed in Sheerness, Kent. The team did not hang about – that evening, the German side took on Sheppey United in front of 1,000 spectators. Whether it was due to the visitors' sea legs, the terrible conditions or the lack of experience and talent in the German side, the Kentish team won 9-0. The press recorded that the German teams would learn a lot from the English clubs on their tour.[5] While newspapers reported the team represented 'the Germany Football Association', these reports were four years premature, as the nationwide *Deutscher Fußball Bund* (DFB – German Football Association) was not founded until 1900.[6] The team had added to their trouncing at the hands of Sheppey United by losing 15-0 to Chatham, Millwall 9-0, and a select XI at Crystal Palace 13-0. The Crystal Palace team was made up mostly of Corinthians and included three England internationals, G.O. Smith, who scored six goals, M.H. Stanborough and Charles Wreford Brown. The German tourists finished their four-game tour 46-0 down. The German sporting press was scathing at the very thought that this scratch side could be perceived as representing

Germany at football. One report even claimed no one had heard of this touring side and invited them to Berlin for a proper match-up.[7] Despite conceding 46 goals, goalkeeper Schlee had done enough to impress Sheppey United and signed forms with them to play in the Southern League.

Contact between Germany and England remained close, despite this most unofficial of tours. In 1899, a team of English professionals toured Germany to play four games, defeating a combined German and Austrian XI 7-0 in Karlsruhe. The 1899 tour had been arranged by another of Germany's footballing pioneers, Walther Bensemann. He had been introduced to football as a student in Switzerland and ended up founding the 'International Football-Club' in Karlsruhe in 1889, aged just 15. He was a passionate advocate for the game and was instrumental in the creation of the VfR Mannheim club and Kickers Frankfurt, as well as the *kicker* magazine in 1920. Bensemann was no stranger to arranging international tours. In 1908, he arranged for a team of German players – including one of the Jestram brothers of BFC Germania fame – to take on a team of English players and a French side in Paris. Bensemann created a Germanified list of football expressions in 1902 so that the locals could use German words, such as *tor* for goal, rather than English equivalents.

## The foundation of the DFB

While Berlin was the undoubted centre of Germany's nascent football scene, the German Footballers' Union was not accepted in other parts of the country. A groundswell for a united national union was by now irresistible, and on 28 January 1900 representatives from 86 clubs attended a summit in Leipzig – another early footballing hub in Germany – to vote on the formation of the *Deutscher*

*Fußball-Bund* – the German Football Association. The vote was passed by 62 to 22 in favour. Walther Bensemann was in attendance, representing the Mannheim club at Leipzig's Mariengarten. The DFB's first president was to be Professor Dr Ferdinand Hueppe, the oldest man present at the age of 48. Hueppe represented Prague, at the time the capital of Bohemia, part of the Austro-Hungarian Empire with a large ethnic German population. The foundation of the DFB was a major step in driving the adoption and respectability of the game in Germany at a time when hostility was rife and paved the way for the sport's popularity to grow.[8] By 1901, German teams were touring England. A Berlin team was beaten 5-1 by Southampton and 6-2 by Aston Villa that year, but a national team was still seven years away. An estimated 600 football clubs existed across the country with close relations with clubs in Prague and Vienna.[9]

In 1903, the DFB established the first German championships. The bronze *Viktoria* trophy – which had been created by the DFB to commemorate the 1900 Summer Olympics, although Germany did not send a football team – would be presented to German champions from 1903 until 1944. Viktoria sits in an almost serene pose, in contrast to her strident pose atop her column in Berlin's Tiergarten. The trophy disappeared in the final months of the Second World War, before reappearing after German reunification. It was housed at DFB headquarters in Frankfurt am Main before moving to the new German Football Museum in Dortmund in 2015.[10] The *Viktoria* was first awarded to VfB Leipzig, inaugural winners of the German Football Championship. In the early set-up, the winners of regional championships entered, with just six teams entering the 1903 knockout. VfB Leipzig – now known as 1. Lokomotive Leipzig – won the final against Prague side DFC Prag at Altona 93's ground

in Hamburg by seven goals to two. There was no final in
1904 due to a protest between clubs, but VfB Leipzig would
win two more championships before the First World War
intervened and football was halted. Viktoria Berlin won two
titles in that period too. English coaches were key to the
development of the German game at this point, with former
Arsenal and Blackburn player William Townley leading
FV Karlsruhe to the 1909 title before moving on to SpVgg
Fürth. In 1904, Corinthian FC took on VfB Leipzig and
SpVgg Fürth and won both matches 4-1. Two years later,
in Berlin, the Corinthians dispatched Germania 11-0 and
Viktoria 12-1.

German championship finals in this pre-war period
were attracting low thousands of spectators, but attendances
would rocket in the post-war period due to massive
social change. SpVgg Fürth, along with 1. FC Nürnberg,
Hamburger SV and Hertha Berlin, were the main contenders
for silverware in the 1920s. FC Bayern München, Germany's
most successful club in the modern era, was founded in 1900
but would not win the German national title until 1932,
after which Germany was to change dramatically.

## The creation of Die Mannschaft

Efforts to create a 'national' football team to represent
Germany had been made prior to the creation of the DFB,
such as the ill-fated 1896 'Duisburg' trip to England and
Walther Bensemann's hosted matches. But it was not until
1908 that a national team created by the official national
football association took to the field to take on one from
another country. The DFB joined FIFA on the day of its
foundation – 21 May 1904 – by telegram. The country
wanted to take part in international matches to develop
the game, but was at the mercy of regional associations.[11]

As there was no national team manager, the DFB could not identify the best players in the country. Each region pushed for the inclusion of its players, so by 5 April 1908, when the first 'official' German national football team took to the field in Basel to face Switzerland, the first XI was drawn from 11 different clubs. It was the speedy Fritz Becker from the FC Frankfurter Kickers (now Eintracht Frankfurt) who scored the first-ever international goal for Germany in that match. He went on to score a second goal in a 5-3 defeat for the Germans. While in England professionalism had been legalised by the Football Association as early as 1885, in Germany, the DFB had a strictly amateur code. The Germans followed up the Swiss loss with a 3-2 defeat to Austria and a 5-1 loss to an England amateur side that formed the crux of Great Britain's gold medal-winning team at the London Olympics that summer. Germany did not send a team to the Olympics that year. Germany notched its first international victory – against the Swiss – in 1909. Even a record 16-0 win against a fledgling Russian team at the 1912 Stockholm Olympics couldn't disguise the fact that Germany – decked in the black and white of Prussia that *Die Mannschaft* are famous around the world for – were some way behind the leading pack.

During the First World War, many British footballers were held as prisoners of war in German camps. These camps included the famous Ruhleben horse racing track near Berlin, where 4,500 men were penned into stables. The POWs created the Ruhleben Football Association and created tournaments to pass the time. Detainees included the prolific former Derby County and England striker, Steve Bloomer, who had moved to the German capital to coach the Berlin Britannia club just weeks before war was declared in August 1914. Also interned at Ruhleben was Fred Pentland who, like Bloomer, had taken up a coaching role in Germany in 1914 for the national Olympic football team. After the war, Pentland went on to coach the French Olympic football team at the 1920 Antwerp games. He then headed to Spain, where he coached a number of clubs, including Athletic Club de Bilbao and Atlético Madrid. England stars Fred Spiksley and Sam Wolstenholme, and Scottish international John Cameron, were also interned at Ruhleben, while in neighbouring Austria, pioneering coach Jimmy Hogan was also detained. After the war, the British football associations were keen to avoid playing the Germans, as relations were still strained after four years of conflict. But in April 1925, the Corinthians returned. The amateurs beat Köln 4-2, Hamburg 4-1 two days later and on the next day drew with Tennis Borussia in Berlin. The tourists returned three years later, beating Hannover and drawing with Hamburg. As relations thawed with Britain, so Germany hosted England in the first official international between the two nations in 1930 in Berlin. Germany came from behind twice to lead 3-2 before ten-man England equalised late on. Germany would not beat England on English soil until 1972.

## What of the German football pioneers?

Konrad Koch continued to teach in Braunschweig and died aged 65 in 1911. His colleague, August Hermann, who played a role in introducing both Association football and basketball into Germany, died aged 70 in 1906 and was inducted into the Lower Saxony Institute of Sport History in 1988. Walther Bensemann's legacy – *kicker* magazine – is Germany's leading football publication. As the son of a Jewish father, Bensemann fled the rise of the Nazis in 1933 and moved to Montreux, Switzerland, and died a year later. As for BFC Germania 1888, the oldest club in

Germany celebrated its 130th birthday in April 2018 with an entertaining 5-4 victory against SSC Südwest II in the tenth tier of German football, the Kreisliga B.

1 https://www.theguardian.com/football/2017/feb/01/which-football-club-champions-have-suffered-the-biggest-fall-from-grace

2 https://www.bfcgermania88.de/verein/chronik.html

3 Hesse, Ulrich, *Tor! The Story of German Football* (London: WSC Books, 2003)

4 https://www.dfb.de/en/about-dfb/

5 *Daily Telegraph & Courier*, 2 September 1896

6 *Sheffield Evening Telegraph*, 1 September 1896

7 *Sporting Life*, 22 September 1896

8 https://www.dfb.de/en/about-dfb/

9 *Lancashire Evening Post*, 1 November 1901 (p5)

10 https://www.dfb.de/news/detail/pokale-auf-reisen-viktoria-und-co-wandern-ins-fussballmuseum-123277/

11 Hesse, Ulrich, *Tor! The Story of German Football* (London: WSC Books, 2003)

# 15.

# Austria

ON THE morning of 23 January 1939, the naked, lifeless body of a man was discovered lying next to his unconscious partner at her Viennese apartment. This man was Matthias Sindelar who, six decades after his death, would be voted Austria's greatest sportsman of the 20th century. Sindelar was found with his unconscious girlfriend, Camilla Castagnola, the 40-year-old owner of the famous Viennese Wesses Roessl restaurant. She died later in hospital. Investigators concluded carbon monoxide poisoning caused the couple's death. The lack of clarity of cause of death at the time has fuelled the rumours that Sindelar was the victim of an assassination and subsequent cover-up. Sindelar, days short of his 36th birthday, had been a fervent opponent of the *Anschluss*, the forced annexation of Austria to Nazi Germany on 12 March 1938. Born Matěj Šindelář in the ethnically Czech Moravia region, the family moved to Vienna when Matěj was just five years old, when his family Germanified his name to Matthias Sindelar. His creativity, pace and poise despite his slim build led him to be nicknamed 'Der Papierene' (The Paper Man) in the Austrian press. Under the capable coaching of Hugo Meisl, with whom Sindelar would fall out, Austria crafted its famous *Wunderteam* of the early 1930s.

The *Wunderteam* was feted for its attractive play and routed Germany twice, 6-0 in Berlin and 5-0 in Vienna. Observers at the Football Association had already warned that the Austrians could match England before the *Wunderteam* ran the Three Lions close at Stamford Bridge in 1932.[1] Sindelar scored in a 4-3 defeat that day and was voted Vienna's most popular man that year. The previous year, he'd netted the fifth in Austria's 5-0 defeat of a Scotland side weakened by the absence of Rangers or Celtic players, but still a strong outfit. It was the first time Scotland had lost to continental opposition. Free-scoring Austria would also put eight goals past its neighbours Switzerland and Hungary in this era. Going into the 1934 World Cup in Italy, the Austrian *Wunderteam* was past its best but still a hard team to beat. The hosts and the Austrians met in the semi-finals in Milan with Austria growing into the tournament. But Meisl was without the influential midfielder Johann Horvath, injured in the previous match, and Sindelar was brutally man-marked out of the game by the *Azzurri*'s Luis Monti, who had represented Argentina at the first World Cup in 1930. The 1934 World Cup is tainted with accusations that Italian dictator Mussolini had arranged for Italy to win the tournament for propaganda purposes. Before the game, Meisl believed his team had no chance and his team was bullied out of the game in the mud of the San Siro. His battered and beleaguered team would lose the fourth-place play-off to Germany, whose new *Fürher*, the Austrian-born Adolf Hitler, had his eyes on reunification with his homeland. First up, though, was Hitler's own sporting propaganda festival, the Berlin Olympics of 1936, where Austria would again come up short against Italy in the final of the football tournament.

Despite Sindelar being Catholic, rumours abounded in the anti-Semitic climate of Germany and Austria at the time that he was Jewish. This rumour was based mainly on his Moravian roots – an area with a high Jewish population – and the fact that he played for FK Austria Wien, labelled by the Nazis as a *Judenklub* (Jewish Club). The Anschluss Match arranged between Germany and Austria for 3 April 1938 at the Prater Stadium in Vienna was, for the Nazis, to be a celebration of the coming together of the two countries. It was also planned to be the last game that Austria would play as an independent football nation before being merged into the greater Germany team. In an act of defiance, the Austrian side ditched its traditional white shirts and black shorts and donned the red and white of the national flag. The organisers had apparently designed the match to finish as a draw, but the Austrian team won 2-0 that day. Sindelar missed a hatful of supposedly simple chances, and some felt he was almost mocking the German players. The Paper Man scored in the second half, and when Sesta put the Austrians two up, Sindelar is reported to have danced in celebration in front of the watching Nazi top brass.

Did the Nazis see this popular footballer, who later refused future World Cup-winning coach Sepp Herberger's approaches to play for the unified German and Austrian team, as such a threat as to have him assassinated? Evidence suggests that Sindelar's neighbours had complained that one of the building's chimneys was blocked, which could have led to the odourless threat of carbon monoxide poisoning.[2] In many ways, Austria's rapid ascent and fall in the 1930s has similarities to that experienced by its former imperial twin, Hungary, two decades later. Like Hungary's 'Golden Team' of the 1950s, the *Wunderteam* was the first continental opponent to beat one of the British powerhouses in Scotland, got deep into the World Cup, and had its Puskás in Sindelar. The fact that Austria was so strong in the 1930s was due in part to the accelerated development of football in the country. In 1925, it became the first European country outside Britain to launch a professional football league, a path that began just three decades before in the exciting cosmopolitan crucible of 1890s Vienna.

## The birth of Austrian football

By 1890, the success of the Austro-Hungarian Empire helped swell Vienna's population to more than two million. The city's coffee shops became the meeting places of *Jung Wien* (Young Vienna) as writers and artists gathered to discuss the topics of the day in Vienna's fashionable cafés. Vienna was confident, vibrant and always ready to try something new.

It was into this environment that British gardeners working for Nathaniel Meyer von Rothschild, of the Rothschild banking group that his grandfather founded, started kicking a ball around. The ball had been provided by Franz Joli, the son of the estate manager who had been educated in Britain. It was a four-a-side match as the English took on the Austrians, and it churned up the Rothschild's lawns. The philanthropic Rothschild allocated some land for them to play on to save his lawn from further damage. In gratitude, the gardeners donned the vertically divided yellow and blue of the Rothschild's racing colours and called themselves First Vienna FC. It was a genuinely international affair reflecting the position of the Austrian capital as a cosmopolitan centre at the end of the 19th century; the founders included Austrian Catholics and Jews, British expats, Germans, and French and Balkan émigrés. The date was 22 August 1894. The club's crest – three legs around a football – was inspired by the *triskelion* flag of designer

William Beale's homeland, the Isle of Man. The president was Jewish accountant Georg Fuchs, and the first captain was Franz Joli himself. Almost immediately, First Vienna FC had a rival. The Vienna Cricket Club had already been established for two years but in August 1894 added its football branch to become Vienna Cricket and Football Club. It is officially just one day younger than First Vienna and became known locally simply as *Cricketer*.

Association football had been played in Austrian schools since 1879, and an organised match took place between the students in Graz in the spring of 1894. However, First Vienna and Vienna Cricket and Football Club are the first recognised clubs founded in the country. The two teams met on 15 November 1894 at First Vienna's Kuglerwiese ground in front of 300 curious spectators. The exclusively British Cricketers ran out 4-0 winners in what is considered Austria's first official football match and won by the same margin at home in the wide-open parklands of Prater two weeks later. Cricketer, dressed in blue and black, had the advantage of playing in football boots and experience of playing at home rather than learning the game from scratch. The third encounter also ended 4-0, but this time in favour of First Vienna. This rivalry was known as the 'Gardeners' against the 'Bankers', as many of the Cricketer team worked in the finance sector. By 1896, the derby had become enough of a draw to attract the British ambassador. Just three years after their first encounter, Vienna Cricket and Football Club's co-founder John Gramlick – who owned a plumbing company in the Austrian capital – suggested the founding of a pioneering international club competition. Named simply the Challenge Cup, the tournament was established exclusively for clubs in the Austro-Hungarian Empire. These teams came almost exclusively from the major cities of Vienna, Budapest and Prague, and ran consistently until 1905, with two further editions in the 1908/09 and 1910/11 seasons. It was a forerunner to the Mitropa Cup that Meisl would launch as secretary of the Austrian Football Association in 1927.

## 'Old Nick' takes Austrian football forward

The most important pioneer in 1890s Austrian football was Mark Nicholson. Nicknamed 'Old Nick', the former professional who had won the FA Cup with West Bromwich Albion in 1892 came to Austria in 1897 to manage the Viennese branch of the Thomas Cook & Son travel agency. On 15 November that year, he debuted for First Vienna against Cricketer and was by some way the standout player. Alexander Juraske is the author of *Blau-Gelb Ist Mein Herz* (My Heart is Blue and Yellow), the biography of First Vienna Football Club. He tells me that Nicholson played a critical role in Viennese football's development. He introduced the goal net, he established the first professional-standard training methods, he wrote newspaper articles about training methods and ordered his players not to drink and smoke, especially in the day before a match. 'His main goal was to bring the native Viennese players to the level of the British expats in Vienna. Therefore, competing against foreign clubs to develop the situation in Vienna was also important for him,' Juraske says. Given the expense of inviting and hosting foreign clubs, Nicholson and others formed a committee – the *Comité zur Veranstaltung von Fußball-Wettspielen* (Committee for the Organisation of Football Competitions) – to raise money to invite foreign clubs to Vienna, especially British clubs.

By 1899, British teams were indeed touring. Oxford University sent a team that demolished a Vienna XI 15-0 on

Easter Sunday. The following day, the Dark Blues romped home 13-0 against a multicultural Viennese team at Prater in front of several thousand spectators. Southampton FC became the first professional side to visit a year later. The Viennese had clearly improved as the margin of defeat to the Saints was just 6-0 this time around. At the turn of the new century, Nicholson's committee had become the *Österreichische Fußball-Union* (Austrian Football Union), with Old Nick as its first president until he returned to England in October 1900. Nicholson had achieved his main objective. As well as giving Austrian football a serious structure, in December 1899 First Vienna FC beat Cricketer without a single British player in its line-up.

## Viennese football mushrooms

Vienna continued to be the hub of footballing activity, with the foundation of Wiener Athletiksport Club (AC) in 1897, who went on to win three Challenge Cups. In the same year, the Erster Wiener Arbeiter Fußball-Club (First Viennese Workers' Football Club) was founded by a group of smelters. The club's founding ethos demonstrates the class divide between those who participated in football in turn-of-the-century Vienna and those who could not. Rather like England two decades previously, the game was splitting into the gentlemen players and working-class men who could play whenever they could. Erster Wiener Arbeiter Fußball-Club invited working-class men from across Vienna to join. The club rebranded two years later as Sportklub Rapid Wien, ditching its red and blue for green and white, and went on to become the country's most successful club. Nineteen hundred was also the year that the first attempts at a league format were established, with the backing of one of Austria's leading newspapers. The *Neue Wiener Tagblatt-Pokal* was a three-division competition for Viennese clubs that ran for three editions between 1900 and 1903. It is considered a forerunner of the future Austrian championship. The top flight, the Erste Klasse, featured four teams at the *Pokal's* launch, including First Vienna, Vienna Cricket and Football Club, Wiener AC and Wiener FC 1898. Meanwhile two parallel second divisions – Zweite Klasse A and Zweite Klasse B – contested one promotion position to the top flight, while the bottom two in the Erste Klasse could drop into Zweite Klasse A or B. As in the Challenge Cup, Wiener AC dominated, winning three *Pokal*s.

In 1901, an international had been played against Switzerland and, in 1904, the national football association was formed, the *Österreichischer Fußball-Bund* (ÖFB – Austrian Football Association). A year later, it was a member of FIFA and Austria was truly on the map as a destination for touring football sides. Both Glasgow giants, Rangers and Celtic, toured in 1904. Celtic beat the hosts 6-1 while Rangers won 7-2, although reports suggest the Gers conceded two goals out of politeness. Rangers' visit, in particular, would leave a lasting impression on football, not just in Austria, but also in neighbouring Hungary. The Scottish passing game was different from the physical English kick-and-rush style of the time. When asked by the Scottish press what the Austrian public made of the two Glaswegian sides, Rangers' tactics and style of play proved most popular.[3] Rangers were also impressed with goalkeeper Karl Pekarna and signed him up. In their summary, the Austrians lament that they have not learned that much from the Scottish professionals, just that they lacked practical experience against stronger teams. The Viennese also felt they had greatly improved in recent years. 'The visit of foreign teams was very important for the sport's development. The Austrian clubs became better and better. Further, foreign players joined Viennese clubs and the typical Austrian playing style derived from the "Scottish combination game",' Juraske tells me.

This Scottish-influenced *Donaufußball* (Danubian football) style was popular throughout the three main Austro-Hungarian capitals of Vienna, Budapest and Prague, and the rivalry between clubs from these three cities would be key to the game's development in Central Europe. First Vienna once played 85 games in one season, just 24 of which were part of the domestic championship and cup; the rest were friendlies aimed at spreading the game. To build on the momentum, Spurs and Everton were offered £600 each to tour in 1905, each playing five Austro-Hungarian sides before two set pieces against each other.[4] The continued improvement in standard was matched by public enthusiasm and by 1907 there were an estimated 300 active football clubs in Austria, 70 of which were in the capital. In May 1908, a Manchester United side featuring Billy Meredith outclassed Vienna Athletic Club 5-0. The following month, England played its first matches away to continental opposition, defeating an Austrian national side made up of players from Vienna and Prague 6-1 at Cricketer Platz in Vienna. A crowd of 3,500 witnessed the historic match, and, two days later, 5,000 fans would witness an even bigger drubbing by England as Austria lost 11-1 at the Hohe Warte Stadion. Spurs' Vivian Woodward bagged four goals.

By now, some players at Vienna Cricket and Football Club were starting to fall out with their own club officials. In 1910, they broke away to form what would go on to become Vienna's second-biggest club – Wiener Amateur Sportverein, now better known as Austria Wien. The capital remained the hub of Austrian football. In 1911, the Lower Austrian Football Association (NÖFV) created the first recognised league championship in the country. The *Österreichische Fußballmeisterschaft* (Austrian Football Championship) launched for the 1911/12 season featured 12 clubs from Vienna, including the two oldest sides, First Vienna and Vienna Cricket and Football Club. Two points were awarded for a win, one for a draw and none for a loss. Rapid won the first title by a point from Wiener Sportklub.

## Austria hits the international stage

By 1912, plans were afoot to send an Austrian team to the Stockholm Olympics under the tutelage of Hugo Meisl. The team just needed the right man to coach them. They found him in Englishman Jimmy Hogan. A Lancastrian born to Irish parents, Hogan had enjoyed a 13-year playing career with Burnley, Fulham, Bolton Wanderers and his hometown, Nelson. Hogan was one of the game's early holistic thinkers. Hogan didn't just pioneer tactics; he would also factor in pitch conditions, player diets, and even which match ball was to be used. Stunned by the Austrians' love of red meat, Hogan got the team prepped on green vegetables and fruit. The Austrians defeated Germany 5-1 in the first round before exiting to the Netherlands 3-1 in the second. Meisl was so hands-on he even refereed Finland's first-round match with Italy.

Hogan's work had only just begun when fate intervened. On 28 June 1914, the heir to the Austro-Hungarian throne, Archduke Franz Ferdinand, was assassinated on a visit to Sarajevo. The descent into war began, and Britain and Austria were on opposing sides. As a foreign national, Hogan was detained but avoided internment due to his friendship with some influential department store owners. They hired him to do odd jobs before the Austrian authorities sent him to Budapest, where he went on to manage the ambitious

MTK Budapest club. Recounting his experience after the war in 1919, Hogan complained at the treatment of him and his family by the Austrian FA and authorities. He had been imprisoned in Austria with common criminals and murderers.[5] By the time Hogan got over his experience and returned to Vienna in 1931 to help Meisl build the *Wunderteam*, Austrian football had exploded. 'During World War One football became a mass phenomenon,' Juraske explains. 'During their military service all men from different social classes came into contact with football. Military saw the benefit from football in the physical training of the soldiers and its help to distract them with sport activities from the war situation.'

## Austrian football comes of age

Defeat in the war led to the exiling of the Habsburgs and the disintegration of the Austro-Hungarian Empire. Vienna now ruled over a country of 6.5 million mainly German speakers instead of its pre-war, multicultural empire of 50 million people. The Treaty of Saint-Germain in 1919 put an end to hopes of a merger with the new German Weimar Republic as the allies prohibited economic or political union, fearing a strong German bloc could re-emerge. It was this prevalent belief in a greater Germany that would lead to the *Anschluss* less than two decades later. A smaller, chastened, Austrian republic was born. Social reforms were enacted, including the introduction of an eight-hour working day. Austrian workers now had more leisure time, and the number of registered players rose from 14,000 before the outbreak of war to 37,000 in 1921.[6] As the game spread, so football became increasingly politicised. Rapid Wien further entrenched its position as the team of the working class, while FK Wiener Amateure and Hakoah Wien – 'Hakoah' being the Hebrew word for 'the strength' – had Jewish connections. New superstars were emerging to be adored by an increasingly attentive public. Long before Sindelar was wowing the Viennese public, Rapid's stocky striker Josef Uridil, who had acquired the nickname 'The Tank' during the war, bulldozed his way through defences. In one famous 1921 match, Rapid trailed Wiener AC 1-5 at half-time and 3-5 with just a quarter of an hour to play, yet won 7-5. The Tank had scored all seven for Rapid. Uridil was Austria's Billy Meredith, as success on the pitch – three straight Austrian championships for Rapid between 1919 and 1921 and again in 1923 – led to lucrative sponsorship deals. He launched his own beer, *Uridil*, among other endorsements, and even had a musical piece written in his honour.

There was money in Austrian football, and in 1924 the top two national divisions went professional, the first European leagues to do so outside of Britain. Wiener Amateure changed its name to FK Austria Wien and Hakoah won the first professional title of the 11-club championship in the 1924/25 season. It would be Hakoah's only title. So strong was Austrian football at this time that First Vienna hammered FC Barcelona 4-1 on a tour of Spain in 1925. Meisl's Danubian style of play epitomises the intellectualism of Central Europe and helped develop superior tactics to the English style of kick-and-rush. Meisl continued to be the shining light in Austrian football during this period as secretary of the ÖFB. He spearheaded the creation of the Mitropa Cup, a tournament that built on the promise of the long-abandoned Challenge Cup, and which was designed for the top professional teams of Central Europe. By now, both Austria's neighbours Hungary and Czechoslovakia had turned professional to deter their top players from defecting to Vienna. The Mitropa Cup's format was mirrored by later pan-European tournaments, and pioneered home and away legs. Two representatives from Austria, Czechoslovakia, Hungary and Yugoslavia could send their respective champions and either league runners-up or cup winners. Rapid Wien would appear in three of the first four tournament finals, losing to Czech side Sparta Praha in 1927 and Hungary's Ferencváros in 1928, before triumphing in 1930. By this time Italian clubs had replaced Yugoslav teams, and the tournament expanded to four teams per country by 1934. The tournament was revived after the Second World War and survived until 1992.

While the Mitropa Cup gave Central European clubs international competition, Meisl spotted a lack of a tournament outside the Olympics for national sides. His suggestion was a Central European International Cup played over a series of games. The trophy was named after ÖFB director and former referee, Josef Gerö. Italy won the first Dr Gerö Cup, held between 1927 and 1930, while the *Wunderteam* triumphed in the second edition held from 1931 to 1932. Elsewhere on the international stage, Austria joined the majority of European nations in turning down the opportunity to take part in the first World Cup in Uruguay in 1930. It is conceivable that Meisl's team could have triumphed there. Hugo Meisl, the man from a wealthy family who turned his back on a banking career to follow his passion for football, should be remembered by history as one of the true pioneers of European football. Along with his friend Jimmy Hogan, he innovated in training and diet, creating one of the most exciting and entertaining sides in world history. In his role within football administration, he created early prototypes of European club and national team competitions and led the march to professionalism in Continental Europe. Austrian football has never again reached the heights of Meisl and Hogan's *Wunderteam*. The country finished third in the 1954 World Cup in neighbouring Switzerland, so the periods immediately before and after the Second World War are the high watermarks for Austrian football.

## First Vienna FC today

Much like Austria's national team, First Vienna's glory days were in the early 1930s, captured forever in grainy black and white. Aside from back-to-back Challenge Cups in 1899 and 1900, the club won all its silverware between 1929 and 1955. In 1931, First Vienna won the double of Austrian championship and Mitropa Cup, creating a unique feat by winning all six matches en route to victory. During the Second World War the club was permitted to keep its English name. Since its sixth and final national title in 1955, the club has largely been left behind by the established Austrian powerhouses within Vienna – Rapid and FK Austria – while regional clubs including Stürm Graz and Red Bull Salzburg have challenged the capital's sides in recent decades. At the time of writing, First Vienna plays in the fifth tier of the Austrian league system. The club had been relegated due to its financial problems and was declared insolvent in spring 2017. The club was saved by an Austrian insurance company, which became the club's sponsor in May 2017. At the Hohe Warte stadium in Vienna, the football club founded in 1894 by British gardeners working for the Rothschild family, you can still hear the fans proclaim in English, 'Vienna 'til I die!' The club is staying at its historic Hohe Warte ground because it has a rental contract with the city of Vienna, who owns the land. The Vienna Cricket and Football Club also still exists near its original home in Prater. It has an athletics and tennis division now but no football section. First Vienna joined the Club of Pioneers in 2018.

1   Smith, Rory, *Mister: The Men Who Taught the World to Beat England at Their Own Game* (London: Simon & Schuster, 2016, p101)

2   https://www.theguardian.com/football/2007/apr/03/sport.comment3

3   *Scottish Referee*, 30 May 1904 (p2)

4   https://footballpink.net/2018-10-19-hugo-meisl-and-the-englishman-who-ruled-vienna/

5   *Sheffield Independent*, 12 March 1919 (p6)

6   Goldblatt, David, *The Ball is Round: A Global History of Football* (London: Penguin, 2007)

# 16.

# Hungary

BUDAPEST'S RUMBACH Sebestyén street is a narrow thoroughfare in the Hungarian capital's Jewish quarter. It seems a pretty out-of-the-way place to stumble across a celebration of what is arguably the most significant moment in the country's sporting history. A mural entitled *6:3* depicts the victory of the *Aranycsapat* (Golden Team) over England at Wembley in November 1953. The 'Match of the Century' was the first home defeat for England to any continental side, and was in many ways a watershed for English football, tactically. This point was driven home in a return fixture in Budapest just six months later when the Golden Team dispatched an England team featuring Billy Wright and Tom Finney 7-1 in front of around 100,000 people. The FA could no longer view the 6-3 as a one-off; England was way behind the best, and the follow-up record defeat just emphasised this fact. The 50m-wide, 30m-high artwork is Hungary's largest mural, which puts the Match of the Century into context. It features Honvéd goalkeeper and captain Gyula Grosics contesting a high ball and a Hungarian shot going in past England keeper Gil Merrick. Both images are surrounded by newspaper cuttings from the time. It was completed on the 60th anniversary of the match, and it took its creator,

Hungarian mural artists Neopaint Works, three weeks and 400 litres of paint to complete. I stumbled across it quite by chance while on a visit to the Hungarian capital and was captivated.

Alongside Ferenc Puskás, that *Aranycsapat* team – also known as the 'Mighty Magyars' in English – included Sandor Kocsis, József Bozsik, Zoltán Czibor and Nándor Hidegkuti. They had won gold at the Helsinki Olympics in 1952 and should really have won the 1954 World Cup in Switzerland, but fell short to Sepp Herberger's West Germany in the final. The Hungarian Revolution of 1956 pretty much signalled the end of Hungarian footballing dominance, with some of the team moving abroad. Puskás, famously, went on to win three European Cups at Real Madrid, while Czibor and Kocsis signed for FC Barcelona. English teams had first come to Hungary at the cusp of the 20th century to teach the locals how to play the game. Half a century later, the Hungarians had returned to teach the English – and the world – a whole new ball game. While England's high point may be 1966, and for Scotland 1967, Hungary's zenith was in the first half of the 1950s, and the national team has not hit those heights since. But where did it all begin for Hungarian football?

## The birth of Hungarian football

Football arrived in Hungary in the last decade of the 19th century, which was an exciting time for the country. In the 1890s, Hungary, as part of the Austro-Hungarian Empire, was part of the second-biggest state in Europe after Russia. The traditional capital of Buda had merged with Pest in 1873 to create a new and vibrant centre of Hungarian administration. Economic growth was stronger than that of Britain and Germany, and the city was quick to adopt new technology and ideas. By the mid-1890s, Budapest had the first underground railway network in Continental Europe. The creation of football clubs and tournaments around the world in the late 19th century had relied in significant part on the presence of a British community. The lack of a strong British presence put football's emergence and spread at a disadvantage in Hungary.

According to Hungarian football historian, Péter Szegedi, it was left to Hungarian travellers to Britain to discover, bring back and promote the game. The first recorded account of a football game in Hungary comes from 1879 when sportswriter László Kosztovits returned from England with a ball and tried to encourage his friends in the town of Szentendre outside Budapest to play but they don't appear to have been impressed. 'This game is not for humans' was their feedback.[1] Kosztovits was ahead of his time by more than a decade. By the early 1890s records show that several schools on the Pest side of the Danube were playing football – although without anyone with hands-on experience of the sport it appears they often played with muddled rules. In one account, a gymnastics teacher named Szaffka Manó introduced a football from England but had mistranslated the rules, mistaking 'kick' for 'hit', resulting in his students doing the opposite of what they should have been and ending up with sore hands. This new sport was initially known as *Angollabda* – English ball. In 1893, the Buda Gymnastics Association was running kickabouts in Buda on the west bank of the Danube. Three years later in the autumn of 1896, sportsman Károly Löwenrosen returned from a stint in England with a football that concerned Hungarian customs officers enough to fine the traveller 11 forints, at the time a princely sum. Löwenrosen had to raise donations from the public to release the ball. According to

Szegedi, Löwenrosen taught anyone who wanted to learn how to play and by All Saints' Day, 1 November 1896, he had organised a full-scale match. The game finished after just 20 minutes due to players kicking *each other*!

Löwenrosen was not alone in importing footballs in 1896. Ferenc Ray, a Hungarian engineer working in Zürich, an exciting football hub at the time, also brought back a football to show to the members of the Budapest Gymnastics Club (*Budapesti Torna Club* – BTC). BTC was a prestigious establishment that had provided three athletes to the Hungarian Olympic team that year. The resulting kickabout resulted in several broken lights and windows. Yet, by May of the following year, two teams of the BTC braved the rain to play an exhibition match in front of 100 spectators, with those in blue and white comprehensively beating their red and white opponents 5-0. Ferenc Ray netted all five goals. Hungarian football was born. Public curiosity was raised further when the Englishmen of Vienna Cricket and Football Club visited to play the BTC on 31 October 1897. That day, 2,000 people turned up to watch. The public was hooked. In 1898, there were 14 matches between gymnasium and academic teams across the Hungarian capital. This figure more than doubled in 1899, and it was around the turn of the new century that Hungary's first dedicated football clubs were founded, some of whom went on to dominate domestic football and forge a name for themselves across Europe and the world.

## Hungary's football giants are formed

In the late 19th century, Újpest was just a small town on the Danube north of Budapest. It has long since been swallowed into District IV of the Hungarian capital as it expanded, but it was here that, in 1885, school teacher János Goll formed

the Újpest Torna Egylet (TE) athletic club. Here, locals
could practise gymnastics and fencing under the motto of
'Soundness, Strength, Harmony'.[2] In 1899, a year in which
31 exhibition football matches were played, Újpest TE added
its footballing arm, Újpest Football Club, which adopted the
purple and white colours of the gym. In 1900, the number
of football matches in Budapest had more than doubled
again to 82. One of these was a 1-1 draw between Újpest
FC and the III Kerületi gymnasium on 29 April 1900. The
two merged a year later and joined the second division of
the newly formed Hungarian League.

Meanwhile, in the southern suburb of Ferencváros a group
of youths known locally as the 'Gang of Eleven' were playing
football in factory grounds. One of the boys had worked in
Prague and seen the British workers play the game there, while
another, István Weisz, played in goal at times for the BTC.
These boys were keen to form a football club and join the
growing number springing up around Budapest but lacked the
funds to get their project off the ground. A local baker, József
Gráf, had connections. Gráf convinced Dr Ferenc Springer, an
influential member of the community, to get on board, and on
3 May 1899 after several discussions the Ferencvárosi Torna
Club (FTC) was founded. While the club's main objective
was to play football, the presence of 'Torna' – gymnastics –
gave it the flexibility to expand into other sports. Springer
was confirmed as club president.[3] The members of the new
Ferencvárosi Torna Club had initially planned to use the red,
white and green colours of the Hungarian flag as inspiration
for their kit. As the BTC already adopted red and white as its
club colours, Ferencváros opted for green and white. An empty
site was secured for a period of six years, albeit smaller than the
standard size of a football pitch, while the club had to store its
goalposts in a nearby café. The site on the Soroksári Út was

developed by members into a usable stadium for 1,500 people and a single open-air shower. The ground opened on 25 March 1900 to a full house against Óbudai, with the visitors winning 1-0. Ferencváros, the club that would go on to become the most successful in domestic Hungarian football, had to wait another week before registering its first win when it trounced the III Kerületi gym team 4-1. Ferencváros used the site for its first decade before moving on, and the site is still a sports club today with a couple of five-a-side football pitches and tennis courts.

## Hungarian football gets organised

By the turn of the new century, it was clear that an organisational body was required to oversee the game's development in Hungary. Matches were being arranged independently between gyms and sports clubs, and they were proving so violent that in 1900 Budapest city council considered banning football altogether. Neither the Hungarian Athletic Association nor the Hungarian National Gymnastics Association wanted the responsibility of running the sport. So, in 1901, 12 clubs got together and formed the Hungarian Football Federation, the *Magyar Labdarúgó Szövetség* (MLSZ). The MLSZ joined FIFA in 1907. In March 1901, the first championship – a two-division set-up called the *Nemzeti Bajnokság* (National Championship) – was established, with BTC winning the first two editions of the tournament. The BTC team could count among its number Alfréd Hajós, one of Hungary's most celebrated sportsmen. While England had the Corinthian Charles Burgess (C.B.) Fry as an exceptional sporting all-rounder, Hungary had Hajós.

Hajós, born to a Jewish family as Arnold Guttmann, was one of an estimated 45,000 Hungarian Jews that changed

*An early photo of Sheffield Football Club, founded 1857 (Credit: Sheffield FC)*

*The foundation plaque of the Football Association, Great Queen Street, London (author)*

*Foundation plaque of the Football League, Manchester city centre (author)*

*Corinthian-Casuals FC return to play Corinthians Paulista, São Paulo, 2015 (Credit: Stuart Tree,* Brothers in Football *film)*

*Lily Parr of the Dick, Kerr Ladies, the first female footballer to be commemorated with a statue (Credit: National Football Museum, Manchester)*

*Hampden Bowling Club, Glasgow, site of the first Hampden Park and scene of early internationals between Scotland and England (author)*

*Queen's Park FC 1880/81, with Andrew Watson back left (Credit: Queen's Park FC)*

*Cathkin Park, Glasgow, former home of Third Lanark (author)*

*Bohemian FC, Dublin's oldest team, taken in 1905 (Credit: Bohemian FC)*

*Le Havre Athletic Club, France's pioneer club, pictured in 1902/03 (Credit: Le Havre Athletic Club)*

*Antwerp FC in 1895 (Credit: Royal Antwerp FC)*

*Opening fixture at Bosuilstadion, Belgium v England 1923 (Credit: Royal Antwerp FC)*

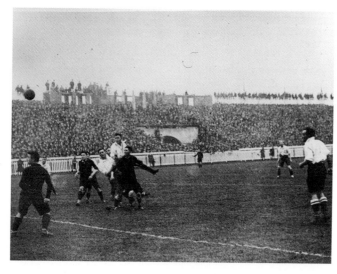

*Early Haarlemsche Football Club (Credit: Koninklijke HFC)*

*Pim Mulier, founder of the Haarlemsche Football Club (Credit: Koninklijke HFC)*

*Albion FC of Montevideo, Uruguay's first football club. William Leslie Poole is centre with the ball (Credit: Albion FC)*

*Alumni Athletic Club, a key club in early Argentine football, pictured in 1910 (Credit unknown)*

*The reformed clubs of Fall River (black) and Fall River Marksmen (red and white) contest the 2020 Taça de Fall River (Credit: Fall River Marksmen FC and Luke Stergiou)*

*The Corinthian Cup, Budapest, pictured in 2019 (Credit: Andy Nunn)*

*Corinthian-Casuals FC in pink and burgundy return to Budapest for the Egri Ebstein Tournament 2019 (Credit: Andy Nunn)*

*William Alexander Mackay, founder of Spain's first football club, Recreativo de Huelva (Credit: Mackay Family Archive)*

*Joan Gamper, co-founder and player, FC Barcelona (Credit: © author unknown/Archivo FC Barcelona)*

The first public match in Portugal, Cascais 1888 (Credit: Arquivo Histórico Municipal de Cascais ref AHMCSC/AESP/CNM/311)

The first Casa Pia Atlético Clube side, 1920. Cándido de Oliveira is standing, third from the right (Credit: Casa Pia Atlético Clube)

James Richardson Spensley, pioneer of Italian football (Credit: fotografici Archivio Storico Fondazione Genoa 1893)

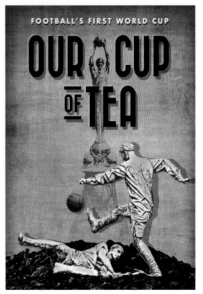

Poster for West Auckland Town FC's 2019 documentary, **Our Cup of Tea** (Credit: West Auckland Town FC)

Hussein Hegazi of Dulwich Hamlet, pictured in 1912 (Credit: Dulwich Hamlet FC)

The football team from South Africa to tour Britain and France in 1899 (Credit: The National Archives, ref. COPY1/442/254)

their name to sound 'more Hungarian' between 1881 and 1919 in the face of rising anti-Semitism, a key feature in the story of Hungarian football in the first half of the 20th century. Hajós – which means 'sailor' in Hungarian – was inspired to swim after his father drowned in the Danube when he was aged 13. He won the 100m and 1,200m freestyle swimming golds at the 1896 Athens Olympics. Two years later he held Hungary's 100m sprint, 400m hurdles and discus titles. He also represented Hungary in its first football international against Austria in Vienna in 1902, spent some years refereeing and went on to coach the Hungarian national team in 1906. Hajós was an architect by trade, and he transferred his love of sport into designing buildings to host games. Hungary's C.B. Fry had become Hungary's Archibald Leitch. He designed Újpest's stadium, opened in 1922, a string of gymnasiums and sports grounds, and the National Swimming Stadium on Margaret Island that now bears his name.

Just one week after the league's foundation, another future giant was born from a gymnasium: Magyar Testgyakorlók Köre Budapest Futball Club – MTK Budapest – who would go on to form the 'Eternal Derby', Hungary's oldest and fiercest rivalry, with Ferencváros. *Magyar Testgyakorlók Köre* in English is 'Hungarian Body Exercise Circle', and the club was founded by mostly liberal middle-class Jews with a view to encouraging assimilation in a climate of growing ethnic tension. MTK's debut finished in a goalless draw with BTC in 1901, not a bad result considering BTC was the dominant force in Hungary at the time. MTK started in the second division.

With a national football association in place and a league established, the next step was for the MLSZ to put a team together to test the strength of the Hungarian game.

The natural opponent was neighbouring Austria, and on 12 October 1902, the two met each other in Vienna with the Austrians demonstrating the gulf in class with a decisive 5-0 victory. In 1902, a team from Oxford University toured. Three years previously, the university had played two games against local sides in both Vienna and Prague, winning by an aggregate of 40-0. In four matches in Budapest in March 1902, Oxford University hammered each of the Hungarian pioneer clubs of Polytechnic Budapest, Muegyetemi FC, Magyar Atlétikai Club and Ferencváros by margins of more than ten goals. The students left Budapest having scored 58 goals without reply in just four games. The heavy defeats did not dampen Hungarian enthusiasm for the game and English sides Richmond Association FC and Surrey Wanderers both toured. The Budapest scene was looking even more promising than in fellow Danubian city, Vienna. By 1903, there were 25 clubs and plenty of enthusiasm. All the Budapest clubs needed was experienced coaches to take their game forward.Steps were taken to address this knowledge gap, with the reporter stating that he'd learned of at least one English coach in the Hungarian capital assisting teams with their development.[4] By 1904, Szaffka Manó – the physical education master we met earlier who had initially apparently misinterpreted the rules – was now publishing one of the first football education and rule books in Hungary.

The Corinthians visited in April 1904, hammering MTK 6-0, BTC 9-0 and Magyar Atlétikai Klub by 12 goals. The tourists were treated with generous hospitality on their tour of the Austro-Hungarian capitals and were so impressed with the spirit of their Hungarian hosts that the club donated a trophy, the Corinthian Cup. This trophy would be fought for by Hungary's best amateur sides for the next three decades. It would also sit in the Hungarian Sport Museum – in storage, not on display – for decades until Corinthian-Casuals FC returned for a summer tournament in 2019. Within three years of Corinthians' 1904 Danubian tour, football had spread so far outside the capital that the first regional leagues were established for the north, south, west and Transylvania. Football had truly gone nationwide and higher-profile touring sides were coming. In May 1908, English champions Manchester United visited Budapest and thrashed Ferencváros 7-0. The physical manner of the visitors' play incensed the crowd so much they started to pelt the visitors with stones. The police had to escort the United players from the ground.[5] While five United players were hit with stones, only one was bruised. It hints at the early volatility of the Hungarian football crowd in a country that would be blighted by hooliganism throughout its history. The English national team followed, and on 10 June 1908 dished out a 7-0 defeat to Hungary in front of 6,500 spectators.

Tensions across the Austro-Hungarian Empire were rising, and both Hungary and Bohemia – part of the modern-day Czech Republic – withdrew from the London Olympic football tournament. In the same year, a third division was added with a fourth in 1910 and a fifth in 1912. By now, both Ferencváros and MTK Budapest, who between them had won every title since 1903, had upgraded their grounds. Ferencváros's new Üllöi úti stadium could hold 40,000 spectators, while MTK's Hungária körúti stadium, completed months later, hosted around the same number and featured an athletics track. By the outbreak of the First World War in 1914, there were 17 clubs in Hungary's top flight, but there was no balance in the Hungarian game; only three teams had won the title – BTC, MTK and

Ferencváros, who had won eight of the 13 championships held. Hungary found itself on the losing side of the war, which led to a massive break-up of the Austro-Hungarian Empire and subsequent economic shock. The war also led to the arrival in Budapest of one of the most influential coaches in history.

## The impact of Jimmy Hogan

Ferencváros's playing style in the first decade of the 20th century reflected the prevailing method in Hungary of the time, 'kick-and-rush', as practised by the physically strong BTC team. MTK recognised it needed to catch up with its green and white rivals and looked to emulate the Scottish style of passing by bringing in Scots players to help them achieve their goal. This change failed to deliver the title, so the club looked up the Danube to Vienna for the solution. Englishman Jimmy Hogan had been working with the Austrian national team at the breakout of hostilities and, as a foreign national, faced internment. MTK vice-president Baron Dirstay negotiated to get Hogan out of Vienna, on condition that he reported to the police daily.[6] The move paid dividends. Armed with the best facilities he had ever seen and some excellent emerging talent, Hogan led MTK to three Hungarian titles in the three seasons he was in charge. MTK would not be dethroned again until 1925. Hogan then returned for two years but could not inspire MTK to catch Ferencváros. By the end of the 1920s Hungarian football had arguably already caught up with the English game. England's 'team of the 20s', Huddersfield Town, which had won three championships that decade, were held 1-1 by Ferencváros in a friendly in 1929.

Hogan helped Hungary ditch the 'kick-and-rush' style that had prevailed and replaced it with the Scottish-style

passing game that Hogan had always admired. During
Hogan's second stint at MTK, the Hungarian FA – fearful
of losing its best players to the newly professional league in
Austria – followed suit and legalised the payment of players.
By the time Hogan left Budapest, the die was cast for what
would become the 'Golden Team', as those playing under
him and witnessing his tactics moved on from playing to
coaching. Gusztáv Sebes, the coach of the Hungarian team
for the Match of the Century, credited their victory to the
way that Hogan had shown them to play.[7] For Hogan's
part, he remained eternally grateful to Hungary for the
experience.[8]

**Ethnicity in the 'Eternal Derby'**

Budapest, situated in the heart of Europe and part of
a large pan-European empire until the end of the First
World War, was a melting pot for people from across the
region. Ferencváros's nickname is 'Fradi', which refers to
the Franzstadt neighbourhood which at the time hosted a
large population of Hungarians of German origin. MTK's
founders were chiefly bourgeoise Jews, and the deliberate
inclusion of the word 'Hungarian' in the club's title displays
the group's determination to assimilate. The fact that both
teams shared every national title contested from 1903 until
1929, when Újpest finally broke the dual hegemony, reflects
the close sporting rivalry of Ferencváros and MTK – known
as the *Örökrangadó* (Eternal Derby) – but it does not tell the
social story. Given that both MTK and Ferencváros fielded
both Jews and gentiles from both working-class and middle-
class backgrounds, it is not accurate to claim that MTK was
exclusively a 'Jewish club' and Ferencváros was Christian.
Still, in an increasingly polarised society both clubs appeared
to take on those perceived identities. After the end of the

First World War, the humiliated former powers of Germany, Austria and Hungary looked for reasons for their defeat. This feeling led increasingly to the 'othering' of ethnic groups. The Hungarians looked for a scapegoat and found it in the prosperous Jewish community.

During the 'White Terror' of 1919–1921 an estimated 3,000 Jews were murdered by mobs who accused the Jewish community of deliberately undermining the war effort. This pogrom would have a major impact on football in the wider European context as many of the early pioneers of the Hungarian game were Jewish and would take their philosophies abroad bringing silverware to the great clubs of Lisbon, Turin and beyond. Jewish players plying their trade in Hungary in the 1920s went on to establish themselves among Europe's elite coaches. Former MTK player Béla Guttmann survived a Nazi labour camp to lead Portuguese club Benfica to European Cup victory twice in the early 1960s. Former Budapesti Atlétikai Klub player Ernö Egri Erbstein, who survived the Holocaust with Guttmann, coached legendary Italian champion side, Il Grande Torino (the Great Torino FC), and died in the Superga air disaster in 1949 that claimed the lives of the entire Torino team.

## Hungary on the international stage

Hungary's first Olympic football appearance was 1912 in Stockholm, having pulled out of the 1908 tournament in London due to political instability. Hungary met Great Britain in its first match and lost 7-0, the same scoreline by which it had lost to England four years previously. Of the 19-man squad, 13 players were drawn from either MTK or Ferencváros. After exiting the tournament, the Hungarians went on to play Russia twice and won 9-0 and

12-0. Budapest had originally been selected to host the Olympics in 1920 but, so soon after the First World War, the losing powers, including Hungary, were not invited to partake and the venue was switched to Antwerp. Hungary did not return to the Olympic tournament until 1924. Then, in Paris, Hungary opened with a 5-0 win against Poland before exiting to a surprise 3-0 defeat by Egypt in the second round. The Hungarians could not compete with the Egyptians' speed and agility.[9] Hungary, who had been one of the favourites going into the tournament and had Guttmann in the squad, went home in disgrace. The country would not take part in the Amsterdam Olympics of 1928 or the first World Cup in Uruguay in 1930, but would take part in the first Central European International Cup, which ran from 1927 until 1930. In 1927, Hungary recorded its highest win – 13-1 – against France in Budapest. Hungary would have to wait for its success – losing both the 1938 and 1954 World Cup finals, but sealed Olympic gold at Helsinki in 1952 with its Golden Team.

## The Hungarian pioneers today

Újpest's cross-town rivalry with Ferencváros has eclipsed the Eternal Derby as Budapest's – and Hungarian football's – premier derby. The club won both pioneering European club tournaments, the Mitropa Cup (1929) and Coupe des Nations (1930), having finally broken the duopoly of MTK and Fradi in the first two decades of Hungary's Nemzeti Bajnokság I. An English language biography of Ernö Erbstein inspired local Budapest sports fans to recreate Erbstein's former club, Budapesti Atlétikai Klub (BAK), in 2018. The original BAK was dissolved in 1947, and after a 70-year hiatus, the club is back! Erbstein's biographer, Dominic Bliss, whose book was translated into Hungarian and inspired BAK's reformation, is now a BAK club ambassador. He helped recreate Corinthians' historic visit in 1904 in the summer of 2019 in the form of the Egri Erbstein Tournament. At stake, the Corinthian Cup, just as it had been at the turn of the 20th century. 'It was a surprise for me and a huge honour that my work had inspired a historic football club to reform, and the emotion was heightened when they asked me to become an ambassador,' Bliss tells me.

The tournament featured BAK, fellow Hungarian sides Testvériség and BEAC, and English non-league side Corinthian-Casuals, the modern incarnation of the Corinthians. BAK lost to Corinthian-Casuals in the first match, meaning the famous English amateurs faced Testvériség in the final. The 200-strong final-day crowd included the British Ambassador to Hungary, members of the Erbstein family and representatives from Torino FC. Corinthian-Casuals triumphed 1-0 and returned to South West London with the Corinthian Cup. Bliss continues: 'It was a fantastic occasion, full of emotion. When I saw Erbstein's daughters, Susanna and Marta, handing over the trophy to the Corinthian-Casuals long-serving captain, Danny Bracken, it was a special moment for me, particularly as scores of Casuals fans had travelled out to Hungary to add something extra to the atmosphere. I'll never forget how that felt.' Hungary's past glories are captured in black and white, ghosts that stare down on passers-by from city walls. But as the reformation of BAK demonstrates, maybe a new spirit is awakening.

1   Szegedi, Péter, *Az első aranykor* (Budapest: Akadémiai Kiadó, 2016)
2   http://www.ujpestfc.hu/club?filter=clubhistory&lang=gb
3   https://www.fradi.hu/klub/tortenet/a-kezdetek
4   *Illustrated Sporting News*, 11 April 1903 (p212)
5   *Manchester Courier and Lancashire General Advertiser*, 25 May 1908 (p10)

6  https://thesefootballtimes.co/2016/01/21/jimmy-hogan-englands-greatest-footballing-pioneer/

7  Ibid.

8  *Sheffield Independent*, 12 March 1919 (p6)

9  *Yorkshire Post and Leeds Intelligencer*, 30 May 1924 (p7)

# 17.

# Czech Republic and Slovakia

ON 20 June 1976, in front of nearly 31,000 people at the Red Star Stadium in Belgrade, Antonín Panenka scored one of the most famous and audacious penalty kicks in history. It was the final of the European Championships. West Germany had just pegged back a two-goal deficit to take Czechoslovakia into extra time and, for the first time in the tournament's history, a penalty shoot-out decided the winner. This West German team had won the World Cup just two years earlier and were defending European champions. The line-up included Franz Beckenbauer, Uli Hoeneß, Berti Vogts and Rainer Bonhof. Panenka had the responsibility of taking the fifth Czechoslovakian penalty. After Hoeneß blazed the Germans' fourth kick over the bar, Panenka found himself with a chance for personal and national glory. Rather than pick a safe spot and place or blast the ball, Panenka sees German keeper Sepp Maier move to his left, so he clips an impudent chip into the centre of the goal. With that one kick, Panenka wrote his name in history. Not only was Panenka the author of a new kind of penalty kick, imitated both successfully and embarrassingly badly by professionals ever since, but he also delivered Czechoslovakia its first piece of major international silverware. The Czechs and Slovaks delivered again four years later, winning the Olympic gold medal at the 1980 games in Moscow, this time against East Germany. One European Championships and one Olympic gold seem like scant return for a footballing nation that had also appeared in two World Cup finals in 1934 and 1962.

## Football arrives in Prague

This territory in the centre of Europe has been a victim of its location: surrounded, occupied, unified, divided, fought over and marched through for centuries. In the 21st century, both the Czech Republic – or Czechia – and Slovakia are modern democracies in the European Union. In the final decades of the 19th century, Prague, in the heart of Bohemia, a small part of a large Austro-Hungarian Empire, was ready for a new sport to break the monotony of German gymnastics. Football caught on like wildfire. Indeed, in the early days of football, Prague was the graveyard of reputations for visiting teams. On 2 November 1892, a group of Prague students formed the Sportovní club Slavia Praha, originally as a cycling club, before adopting the new round-ball game. The club better known in English as Slavia Prague donned red and white halved shirts and a red five-pointed star crest. The rumour is the founders did not have enough cloth to make a full-colour kit – hence the shirt's nickname as the 'stitched together' – but Slavia claims a world record for the longest period of unchanged kit since debuting this shirt in March 1896. On 16 November 1893, the Athletic Club Královské Vinohrady was formed, and its ground was in Holešovice. Nine months later it changed its name to Sparta Praha, and the club would don black shirts with a large white 'S' on the chest. Also founded in 1893 was Academic Prague, which would later become CFK Kickers Praha.

Within three years of football first being played in Prague, matches were arranged with Viennese clubs, where the game had also just been introduced. On 7 April 1895, the Cricketer club of Vienna lost 2-0 to a team referred to as 'the Prague Football Club'.[1] The 29 March 1896 saw the first meeting of Slavia and Sparta in what would become the fiercest rivalry in Czech football. The first 'Prague S' derby ended with a 1-0 win for Sparta. Within two months, the two clubs had a new rival as the sizeable German-Jewish community formed its own club, the Deutscher Football Club – DFC Prag. The club traversed the Bohemian and German worlds, playing a key role in the creation of the German Football Association, the DFB. The Prague club's founder, Ferdinand Hueppe, would serve as the DFB's first president. Hueppe, originally from Dresden, was a professor at Charles University in Prague. The Bohemian side could partake in German tournaments, but it could not provide players to the German national side. Some prestigious names would turn out for Deutscher FC, including the remarkable all-rounder Karel Koželuh, who went on to represent both Austria and Czechoslovakia at football, win a European Championship at ice hockey with Czechoslovakia, and rank number one in world tennis.

There was enough of a bourgeoning soccer scene in Prague by 1896 to start up the unofficial Czech and Moravian Championship, which would run nine times until 1902. The first tournaments included a spring and autumn tournament in both 1896 and 1897, with Kickers becoming the first-ever champions in the spring of 1896 and Deutscher winning the autumn edition. This was followed by six straight triumphs for Slavia. ČAFC Vinohrady won the final edition in 1902. With the middle-class academic sides of Kickers and Slavia, the working-class team of Sparta, and the German-Jewish side in Deutscher, partisanship was already developing and sometimes overspilling into violence. In January 1898, players of two teams made up of English residents and German Bohemians were attacked by a mob of stone-throwing 'savage roughs' during a match at Kaiser Meadow. The players fled to the clubhouse, which was pelted.[2] One of the chief instigators that was arrested was apparently the *burgomeister* (mayor) of a nearby town, who had recently demolished the German schoolhouse there. Other contemporary British accounts seem to imply that the German community was the actual target, as British visitors as demonstrators of the game had been generally well received. The writer put the incident down to a case of guilt by association for being among the German community in Bohemia at a time of heightened tension.[3] Football was already a lightning rod for ethnic tensions. In 1899, two German student clubs – Unitas and Urania – merged to form DFC Germania Prag. Like its similar-sounding German-Jewish compatriots, the club would maintain membership of the German DFB until the club folded in 1903 after losing its home ground.

## The 'exponents of the game' arrive

The tense situation in Bohemia did not deter the first British side to tour the region in March 1899. The Dark Blues of Oxford University toured Prague and Vienna, with the Prague sides of Slavia and Deutscher putting up a much better fight than their Austrian neighbours. The visitors beat Slavia 3-0 before dispatching Deutscher 9-0 the following day. These results compare favourably with the students' 15-0 and 13-0 routs of two Viennese XI sides. Observers of the Prague matches noted the huge rivalry that had already developed between the two main Prague sides, along with the sizeable crowd of 7,000. One English reporter recorded a 'tremendous rivalry' between Slavia and Deutscher, and the houses overlooking the ground were filled with fans of the 'Sportovni Club' (Slavia), who appear to have been delighted with Oxford's 9-0 trouncing of Deutscher. The match was a one-sided affair, with the Oxford goalkeeper handling the ball just three times while the hosts resorted to rough play.[4] The Deutscher club's pride was evidently dented somewhat, having established a reputation already as being among the best sides on the continent. To mark the opening of its new Eden Stadium in the summer of 2008, Slavia invited Oxford University back to Prague to play an exhibition match. The two had last played each other in 1936, and for the unveiling of the 21,000-capacity ground, Slavia fielded former players Patrick Berger, Vladimír Šmicer and Pavel Kuka. Slavia beat the amateurs of Oxford University 5-0 in front of 14,000 fans.

By the close of the 19th century, with Czech football less than a decade old, English reporters were waxing lyrical about the health of the game there. The *Illustrated Sporting and Dramatic News* reporter stated the best all-round play he had seen on his European tour had been in Prague, and the defence was the best he had seen.[5] Oxford University had paved the way for other British clubs to tour Prague. In 1901, a match between Slavia Prague and the British Civil Service Football Club attracted 5,000 spectators in Bohemia. Players battled the wind with the visitors winning by five goals to nil. Observers reported that the Slavia players had improved, even to the level of senior London clubs.[6] Also in 1901, Slavia ran a visiting Cambridge University side close, losing just 1-0, and a year later Deutscher improved markedly on its previous outing against Oxford University, losing just 4-1 this time. The Czechs were getting good at this game. Good enough to establish their own Football Association. But were they good enough for the Corinthians?

## Bohemian football on the rise

The famous English amateur side Corinthians visited Prague as part of its Austro-Hungarian tour in April 1904. It was the first tour the Corinthians made in Continental Europe. After three huge wins in Budapest and another in Vienna, Slavia pushed the visitors the closest, losing 7-4 and 4-1. Slavia also beat a returning Civil Service team twice in 1904. That same year, Glasgow Celtic came to Prague, beating Deutscher FC 3-0 and Slavia 4-1. The former Celtic player John 'Jake' Madden – a three-time Scottish title winner with the Bhoys – was so impressed with the technical skills of the Slavia players that he agreed to become the club's first professional manager rather than return to working in the shipyards in Glasgow. He would stay for a quarter of a century and lead the club to four Czechoslovakian titles, despite never having fully mastered the language. In this period, the Casuals also came and notched two wins, and Everton three, while in the Prague suburb of Vršovice, a new club was founded – AFK Vršovice – later renamed as Bohemians.

In 1906, Sparta's president, Dr Petrik, visited London and was so impressed by the Woolwich Arsenal's performance that he chose that Sparta should ditch its colours and wear red shirts with white sleeves, although the club retained black socks. The Arsenal would visit the following year, beating Madden's Slavia twice in high-scoring games and, in 1908, Manchester United repeated the feat. Crystal Palace ventured beyond Prague after beating Slavia twice and travelled to Hradec Kralove, Smichov and Kladno. The Corinthians returned five years later to find the standard of

Czech football had improved markedly. In front of 15,000 spectators, Corinthians survived a last-minute penalty shout against Slavia to finish goalless but beat the same opposition 3-1 the following day. However, Slavia would make history in 1912 when Corinthians visited for the third time. Travelling without a recognised full-back, the Englishmen cruised past Slavia 5-1 in the first encounter on 7 April. On the following day, however, and up against a referee who awarded two penalties, Corinthians finally tasted defeat on the continent, going down 3-1 to Slavia. Two days later, the team lost again, 4-2 to a combined Bohemia side.

By the end of the 20th century's first decade, Slavia was beating visiting teams regularly. Aberdeen, Ipswich Town, Jesus College Oxford, Amateur FA London, London Nomads, London University and New Crusaders all fell victim to the 'stitched-together' club. Another Scot, former Airdrieonians and Woolwich Arsenal player John Dick, arrived in 1912 to coach Deutscher FC. Deutscher had previously played under the German DFB's auspices, but when the DFB joined FIFA in 1904 that came to an end, and the club switched to the Austrian FA. But world events were soon set to change Bohemian football forever.

## The birth of Czechoslovakia

In the late summer of 1914, Europe collapsed into war following the assassination of Archduke Franz Ferdinand by Serb nationalists in Sarajevo. Around a million Czechs fought for the Austro-Hungarian Empire on both the western and eastern front, making up nearly 20 per cent of the total Austro-Hungarian army.[7] Yet some Czechs fought with the Allies in France, Italy and Russia with the aim to push for independence in the event of an Allied victory. Driven by Tomáš Masaryk and his future deputy, Edvard Beneš, the movement for an independent Czech land partnered with neighbouring Slovakia gathered pace. In October 1918, this became a reality. This new country – Czechoslovakia – married the industrial west of Bohemia and Moravia with the more agricultural Slovakia to the east.

There was already a football culture in Slovakia before unification. Ferenc Ray, who had encountered football when studying in Switzerland and appears in the Hungarian pioneer story with the BTC club, brought a real football from England to Eperjes (modern-day Presov). In December 1896, the first documented kickabout of any description in Slovakia occurred. It was Ray who taught the locals the rules. Slovakia's first football club was founded in Eperjes in May 1898 as the footballing arm of the Eperjesi Torna es Vivo Egyesület (ETVE) sports club and was founded by Ferenc Pethe, a professor of Latin. The Pozsonyi Torna Egyesület (PTE) club was also founded in Bratislava in 1898, a later incarnation of which would appear in the Champions League in the 21st century as FC Artmedia. Slovakian football journalist Mojmir Staško informs me that the relationship with the emerging clubs from nearby Vienna and Budapest was instrumental in the development of football in Slovakia, more so than the Prague clubs. 'The first documented match in Slovakian territory took place in Eperjes on 25 May 1898 between two teams from Budapest – BTC Budapest and Óbudai TE,' Staško says. Ferenc Ray had also introduced football to the BTC club in 1896, and the Eperjes exhibition match appears to have inspired the foundation of both ETVE and PTE. 'The first match between two Slovak teams was between PTE and ETVE in Pozsonyi on 22 May 1899,' Staško adds. 'PTE won 2-1.' Games were played fairly regularly with Viennese and Budapest teams to develop the Slovakian clubs. After the First World War, a club would emerge that would go on to dominate the domestic game. On 3 May 1919, 1. Čs.Š.K. Bratislava – later renamed Slovan – was founded. Within a decade the team was good enough to thrash Newcastle United 8-1.

Following unification between the two nations, the first test of the new Czechoslovakian national football team came at the 1920 Olympics in Antwerp. The entire team was made up of Czech amateurs, and all but six of the 19-man squad played for Sparta. Slavia, Viktoria Žižkov and Union Žižkov all provided two players each. Czechoslovakia opened with a 7-0 drubbing of another new nation formed out of the ashes of the Habsburg Austro-Hungarian Empire – Yugoslavia. There was a hat-trick apiece for Slavia's Jan Vanik and Sparta's Antonín Janda-Očko in front of 600 spectators at the Stadion Broodstraat. The next day, in Brussels, Janda-Očko bagged another hat-trick and Vanik one more goal as the Czechs beat Norway 4-0. Two days later, on 31 August at the Olympic Stadium in Antwerp, it was Sparta's Otakar Škvajn-Mazal's turn to bag a hat-trick. Viktoria Žižkov's Karel Steiner added another as the Czechoslovakians brushed the French aside 4-1 to reach the final. A Belgian record crowd of 35,000 turned up at the Olympic Stadium in Antwerp on 2 September for the final between the free-scoring Czechoslovakians and the hosts, Belgium, who themselves had netted three times apiece in both their semi- and quarter-final matches. What unfolded from this eagerly anticipated match was, in fact, a fiasco. After a fast opening exchange, the Belgians were awarded an early penalty, which Robert Coppée duly dispatched. On the half-hour mark, Henri Larnoe doubled the hosts' lead with a contentious second. The Czechs were unhappy with the officiating of 65-year-old Englishman, John Lewis, and his supporting linesmen, which included former Corinthian Charles Wreford Brown. Czech left-back Steiner lost his cool and kicked at Coppée just before half-time. Lewis sent him off and the incensed Czechoslovakians all walked off in protest. The match – and the gold medal – was awarded to Belgium. Match reports imply that Czechoslovakia had missed a number of chances in front of goal, so perhaps frustration got the better of the players. Nearly a year later, the Czechoslovakian FA wrote to Mr Lewis to express regret over walking off the pitch and admitting it was unsporting. Lewis accepted the apology and said he wished the game well in the country.[8]

The Czechoslovakian team was back for the 1924 Olympics in Paris, thrashing Turkey 5-2 at the Stade Bergeyre in the first round before falling to the Swiss after a replay. Meanwhile, at home, football was getting organised. In 1925, the First League was founded featuring ten clubs playing each other once. Madden's Slavia topped the first table, winning seven matches, drawing one and losing just once. Slavia's 1920 Olympic hero Jan Vanik top-scored with 13. Slavia and Sparta would dominate title wins right up to 1938, when German occupation brought further changes. Only Viktoria Žižkov in the 1927/28 season managed to break the Slavia-Sparta hegemony. In 1927, AFK Vršovice became an unlikely ambassador for the Czechoslovakian game. With the Australian FA keen to spread the game down under, several European clubs were invited – but declined – to make the long trip to Australia. Sparta were among those to decline but AFK Vršovice answered the call, rebranding as the 'Bohemians' for the four-month tour. Bohemians won 15, drew two and lost three, and made enough of an impression for the Australians to gift Bohemians two kangaroos to take back to Prague with them. The club's crest now features a kangaroo, and the club is known as the *Klokani* – the Kangaroos.[9]

The 1929/30 season would be the Scotsman Madden's last at Slavia. He finished with a perfect 14 wins from 14 games. The 3-2 win over Sparta was the icing on the cake for the 65-year-old. In his 25 years at Slavia, during which he had earned the nickname 'Dědek' (Codger), Madden had transformed Czech football. He had introduced new training, dietary and hygiene methods for his players. He won 134 of his 169 competitive matches in charge of Slavia, losing just 23. He also managed the 'Bohemian' national side against England in 1908, and his team was made up entirely of Slavia players. Madden arrived aged 40, sporting a classic Victorian-legacy moustache. By his retirement, he was grey and his moustache a lot less pronounced, but he retained his disciplinarian edge, earning the respect of his players. He married a local woman 17 years his junior, but their son tragically died by suicide.[10] Madden, however, has been dubbed 'the father of Czech football'. He has a stand named after him at Slavia's Eden Arena and his image appears on Slavia fan banners.

## The pioneer clubs today

In contrast to many countries, the pioneer clubs in the Czech Republic – Slavia and Sparta – continue to dominate. Sparta has won 33 Czech or Czechoslovak First League titles, compared to Slavia's 19. Sparta leads Slavia in Czech Cup wins too, by 14 to nine. DFC Prag enjoyed success, winning the Bohemian championship in 1896 and 1917, and also competed in Germany, finishing second in the inaugural German championship in 1903. After the Nazi occupation in March 1939, many of its Jewish members either fled abroad or died in concentration camps during the Second World War. In 2016, a new DFC Prag was established.

1 *Illustrated Sporting and Dramatic News*, 11 May 1895 (p9)
2 *Liverpool Echo*, 8 January 1898 (p3)
3 *St. James's Gazette*, 7 January 1898
4 *Leeds Mercury*, 31 March 1899 (p3)
5 *Illustrated Sporting and Dramatic News,* 9 December 1899 (p52)
6 *London Daily News*, 8 October 1901 (p7)
7 https://www.radio.cz/en/section/czech-history/many-czech-wwi-graves-neglected-says-member-of-history-buffs-group
8 *Birmingham Daily Gazette*, 6 August 1921 (p6)
9 https://www.theguardian.com/football/2010/sep/22/why-do-club-prague-kangaroo-crest
10 https://en.slavia.cz/clanek.asp?id=Celtic-Slavia-and-Football-The-story-of-John-William-Madden-112

# 18.

# Spain

IN MARCH of 2016, Spain's oldest football club, Real Club Recreativo de Huelva, stood on the brink of extinction. As debts spiralled, fans from across the country packed the 21,670-capacity Estadio Nuevo Colombino in the southern port city of Huelva to support the team and protest against the running of the club. Real Club Recreativo de Huelva – or 'Recre', for short – has rarely appeared in the top flight since its foundation in December 1889. Recre usually flits between the second and third tiers of the Spanish league system, drawing in an average crowd of just a few thousand. But something was stirring in the spring of 2016 as the team faced a crunch survival match in Segunda B, Spain's third tier, against a Granada B side. With tickets priced at just one euro, the game sold out within 24 hours. Local buses carried fans for free. Goodwill messages came in from clubs across Spain as fans wished Recre to survive. If ever there was a public display of what Recreativo de Huelva means to Spanish football, this was it. Recre saw out that season, and in March 2018 it was confirmed that the club would be sold for just one euro to a buyer, provided the club's debts were paid. Recreativo is officially recognised by the

Royal Spanish Football Federation (RFEF) as the original Spanish football club, *El Decano*. This translates as 'Dean' or 'Doyen': the most experienced or revered person in an academic institution. Like HAC in France or Royal Antwerp in Belgium, Recre is Spain's doyen.

Huelva – pronounced 'Well-ba' – is nestled in the south-west corner of Spain, not far from the Portuguese border. It's believed that people have lived here at the confluence of the Odiel and Tinto rivers for more than 5,000 years. The city has a long naval tradition. Huelva, like the home of Italy's first football club, Genoa Cricket and Football Club, has a strong connection to Christopher Columbus. It was from Huelva that the Genoese navigator Columbus set sail for India but landed in what became known later as the Americas. The two port cities of Huelva and Genoa are twinned. Huelva is perhaps an inauspicious place for football to gain a foothold in Spain, a country that would go on to give more than most to the game. But Huelva's position as a port city was decisive in attracting that often essential ingredient in the spreading of football – British merchant expats. The Tinto river's upstream copper deposits attracted British speculators and settlers who would go on to play, develop and spread the game across the Iberian Peninsula. When the British Rio Tinto Company Limited purchased the copper mines in 1873, there was an even greater influx of British workers. These workers needed pastimes, of course, and were keen to cling to the customs they were used to back home.

**The first football match in Spain**

A match took place as early as 2 November 1870 in the Andalusian town of Jeréz de la Frontera, a place renowned for sherry and its expert horsemanship. The town's *El*

*Progreso* newspaper carried a small snippet which, in Spanish, announced that a cricket match would be played that day starting at midday sharp in the Hippodrome, followed by *un rato de football* – a bit of football.[1] However, we don't know for sure if the 'bit of football' the paper was talking about referred to Rugby or Association rules because the date falls between the formations of the Football Association (1863) and the Rugby Football Union (1871) and versions of the game were fairly fluid. The next earliest record of a football match taking place on Spanish soil occurred on 10 September 1874, when a team of railway engineers building a line from Huelva to the mines at Rio Tinto took on a team skippered by Captain W.F. Adams. Four years later, the 'English Club' was founded to promote sports and activities among the by now sizeable British community in Huelva. These sports included cricket, tennis, golf and polo.

## Send for the doctor ...

In the early 1880s, a young Edinburgh doctor, William Alexander Mackay, arrived in Huelva as an employee of the Rio Tinto mining company. At the time, it was the largest mining company in the world. It had been extracting copper from the land around Huelva for almost a decade. Mackay was born in 1860 at Lybster, Caithness, in the far north of Scotland, and was the youngest son of a Presbyterian minister, Reverend John Mackay. Aged 14, William moved to Edinburgh to study at the Royal High School, one of the oldest schools in the world. The school's famous alumni include Alexander Graham Bell, the inventor of the telephone, banker Thomas Coutts, and author Walter Scott. It was at this prestigious school that his early sporting prowess began to show, and he became captain of the cricket team. He continued his education at the University of Edinburgh, where he studied to become a doctor and joined the newly formed Edinburgh University Association Football Club.

William's older brother John was also a doctor and had moved to Spain in 1879 to head up Rio Tinto's medical department. But John needed help, and in 1882 sent a telegram to his younger brother, who had graduated that year. Today, William Alexander Mackay's great-granddaughter, Charlotte Mackay, is Recre's UK club ambassador, and she picks up the story: '[William] had a call from his brother who was already in Huelva for the Rio Tinto Mining Company, and he asked him to join him as there was a lot of illness amongst the employees,' she tells me. 'My great-grandfather was brought up in Scotland with the understanding that football, and sport in general, can play a role with the recuperation from illness. He had this medical interest in sport and thought about how he could incorporate it into his work.'

From his arrival in the Andalusian port, Mackay threw himself into the local sporting life of the British expatriate community and took an active role within the English Club. Alejandro López is a Recre historian. López informs me that Mackay stayed in the newly opened Hotel Colón, the swankiest residence in the city in the 1880s and which later became the offices of the Rio Tinto company in Huelva. Here, Mackay tended to Rio Tinto employees and British sailors who loaded the ore. He also treated the poor for free on Thursdays, which gives us a clear gauge of the man's sense of purpose. López says that to play football and cricket, the expatriate Brits marked out a large area of marshland in front of a gasworks owned by Scotsman Charles Adam. I asked López what the locals made of this new game being played in their paddocks. 'A lot of young men from the higher social classes in Huelva were curious for the game and liked to imitate all the things that arrived from Great Britain,' he explains. 'For the rest of the population, they viewed the sports as "English oddities", watching adult foreigners dressed in long johns chasing a ball.' However, the locals did show an interest, and some even asked to join in. Dr Mackay, who by now was well settled in Huelva, welcomed them in.

## The foundation of Recre

On 18 December 1889, the first of two meetings took place at the Huelva Recreation Club, known in Spanish as Club Recreativo de Huelva, with the second club meeting held on 23 December. Charles Adam, an esteemed figure in the port and several years Mackay's senior, owned the land on which the team played and became the club's first president. In many expatriate communities around the world, the British clubs were *for* the British, but Recreativo opened its doors to the local Spanish population. Young local players included the translator José Garcia Almansa, Alfonso Le Bourg, Ildefonso Martínez and José Coto. Both British and Spanish surnames appear in team sheets from the outset, reflecting the cultural mix of the first 32 British and Spanish *socios*, or members. It was to be distinctive from its sister association, the exclusive English Club. Tour guides of the time even recommended Club Recreativo as a place to meet great sportsmen. But when you're the first football club in a country, against whom do you play? Recre played against teams of directors and engineers of the Rio Tinto mines, versus teams from the nearby mines of Tharsis and against seamen from visiting British ships. That was until 1890, when – just up the sandy Andalusian track – a new kid arrived on the block ...

## Sevilla FC

There are few cities on earth that offer as much character and flair as Seville. The many people who have passed through this city – Romans, Visigoths, Moors, Christians and Roma – have all left their own indelible mark on the architecture and nature of the city. Seville is Spain's fourth-largest city by population, and the warmest city in Europe by average temperature. You can expect blistering 40°C+ days in summer and mild sunny days even in the winter. It's really difficult to talk about Seville without descending unwittingly into cliché. It's mesmerising, spellbinding; it's the home of all the things one associates with Spain: bullfighting, Carmen, flamenco … and *fútbol*.

Sevilla Football Club was formed just one month after Recreativo de Huelva, on 25 January 1890, 'after a deal of talk and a limited consumption of small beer'.[2] As the anglicised name implies, it was a mixed project between Spaniards and Brits – principally Edward Johnson (president), Isaiah White (secretary) and club captain Hugo MacColl. The team started with a five-a-side kickabout at the Racecourse Club on a Sunday morning. In Britain, workers enjoyed Saturday afternoon off, which had proven to be a catalyst for the game in its home country. The same could not be said of Spain, but it appears the players managed to gain concessions from their employers to play. The Seville team initiated contact with their compatriots in Huelva and invited them to travel inland and meet them for a game of football. Saturday, 8 March 1890 marks the very first recorded competitive match between two established football clubs in Spain at the Tablada Hippodrome, Seville. The weather was chilly but 'glorious' that day, and a small crowd of around 150 people had gathered to watch. Then the rain came down, but it didn't deter them from a 4.45pm start.

The *Dundee Courier* was the first newspaper in Britain to report the Sevilla–Recre match.[3] The umpires – Sevilla FC's English doctor and Mackay as Huelva's secretary, along with the British Vice Consul – took on refereeing duties 'to everyone's satisfaction'. Neither Sevilla FC nor Recre had acquired a kit at this point, with the players presenting 'a motley appearance, all kinds of costumes being in requisition'. Sevilla FC's left-winger had never been a part of a sports team and is reported to have donned a 'fantastic patterned suit' of pyjamas, drawing the derision of the crowd and earning the title 'Clown Yugles'. Sevilla FC's Ritson has the distinction of scoring the first recorded goal on Spanish soil, followed shortly by none other than the Clown Yugles. And that's how it finished: Sevilla FC 2-0 Recreativo de Huelva. The occasion that this was most probably the first football match in Spain was not lost on either party, and the Suizo Restaurant hosted 30 players and staff post-match. Sevilla FC's president Edward Johnston toasted the British and Spanish monarchies, and the two clubs promised a rematch. Huelva's team featured two Spaniards – Señores Duclós and Coto – while the Sevilla team was made entirely of British expats who worked for Seville-based employers, such as Seville Water Works. The *Dundee Courier* predicts a great future for football in Spain where British communities exist. But it would not be long before non-Brits took up the footballing cause in Spain …

## Other Andalusian pioneers

Recreativo can claim to be the first sports club to play football in Spain, while Sevilla FC can argue to be the first club formed *exclusively* to play the game. For the first decade, just Sevilla FC, Recre and a team from the town of Riotinto were active in Andalusia. Travelling around Spain – Europe's second-most mountainous country after Switzerland – was not simple in those days so, understandably, matches stayed local. Seville's other major club, Real Betis Balompié, was not formed until 1907. While Sevilla FC took the English word 'football' and used its phonetic equivalent *fútbol* – the widely adopted word for the sport in Spain – Real Betis used the literal Spanish translation, matching *balón* (ball) and *pie* (foot) to create *balompié* (pronounced bal-om-pee-ay). Betis's green and white colours were inspired by Celtic. One of the club's founders, Manuel Asensio Ramos, had studied in Glasgow and watched Celtic regularly.[4] Andalusia's flag is also green and white, and Betis takes its name from the Roman name for the river Guadalquivir that runs through the city.

Sevilla FC and Real Betis have been fierce rivals since the get-go. In 1915, the first-ever Seville derby had to be abandoned due to a pitch invasion. Sevilla FC were winning 4-3. A century later, Sevilla FC had won 45 per cent of derbies and Betis 31 per cent. Real Betis won its only title in 1935 under the stewardship of the remarkable Irishman, Patrick O'Connell, who left at the end of that season to coach FC Barcelona. The following year Spain descended into a bloody three-year civil war, resulting in a fascist dictatorship under Francisco Franco that lasted until 1975. O'Connell is credited with saving Barça from financial collapse during the early years of the Franco regime, by shipping the team away on a fundraising North American tour. Meanwhile, Sevilla FC was something of a late bloomer. It won its first and only La Liga title in 1946, but in the first two decades of the 21st century its trophy cabinet positively bulged. The club won five Europa League titles between 2006 and 2016 and two Copa del Rey titles in 2007 and 2010. It's an impressive return for a period of football dominated economically by the traditional Spanish duopoly of Real Madrid and FC Barcelona.

According to a study by Spain's Centre of Sociological Investigations (CIS) in 2014, Real Betis is Spain's fifth-most-supported football club (3.2 per cent of the population), behind Real Madrid, FC Barcelona, Atlético de Madrid and Valencia CF. This compares with Sevilla FC's national fan base of 1.1 per cent.[5] As in many city rivalries, a juxtaposition had to be established to differentiate the teams. The story is that Sevilla FC is the upmarket team and Betis is the working-class team founded in the characterful Triana district, but there is no real class divide between fans. Fandom often depends on family tradition but, as you can imagine, *El Gran Derbi* (The Great Derby) can divide friendships and families.

## The first football stadium in Spain

Each year in Huelva, the city gathers to celebrate a week-long party – *Las Fiestas Colombinas* (The Columbus Festivals). On 3 August 1492, Christopher Columbus – aided by the three Pinzón brothers from Huelva – departed on his great ocean adventure from Palos de la Frontera on three ships named *Niña*, *Pinta* and *Santa María*; 3 August 1892 marked the 400th anniversary of Columbus's departure to 'discover' America, and for the great and good of Huelva, this was a big deal. Recre had committed to organise parties and competitions during 1892 as part of the festivities. Huge crowds were anticipated to attend, and to accommodate them it was agreed that the club should build its own sports ground based on those in Britain.[6] Recreativo's board of directors met at the Hotel Colón on 9 December 1891 to decide on what would be Spain's very first sports venue designed to practise football – along with cricket and cycling. By the end of

January 1892, the land between the Alameda Sundheim and the railway line that belonged to the Rio Tinto company was transferred. This land was conveniently close to the Hotel Colón and the hub of official events around the *Colombinas*.

*El Velódromo* – The Velodrome – was constructed during the first months of 1892 under the supervision of William Alexander Mackay and Charles Adam. The ground was inaugurated on 13 August 1892, with a programme of sports events, featuring cricket, tennis, athletics, cycling and equestrianism. Football at *El Velódromo* would have to wait until October that year for the culmination of festivities when the Spanish royal family were due to visit. The British would consider it unthinkable to play football at the height of the Andalusian summer when temperatures average in the early- to mid-30 degrees centigrade. This programme included a match against nearby Gibraltar and the Rio Tinto club. *El Velódromo* would be Recre's home ground for its first six decades.

## Meanwhile, in the north ...

While Spain's earliest kickabouts were taking place in Andalusia, in the north the game was starting to get attention. As early as 3 May 1894, local students took on a group of British workers in the Basque city of Bilbao. The city is the largest on the Atlantic north coast of Spain, and a key access port for the whole country. It therefore comes as little surprise that British workers could be seen kicking a ball around the docks at Bilbao, much as they were in the ports of Montevideo and Buenos Aires at this time. The field in which they played became known as *La Campa de Los Ingleses* – The Englishmen's Field. The Guggenheim Museum now stands nearby. This new game piqued the interest of the locals, and when the students of the Zamacois gymnasium decided to take on the 'foreigners', it attracted something of an audience. The British team won by six goals to nil in this first match at Lamaiko on the east bank of Bilbao's Nervión river.[7]

Bilbao was at the forefront of industrialisation in Spain, along with Catalonia, in a country still very much stuck in a backward and unproductive agrarian economy. Poverty was rife and, in the summer of 1898, Spain was at war with the United States in the Caribbean and the Philippines. The US stepped in to support the *Cuba Libre* (Free Cuba) movement to protect American interests in Cuban tobacco and sugar. The loss of Spain's last colonies marked a new nadir in Spanish history. This defeat was to leave a profound impact on the future dictator, General Francisco Franco, who as a child witnessed the remnant of the defeated Spanish fleet limp into his home town port of El Ferrol in Galicia. Four centuries of Spanish rule in the Americas was over. Meanwhile, in Bilbao, there were shipyards, railways, steel mills and – importantly – a powerful business class who would be critical to the adoption of football. All things 'English' were all the rage among these classes, and football became a curio to add to the Basque sporting culture of lawn tennis and cycling, along with the local game *pelota*, a squash-like game that involves a big basket glove, a ball and a wall. Thirty-three Zamacois gymnasium members formed a team in 1898 to practise and discuss football – Athletic Club was born. Meanwhile, another group of students went on to form Bilbao Football Club in 1900, charging its members 200 pesetas a year to take part in training and matches.

Bilbao FC became Athletic Club's main rival, with some matches at Lamaiko attracting crowds of 3,000 spectators at the turn of the 20th century. That was until May 1902, when the first state tournament was organised in Madrid to mark King Alfonso XIII's coronation. To give themselves the best possible chance in the *Copa de la Coronación* (Coronation Cup), Athletic and Bilbao formed a joint team named 'Bizcaya' (Biscay). The other teams taking part were FC Barcelona (founded 29 November 1899), Club Español de Foot-ball (founded 28 October 1900 – now RCD Espanyol), Madrid Football Club (founded 6 March 1902 – now Real Madrid CF), and the New Foot-Ball Club, which was active in Madrid between 1897 and 1903. The Coronation Cup is not recognised by the Royal Spanish Football Association as the first season of the *Copa del Rey* (King's Cup), which commenced the following year, but it is the very first football tournament to have been contested in Spain. On 13 May 1902, Bizcaya thrashed Club Español at the Madrid Hippodrome 5-1, with a hat-trick for Walter Evans. That same day at the same venue marks the first recorded contest between FC Barcelona and Madrid FC. Barça won 3-1, including a penalty goal for the club's co-founder, Joan Gamper. In the semi-finals, Bizcaya hammered New Foot-Ball Club 8-1, with William Dyer scoring four, before dispatching FC Barcelona the following day in the final by two goals to one. The *Copa de la Coronación* trophy – a silver vase-like urn standing on a round black plinth – is now on show at the Athletic Club museum in Bilbao.

Thanks in part to their joint success, Bilbao FC decided to dissolve itself in 1903 and merge its membership with Athletic, adopting the name Athletic Club de Bilbao. Under the watchful eye of English manager, Mr Shepherd, Athletic Club won the first *Copa del Rey* tournament in 1903 and retained the trophy in 1904. In 1910, the club changed its colours from blue and white halves to its famous red and white stripes. The origins of this move are the subject of some debate. Athletic Club's kit is similar to both Southampton and Sunderland in England. All three clubs wear red and white stripes, and black shorts. All three cities are also major ports. The most plausible explanation is that Athletic Club's Juan Elorduy was asked to bring back Blackburn Rovers shirts from his trip to London. Rovers' blue and white halves matched Athletic's shirts at the time. Elorduy failed to find any Blackburn Rovers shirts in London, so instead purchased 50 Southampton FC shirts before embarking on his boat from the port. The red and white stripes matched the colours of the city of Bilbao and – at the time in Spain – only Sporting Gijón, another northern city with a maritime tradition, wore a similar kit. On 13 November 1910, Athletic Club adopted the red and white stripes in perpetuity. Soon after, the club's Madrid branch – nowadays known as Club Atlético de Madrid – did the same.[8]

Interest in the northern game was growing fast. In 1911, Corinthians came to the Basque Country to play three exhibition matches in San Sebastian. In the first, they beat fellow touring amateur side London Nomads 7-0 in front of 3,500 spectators. Two days later, Corinthians fielded a weaker side against a local team, running out 3-1 winners before again trouncing Nomads 6-0. Back in Bilbao, changes were afoot. Despite its foundation by Englishmen, in 1912 the club adopted its famous *cantera* (homegrown) system, which it still maintains. Under this unwritten rule the club will only sign players who were born or brought up in the Basque Country. This policy has since been expanded to include players with at least one Basque parent or even further back in the player's lineage. Athletic Club de Bilbao's position as a beacon for Basque nationalism had been born. The last time a player with a non-Basque connection played for the club was 1919. French international left-back Bixente

Lizarazu became the first French-born Basque to don the red and white strips in 1996. In 2015, Iñaki Williams – born in Bilbao to Ghanaian parents – became the first black player to score for the club in its history.

In 1913, the Basque outfit put down roots and made a piece of Spanish football history with the construction of the San Mamés stadium, the first purpose-built football arena in Spain. It was built in just seven months and inaugurated in front of King Alfonso XIII with a tournament that featured fellow Basques, Real Unión, who had recently rebranded from Racing Club de Irún, and London's Shepherd's Bush FC, which existed until 1915. The first goal scored at the San Mamés went to Bilbao striker Rafael Moreno, known as 'Pichichi' due to his slight build, who went on to assume legendary status. Moreno was to be part of Spain's first national team in 1920 and won four *Copa del Reys* with Athletic Club before his untimely death from typhus. Spanish sports paper *Marca* named its award for the top goalscorer in La Liga the *Trofeo Pichichi* (Pichichi Trophy), still synonymous with the top scorer in the Spanish league to this day, and there is a bust of him at the new San Mamés. The San Mamés was Spain's first arena built solely to host football matches and became famous for its boisterous atmosphere. It was replaced by the new San Mamés a century later.

Athletic Club de Bilbao dominated the growing Spanish football scene, missing out on the Copa del Rey only twice between 1910 and 1916 under English coaches, Messrs Shepherd and Barnes. Since the formation of La Liga in 1928, Athletic Club de Bilbao has never been relegated, a feat equalled only by Real Madrid and FC Barcelona. Around the same time that the original Athletic Club was founded in 1898, across in Catalonia something was stirring.

## The Catalan uprising

The small Catalan fishing port of Palamós lies roughly halfway between the French border to the north and Barcelona to the south. Yet the townsfolk were fielding a football team before fellow Catalans FC Barcelona and Espanyol, 100km down the coast. Gaspar Matas Danés was a student returning from England. He established Palamós Foot-ball Club aged just 20 with some friends and is credited with introducing the sport into Catalonia. Palamós's first 'proper' match was against a group of English sailors in 1898, with the Catalans winning 2-1.[9] Matas has a street named after him in his hometown. Several other clubs were formed in Catalonia the following year, including Català SC and FC Barcelona. Sociedad Española de Football was founded in 1900 by Angel Rodríguez as a club for students at the University of Barcelona. The patriotic title was a response to differentiate the institution from other clubs around Barcelona, which were often dominated by foreigners, particularly FC Barcelona, founded by the Swiss Hans Gamper. Gamper later changed his name to Joan Gamper in order to blend in with the local Catalan language and community. The Swiss placed an advert in the *Deportes* (Sports) newspaper on 22 October 1899 requesting that players who were interested in playing football present themselves at the newspaper's headquarters at a stipulated day and time. Enough recruits came forward for Gamper to host the inaugural team meeting at the Solé gymnasium the following month. The origins of the blue and maroon *blaugrana* shirts are the cause of some debate, but are said to be inspired by the colours of the Merchant Taylors' School in England, as suggested by the influential Anglo-Catalan family, the Wittys.[10] Blue and maroon are also the colours of FC Basel, where Gamper had played.

By late 1900, there were enough clubs in Spain to establish the *Football Associació de Catalunya* (Football Association of Catalonia). Alfons Macaya i Sanmartí, president of one of those sides – Hispania Athletic Club – suggested a round-robin competition for Catalan teams. He donated a humble grail-like trophy for individual winners and a wonderfully ornate trophy crafted in London for whoever won it three times. Macaya was in it for the long haul. Six clubs took part in the first edition in 1901, which Hispania AC won. This tournament was the first football league in the whole of Spain.

FC Barcelona got their first piece of silverware the following year. Espanyol won the third and final edition of the *Copa Macaya* in 1903, but by then the *Copa de Coronación* had been staged in Madrid, plus another tournament – the *Copa de Barcelona* (Barcelona Cup) had been held and won by FC Barcelona. The Copa Macaya became the *Campionat de Catalunya de Futbol*. The Catalonia-wide league tournament ran right up to 1940 when it fell victim to the new Franco regime. Espanyol won the first edition and FC Barcelona the second.

## Spanish football gets royal approval

In April 1906, Recreativo de Huelva attended the Copa del Rey in Madrid. Only Madrid FC and Athletic Club de Bilbao also took part. Athletic's line-up comprised of entirely Spanish and Basque names, while Recre's team was still mainly British, but the Anglo influence was clearly on the wane at both pioneering clubs. Recre returned for the 1907 edition without a single Briton but finished bottom in a tournament won by Madrid FC in front of 6,000 people at the Hippodrome. By 1909, Spanish football started to come together with the foundation of the *Federación Española de Foot-ball,* the Spanish Football Federation. With its representative Francisco Pérez de Guzmán in attendance, Recre was a founder member and the only Andalusian club present. In this pivotal year for the club, Recre helped establish the Andalusian championship – an initiative that Mackay, now club president, had promoted – which was held in Huelva. The Andalusian championship ran between 1909 and 1918 and featured Sevilla FC and Español FC from just down the coast in Cádiz. Also in 1909 Recre adopted its famous blue and white stripes. The kit was bought in London. Before that, the team had played in white shirts. By the following year, Recre had their first taste of international football, hosting Lisbon's Sporting Clube de Portugal. In a later return fixture, Recre became the first Spanish team to win away in Portugal.

One constant fixture throughout the early growth of the game in Spain was King Alfonso XIII. He had come to the throne at birth, as his father, Alfonso XII, died shortly after his mother, Maria Christina of Austria, became pregnant. Maria Christina acted as regent until his 16th birthday in 1902. The festivities for his coronation included, as we have seen already, the *Copa de la Coronación* in Madrid, the first such nationwide football tournament in Spain. Alfonso XIII's reign was marked by pivotal crises in Spanish history. It culminated in the ultimate demise of the monarchy with the emergence of the Second Republic in 1931. Alfonso fled the country, and Spanish royalty was over until his grandson, Juan Carlos, stood in to replace Franco following the dictator's death in 1975.

In 1912, the king donated a trophy for the centenary celebrations of the Courts of Cádiz, the next major port east of Huelva. Recre won the tournament, defeating the local side Español FC by three goals to nil. As in Romania and

Denmark, royal approval was key to promoting the game in Spain. A year and a half after its foundation in January 1907, Club Deportivo de la Coruña in Galicia became the first Spanish club to be bestowed with the title *Real* (Royal) after the king was made honorary president.[11] In 1913, Spanish football's governing body, the *Federación Española de Clubs de Football* (Spanish Federation of Football Clubs), gained royal approval four years after its foundation, now known as the *Real Federación Española de Fútbol (*Royal Spanish Football Federation – RFEF). In March 1915, Mackay – still president of Recre – went in person to petition the king to accept the honorary presidency of his club. Alfonso accepted, and at that moment Recre became 'Real Club Recreativo de Huelva'.

## The creation of the Spanish national side

Although Spain had joined FIFA in 1904 via Madrid FC, the country would not play an international team for another 16 years, when a Spanish national team was put together to contest the 1920 Olympic tournament. The Spanish team was managed by former FC Barcelona defender Francisco Bru Sanz, who had won the Copa del Rey and four Catalan championships with Barça and two further regional championships with cross-town rivals Espanyol. The 22-man Olympic squad included 13 Basque-based players, four FC Barcelona players, and the rest from Asturias and Galicia. Among the squad were Pichichi, and teenage Barça stars José Samitier in midfield and goalkeeper Ricardo Zamora. They all travelled in third-class rail carriages during the long trip to Belgium. Spain made their debut at Le Stade Joseph Marien in Brussels, home of Royale Union Saint-Gilloise, on 28 August 1920, beating the much-fancied Danes by a 54th-minute goal from Real Unión striker Patricio Arabolaza.

Spain moved on to the Olympic Stadium in Antwerp the next day for the quarter-final with hosts, Belgium, and found themselves 3-0 down after an hour to a Robert Coppée hat-trick before pulling one back. The 3-1 defeat meant Spain entered a silver and bronze medal competition because Belgium's co-finalists, Czechoslovakia, had walked off the pitch in protest at the officials' decision-making, thus forfeiting the silver medal. The Spanish team defeated the Swedes 2-1 in the first round and the Italians 2-0 in the second. In the silver medal decider, the Spanish side defeated the Netherlands 3-1 with two goals from Barça striker Félix Sesúmaga and a third from Pichichi to clinch the silver medal. It would be Pichichi's only international goal; within two years he died from typhus, aged just 29. Spain's first tournament had resulted in success. Still, *La Roja* (the Reds) did not add to the trophy cabinet until 1964 with a European Championship win. Leaving Belgium, the team was detained at the border as Zamora attempted to smuggle out a case of Cuban cigars.[12] Spain would disappoint at the 1924 Olympics and were dumped out of the 1928 tournament 7-1 by Italy at the quarter-final stage.

## Creation of La Liga

By the mid-1920s, Spain had a national cup competition in the *Copa del Rey* and a national team, but no national league. The league system was still regionalised. Keen to capitalise on growing interest in the sport, José María Acha Larrea, vice-president of the Basque club Arenas Club de Getxo, proposed a professional national league. Supporters of the idea fell into two camps: those who wanted a larger championship and those who wanted a smaller one. Divided, neither could garner public interest, so in November 1928 the two groups reached agreement. The national championship,

*El Campeonato Nacional de Liga de Primera* (National Premier Championship) – abbreviated to *La Liga* – would consist of the six Copa del Rey winners – Arenas de Getxo, Athletic Club de Bilbao, FC Barcelona, Real Madrid, Real Sociedad and Real Unión – and three runners-up – Athletic Club de Madrid, and Barcelona clubs Espanyol and Club Deportivo Europa. The tenth spot would be decided by the winner of a ten-team knockout tournament, while the other nine participants would form La Segunda División, the second tier. Racing Santander pipped Sevilla FC in the competition to take the final spot in the inaugural La Liga season.

On 10 February 1929, José Prats of Espanyol scored the very first La Liga goal after just five minutes in his side's 3-2 victory over Real Unión at the Estadio de Sarría in Barcelona. Seven thousand fans had paid just a couple of pesetas to enter.[13] The Irún side's goalkeeper that day who conceded La Liga's first-ever goal was Antonio Emery, grandfather of future Valencia, Sevilla, PSG and Arsenal coach, Unai Emery. Fittingly, the first La Liga championship would feature a close contest between FC Barcelona and Real Madrid, with the Catalans clinching the title in the last round with victory against Real Unión. Racing Santander, the qualifier, had to enter a competition with the Segunda División champions – Sevilla – and, for the second time, the two were battling out for a place in Spain's new top flight. Again, Racing Santander won over two legs to retain its place.

England scheduled its first visit to play Spain on 16 May 1929, the third leg of a tour that included a 4-1 victory over France and 5-1 thumping of Belgium. Anticipation for the match led to eager Spaniards queuing around the block for tickets at the RFEF offices, and the Estadio Metropolitano

– no relation to the current Wanda Metropolitano, other than Atlético de Madrid also played there – could have sold out twice over. 'Spain has taken to football with as much success as her South American cousins, the Uruguayans and the Argentinians,' British media reported.[14] The lucky 25,000 spectators witnessed a piece of history as Spain overturned a 2-0 deficit to win 4-3 and become the first continental opposition to defeat England. At the final whistle, the ecstatic crowd rushed on to the pitch to embrace the players. Spain's assistant that day was Fred Pentland, the Englishman who managed Athletic Club, Racing Santander, Atlético de Madrid and Real Oviedo over a 15-year spell in Spain. Pentland had insisted on the game being played in the middle of the day to give Spain an advantage, which seemed to pay off as England wilted. Tragically, José María Acha Larrea, president of the Arenas club and driving force behind the creation of La Liga, was killed in a car crash north of Madrid on his way to watch the match. England and Spain met again two years later at Highbury, with the home side hitting seven past Zamora in a 7-1 win. By this time, Spain's internal divisions were beginning to unpick a fragile peace that would eventually lead to the outbreak of civil war in 1936 and suspension of La Liga.

Two years before hostilities broke out between the rebel Nationalist forces and the Republican government, *La Roja* made its World Cup debut in the second tournament in Italy. Spain raced into a 3-0 lead within half an hour against Brazil at the Stadio Luigi Ferraris in Genoa. The Brazilians threatened to come back in the second half with a goal on 55 minutes from Leônidas, and Zamora saved a penalty to snuff out the Brazilian revival and send Spain through. Zamora would receive little protection from the officials when Spain met the hosts in the quarter-final in Florence. A 1-1 draw required a replay, which the Italians won 1-0. A long spell as World Cup 'dark horses' had begun, and Spain would not lift the World Cup for another 76 years.

## The pioneers today

William Alexander Mackay presided over affairs at Recreativo until 1924. Mackay had resisted professionalism as president but – as in England nearly half a century earlier – the move to paying players became unavoidable. Mackay's legacy is preserved. In 1923, he was made an 'adopted son' of the city and the street where he lived is now named after him. Following his retirement, the doctor returned to Scotland, where he died aged 67 on 14 July 1927 in the Highlands. As the game spread across Spain, Recreativo, from its small enclave on the south-western edge of the peninsula, struggled to compete. At the time of writing, the club has only spent a total of five seasons in the top flight of Spanish football and never won the title. Its recent zenith was probably a 3-0 away win at the Bernabeu in 2006 versus David Beckham's *Galácticos*. That Recre team featured Santi Cazorla, who went on to make a name for himself at Villarreal and Arsenal, and forward Florent Sinama-Pongolle, once of Liverpool. The club anthem reads *Tu leyenda será siempre la primera* (Your legend will always be the first), which no other Spanish club can claim.

How does the future look for Recre, Spain's 'grand old man'? Andrew Gillan, a football blogger originally from Northern Ireland, was a season ticket holder at Recre. According to Gillan, the fans' pride in being the original team in Spain resonates through terrace song. In 2016, 'On the pitch, the club went through a huge number of players, struggling to field a settled side for ages and generally struggled for goals, but eventually did just enough to stay up with a week to spare,' Gillan tells me. 'The game where they clinched their Segunda B [third tier] status was the sixth-best-attended game in Spain that weekend, which gives a hint of the potential there. Falling into the Tercera División [fourth tier of Spanish football] would have been disastrous for the club and in my three seasons living there, Recre always did just about enough to avoid falling through the trapdoor,' Gillan adds.

The 2018/19 season was much better: a strong run of form late in the season saw Recre top their group and qualify for the promotion play-offs for the first time since they returned to this level in 2015. 'Unfortunately, they were heavily beaten by Fuenlabrada in the first leg of their tie and never recovered their earlier momentum. The summer saw the coach depart and the vast majority of the squad picked off by wealthier clubs meaning the new manager coming in would have to start over again with a blank canvas,' according to Gillan. 'Segunda B is notoriously difficult to get out of and Recre could be in for a few more years of struggle before finally seeing light at the end of the tunnel.' In July 2018, Recre's veterans' team took on Mackay's hometown side of Lybster at the Nuevo Colombino, winning 5-0 in a testimonial to celebrate the life and legacy of the father of not only Recreativo de Huelva but also of the first football in Spain itself. For Recre, the job of building its profile outside of Spain as pioneer of the sport in one of the game's most successful countries continues. 'We're trying to build bridges internationally, trying to get the word out there about the origins of football in Huelva,' Charlotte Mackay tells me. There's life in the grand old man yet.

1  *El Progreso de Jeréz de la Frontera*, 2 November 1870
2  *Dundee Courier*, 17 March 1890

3  Ibid.

4  https://www.dailyrecord.co.uk/sport/football/football-news/celtic-tribute-kit-unveiled-real-9831735

5  https://elcorreoweb.es/historico/el-betis-es-el-sexto-equipo-con-mas-seguidores-de-espana-IBEC709908

6  http://www.recreativohuelva.com/2017/08/13/el-velodromo-cumple-125-anos/

7  http://www.athletic-club.eus/en/1898-1913.html

8  https://as.com/futbol/2016/10/25/primera/1477428364_550337.html

9  http://palamoscf.cat/el-club/historia/

10  Ball, Phil, *Morbo: The Story of Spanish Football* (London: WSC Books Ltd., 2002, p106)

11  https://www.rcdeportivo.es/rcdeportivo/historia/el-depor-nace-en-un-gimnasio

12  https://thesefootballtimes.co/2019/02/13/how-ricardo-zamora-became-spanish-footballs-first-idol-and-blazed-a-path-for-future-goalkeeping-greats/

13  https://thesefootballtimes.co/2019/02/08/how-90-years-of-laliga-growth-and-some-odd-quirks-gave-us-24895-games-71149-goals-and-63-different-clubs/

14  *Hartlepool Northern Daily Mail*, 15 May 1929 (p7)

# 19.

# Portugal

AT EURO 2016, I lucked out by scoring a ticket for what turned out to be the match of the tournament: Portugal versus Hungary in Lyon. Sat among the Portuguese fans decked in that beautiful port wine red shirt of Portugal, we enjoyed a friendly, family atmosphere which was very different to the experience the Hungarian ultras had given us prematch. Two of the best goals in the 3-3 group match draw were scored at our end, including a deft flick from Cristiano Ronaldo. The Portuguese national side, *A Seleção* (Selection) sneaked into the second round with three draws. Third place would usually mean elimination at any previous tournament, but due to the 24-team set-up at Euro 2016 this was enough for Portugal to proceed – and set a course for the final. In the final a couple of weeks later in Paris, Portugal slammed the door shut on France's talented attack for 120 minutes despite losing Cristiano early on. It wasn't a vintage final – major tournament finals rarely are in the modern era – but in those dying seconds of the match Eder swung his long legs and lashed a shot from outside the box past the despairing Hugo Lloris in the French goal. The Stade de France was stunned. France won the European

Championships at home in 1984 and the World Cup in 1998. This was *their* time and Eder – once of Swansea City – had snatched it cruelly from them.

The 2016 European Championship was the first trophy in Portugal's international history after coming close at its home tournament in 2004 and featuring in numerous tournament semi-finals. For its contribution to world football, Portugal deserves this silverware. Despite the gravitation of power towards Europe's 'Big Five' leagues in England, Spain, Germany, Italy and France, Portugal's own 'Big Three' clubs – *Os Três Grandes* of Benfica, FC Porto and Sporting – can hold their own. Portuguese players have always graced the major leagues and have a reputation for flair. When the *Seleção* paraded the European Championship trophy to a joyful crowd of thousands in Lisbon, it marked the pinnacle of a relationship with football that first started in 1875. Once again, it was an Englishman that introduced the game to a new territory.

## Portugal's first football match

Madeira loves a good football monument. The Atlantic island's most famous footballing son, Cristiano Ronaldo, has two. The first, a 3.4m-high statue of Ronaldo's famous stance as he prepares to strike a free kick, stands outside the entrance to the footballer's museum, Museu CR7 in the Madeiran capital, Funchal. The museum was completed while Ronaldo was still playing and is used to house mementoes of his successes. The second is a replacement for the much-ridiculed bust of Ronaldo hosted inside Funchal's airport, which was also named in his honour. But there is another small monument in the town of Camacha, inland from Funchal, that is even more significant. It's a wall of sandy-grey blocks featuring the words in Portuguese announcing that, 'Here, football was played for the first time in Portugal, 1875, Camacha.' The wall, complete with a curved brass figurine, stands in what is now the park of Largo da Acharda. It was here that 18-year-old Madeira-born Anglo-Portuguese Harry Hinton, who had brought a ball back with him from his studies in England, orchestrated Portugal's first football match. Hinton's family was drawn to Madeira for its climate and was involved in the banana and sugar trades. As an island with close links to England, it is probably not surprising that this should be where English sailors and expats got together with some locals and had what was probably no more than an informal kickabout. Hinton's ball was made of animal bladder, and he records that the ball got damaged several times during that first game.

## Football hits the mainland

Statues aside, it is probably fitting that Madeira's role in the development of the Portuguese game is recognised, but the game largely disappears from the record for more than a decade. It is likely that British sailors – as elsewhere in the world – would have been intriguing the locals with their dockside kickabouts during this period. It isn't until late 1888 that we see another firm record of a match. Interestingly, this was led locally. In the seaside residence of Cascais, west of Lisbon, the aristocratic Pinto Basto family arranged a game. Like Harry Hinton before them, brothers Eduardo and Frederico Pinto Basto had been studying in England, and they brought a ball back with them to arrange a game. Another Pinto Basto brother, Guilherme, was highly influential in organising a match between friends in the highest echelons of Portuguese society. Lisbon-based journalist Filipe d'Avillez is a descendant of António d'Avillez, who played in the game alongside the Pinto Basto brothers.

'The game was played in Cascais, where the King spent his holidays,' d'Avillez informs me. 'The d'Avillezes were an important family in Cascais, so it was only natural that they would have a couple of players in that match.' Again, this match was informal. Sports historian Ricardo Serrado has written two volumes titled *História do Futebol Português* (The History of Portuguese Football). He told me we should consider the first 'formal match' in Portugal to be the one that took place in Campo Pequeno, Lisbon, in January 1889. This game featured field markings and goalposts, lasted 90 minutes and featured a Portuguese team against a British team made up of players working on the installation of a submarine cable in Carcavelos, the Graham port house, and other expats. The Portuguese team won 2-1, which demonstrates that quite a bit of football had been played between 1875 and 1889.

In 1890, Britain and Portugal came to loggerheads over their respective colonial ambitions in Africa in an event known as the British Ultimatum. It created tension between Brits in Portugal and the locals that lasted decades and is now immortalised in the words of the Portuguese national anthem. The British Carcavelos team went unbeaten from 1894 until 1907, when Sport Lisboa beat Carcavelos 2-1 for the Lisbon Championship. The public went wild! By then, matches in Lisbon were attended by crowds of more than 3,000 people. Serrado adds: 'There are some indications that the match between Sport Lisboa and Carcavelos was viewed by 8,000 people, principally because of two factors: 1) this game pitted the best Portuguese team against the best team in all Lisbon and, subsequently, in the whole country – the unbeatable 'masters' of Carcavelos; 2) because of that, this match was considered a game between Portugal and England. An opportunity for Portugal to take revenge from the

Ultimatum of 1890.' Indeed, due to the strained relationship with Britain, some in Portugal called for their countrymen to give up this English *jogo do coiçe* (kick game). 'Nevertheless, if this happened, it was for a short time and with low impact, because the game grew after 1890 and by 1908 it was the main sport in Lisbon, by far,' Serrado explains.

## Portugal's first football club

There is some debate over who was the first dedicated football club in Portugal. According to Serrado, the very first sports club in Portugal is the Real Ginásio Club (Royal Gymnastic Club – known as Ginásio Clube Português since the fall of the monarchy in 1910), which was formed in 1875 and started playing football in 1889.[1] 'Between 1890 and 1894 dozens of clubs were formed in Lisbon, but the most powerful football club was the Club Lisbonense, which no longer exists. However, between 1890 and 1894 was the most popular football team in the country,' Serrado adds. One of the oldest existing clubs still playing in the top leagues is Associação Académica de Coimbra. Although founded in 1887, the sports academy didn't start playing football until comparatively late in 1912. The year 1889 was the kick-start year for Portuguese football. It is from here the country gets the football bug and the game really took off, especially in Lisbon, where a season of sorts ran between local teams from September to April. In Porto, there were only two teams in the early days – Football Club Porto and Oporto Cricket Club. FC Porto had been founded by port wine merchant and sports enthusiast, António Nicolau d'Almeida.[2] In 1893, the Associação Naval 1 de Maio club was founded in Figueira da Foz near Coimbra. It folded in 2017 due to financial difficulties and has since been revived as Naval 1893.

By 1894, Portugal had a cup competition – the *Cup d'el Rey* – between the best teams from cities around the country at Campo Alegre in Porto. In that first year, that meant just Club Lisbonense from the capital and FC Porto took part on 2 March. King Carlos I and Queen Amélia were in attendance to see the Lisbon side win 1-0. The cup competition still exists as the *Taça de Portugal* (Portugal Cup). 'In reality, that game was considered by all as a Lisbon versus Porto – the first and second cities of Portugal, respectively,' Serrado tells me. FC Porto then went into a period of inactivity before being revived in 1906 under José Monteiro da Costa as a multisports entity, including football. The other two in Portugal's 'Big Three'– Sporting Clube de Portugal and Sport Lisboa e Benfica – were also founded in the period 1906–08. Benfica was formed by a merger of the Belém-based Sport Lisboa club, founded in 1904, and Sport Benfica, established in 1906. Across Porto, the English brothers Harry and Dick Lowe from the William Graham factory established The Boavista Footballers in 1903 for both British and Portuguese staff to play. Now known as Boavista Futebol Clube, the famous *Axadrezados* (Chequers) have played at the same ground since 1910 and won the Primeira Liga title in 2000/01.

In the first decade of the 20th century, football in Portugal began to formalise. The first national league was created in 1908 and the *Associação de Futebol de Lisboa* (Lisbon Football Association) was created two years later, followed by local associations in Portalegre and Porto. Finally, in 1914, the *União Portuguesa de Futebol* (UPF – Portuguese Football Union) was formed. On 26 August that year, it became affiliated with FIFA. Then the First World War interrupted matters. Portugal managed to remain neutral until 1916 before coming in on the side of the Allies. The disruption of war meant that, despite having been founded in 1914, the UPF could not arrange a first national team match until 1921. The first *Seleção* headed to Madrid in December that year to take on Spain at the Campo de la Calle O'Donnell. A crowd of 14,000 saw Spain win 3-1 with two goals from FC Barcelona's Paulino Alcántara and one from Manuel Meana of Sporting Gijón. The scorer of Portugal's first international goal was Alberto Augusto, who netted from the penalty spot on 75 minutes.

## Casa Pia: Portugal's early talent factory

All of the players that had formed part of the Lisbon side that beat the British side Carcavelos for the first time in 1898 had been students of the *Real Casa Pia de Lisboa* (Royal Pious House of Lisbon). This breakthrough moment in Portugal's sporting history was not formed from the Portuguese upper classes; it was made up of orphans. The establishment was founded in 1780 in Lisbon's São Jorge castle by the Chief of Police of the Court of the Kingdom, Diogo Inácio de Pina Manique (1733–1805). It was named Real Casa Pia de Lisboa after Queen Dona María I, 'The Pious', who was monarch of Portugal at the time of the institution's founding. Casa Pia's aims were to instruct, educate and support abandoned and difficult children in the city of Lisbon following the 1755 earthquake. Similar to the English ethos of muscular Christianity, the institution believed in physical as well as spiritual education of its students. Casa Pia, based in the west of Lisbon, built Portugal's first gym. It introduced football into the curriculum in 1893, despite popular opposition to English things following the British Ultimatum of 1890. With the 1898 victory, Casa Pia students had won over the public for the new game, helping establish football into wider Portuguese society.[3]

Former Casa Pia students went on to form football clubs that would eventually lead to the foundation of Sport Lisboa e Benfica, but it was not until the summer of 1920 that two Benfica players who had studied at Casa Pia set up the Casa Pia Atlético Clube. One of the co-founders was Cândido de Oliveira, who would later coach the Portuguese national side at the 1928 Amsterdam Olympics. Oliveira had been orphaned young and sent to Casa Pia, where he learned football and joined Benfica in 1914.[4] The impact of this new club posed a genuine threat to Benfica's fledgling dominance of the Lisbon game as Casa Pia Atlético Clube won every game en route to the Lisbon Championship in its first season. 'Casa Pia was responsible for making the game popular among the lower working classes, and that's how the game really took off in Portugal,' Filipe d'Avillez tells me. 'Being mostly orphans, the students developed a tremendous *esprit de corps* and this, which they referred to as *mística* (mystique), is the origin of the *mística* which Benfica fans say characterises the club and its members.' The list of 18 founders is a real 'who's who' of the time: journalists, poets and writers, an Olympic swimmer, and António Pinho, who was capped 12 times by Portugal.

The *Cruz de Cristo* (Cross of Christ) on Casa Pia Atlético Clube's crest was designed by the painter Pedro Guedes, the first captain of the Real Casa Pia de Lisboa team. Guedes was in the 1898 Portuguese team that defeated the previously invincible English masters of the Carcavelos Club for the first time. The adoption of the emblem, which had been sported by Pina Manique himself, was made on the suggestion of *Casapiano* journalist Ribeiro dos Reis, founder of the sports newspaper *A Bola* (The Ball). Casa Pia also flew the flag abroad, appearing in tournaments in France and Spain in the early 1920s. In 1906, the former

Casa Pia student and Sport Lisboa player, Francisco dos Santos, became the first Portuguese footballer to play abroad with two seasons at Lazio in Rome while he studied at the Academy of Fine Arts.

## Football unites the country

By 1922, Portugal had its own championship, which had an elimination format. Portugal was an underdeveloped country by European standards at this time, so did not enjoy the benefits of an extensive transport network, as existed in England, for example. So, power was concentrated in the capital and Porto, and not dispersed across the land as in England, Germany, Italy or Spain. FC Porto won the first edition on 18 June 1922 with a 3-1 win over Sporting. The knockout *Campeonato de Portugal* was replaced by a league format in 1934 and the *Taça de Portugal* continued as the premier elimination tournament. FC Porto also won the first league format in the 1934/35 season. To date, the Portuguese championship has been dominated by SL Benfica, Sporting and FC Porto, with just two other sides winning the title – Belenenses of Belém in 1946 and Boavista of Porto in 2001.

In 1922, Spain visited for Portugal's first home match at the Estádio do Lumiar, attracting a crowd of 20,000. The margin of defeat for the *Seleção* was narrowed to 2-1 from their previous encounter. The UPF rebranded as the *Federação Portuguesa de Futebol* (Portuguese Football Federation – FPF) in 1926, and over that Easter the Casuals visited from London, drawing 1-1 with Benfica and 2-2 with Sporting. But Portugal would soon descend into chaos. The 'May Revolution' was a coup d'état led by the military to overthrow the unstable First Republic and ushered in 48 years of dictatorship under the *Estado Novo* (New State). When the former governor of Madeira, Dr Amenco da Silva, arrived in London in 1927 after being imprisoned in the Avenida Palace Hotel in Lisbon, he described the revolution as a 'gentlemanly affair' as government troops and rebels did their best to avoid shooting innocent people. According to a report in the *Forfar Dispatch*, da Silva credited this 'sporting spirit' to the effect of football in Portugal. Da Silva reported that over the previous decade the Portuguese had become 'fanatics about football' with crowds of more than 20,000 at matches in the larger cities. He argued that the Madeiran team that he was president of could beat any side, except the British clubs.[5]

A year later, the Portuguese team was able to test that theory with its Olympic debut in Amsterdam, having enjoyed solid warm-up performances, drawing with Spain, France and Argentina, and beating a strong Italy side 4-1. In its qualifying match against Chile, Portugal played in front of a small crowd of 2,309 at the Olympic Stadium. Within half an hour, the Chileans were 2-0 up through Saavedra and Carbonell, but Portugal were level by half-time with two goals in two minutes from Vitor Silva of Benfica and Soares Pepe of Belenenses. Two further goals in the second half gave Portugal its first victory at a major tournament and sent the *Seleção* into the first round proper, where the team defeated Yugoslavia 2-1 with a last-gasp strike from Belenenses's Augusto Silva. Pictures appeared in the British press of Portuguese fans flooding on to the pitch and kissing the players at the final whistle. Led by Casa Pia's co-founder, Cândido de Oliveira, Portugal felt confident going into its quarter-final with Egypt in the Olympic Stadium in Amsterdam. But in the evening kick-off in front of just 3,448 spectators, Portugal trailed 2-0 just after half-time. With 14 minutes to go, Vitor Silva pulled one back, but it was not enough. The Egyptians had proven to be faster and fitter. Egypt fell 6-0 to Argentina in the semi-final, a team the Portuguese had drawn with just weeks earlier. Following the shock defeat, Oliveira resigned only to return in 1935 after a spell studying coaching at Arsenal, England's leading club at the time.

## The Portuguese pioneers today

Portugal's representative in the Club of Pioneers, Sheffield FC's initiative for the oldest club in each country, is Associação Académica de Coimbra. This students' union sports club was established on 3 November 1887 and was admitted to the Club of Pioneers on its 130th anniversary.[6] The club did not play a football match until January 1912, beating Ginásio Club de Coimbra 1-0.[7] Portugal has developed some wonderful players over the decades and many of these have featured on the wing: Ronaldo, Eusébio, Luis Figo, Rui Costa, Ricardo Quaresma, Nani, Simão Sabrosa, Paulo Futre and others. The attractive style for which Portugal's 'Golden Generation' of the early 2000s were known didn't culminate in victory in the country's home Euros in 2004, losing in the final to a negative Greek team, but – ironically – it was the Greek-style defensive approach that led *A Seleção* to glory in 2016. And to think, it all started with Harry Hinton's kickabout in Camacha.

1   http://gcp.pt/gcp/historia-e-patrimonio/momentos-historicos/1880-1889
2   https://www.fcporto.pt/en/club/history
3   https://casapiaac.pt/pagina-exemplo/historial/
4   https://portugoal.net/classics-topmenu/550-candido-de-oliveira-portugal-s-football-pioneer
5   *Forfar Dispatch*, 17 February 1927 (p2)
6   http://www.academica-oaf.pt/home/fans/club-of-pioneers/
7   http://www.academica-oaf.pt/home/2018-07-18-15-13-58/historia/

# 20.

# Italy

THE DESTINY of Genoa and its people has always been linked to the sea. The Liguria port was the birthplace of navigator Christopher Columbus. It was also the launch pad of revolutionary Giuseppe Garibaldi's Expedition of the Thousand, a key event in Italy's unification, the *Risorgimento*. Genoa was also the departure port for hundreds of Italian émigrés seeking a new life in the Americas. Many of them would never see their homeland again. Yet, just as Genoa was the scene of mass exodus, a new community was on its way into the country. It was a group of British merchants. They had a ball and a rule book with them, and they were about to redefine Italy's sporting and cultural landscape forever. The key to how football gained a foothold in Genoa is due in large part to its location. Genoa has long been a key port on the Italian peninsula, and the city's relationship with England goes back centuries.

Despite its current standing as one of the leading footballing powers with one of its best leagues, Serie A, Italy was a relative late starter. Records of Association football clubs do not emerge until the 1880s and 1890s.[1] However, games had taken place in port cities such as Livorno, Palermo, Naples

313

and Genoa as British ships stopped off there on their way to the Suez Canal. Visitors to that part of the Mediterranean will notice the prevalence of a red cross on a white background – the cross of St George. It features in the flags of Catalonia in north-east Spain, as well as Sardinia, and the dragonslayer is also the patron saint of much of northern Italy, including the city states of Milan, Venice and Genoa. Genoa has been using the cross of St George as its flag since at least 1218. One of the many rumours as to how it ended up being used by the English is that the port lent its flag to English ships trading in the area at the time of the Crusades so they could sail without fear of piracy. Back in England, the flag stuck, although plenty of other theories exist as to how England adopted this popular Mediterranean saint. At the hotel I stayed in on my first visit to the city, the Genoa team bus was parked outside, attracting selfie seekers and other curious visitors like me. Emblazoned on the side of it were the words 'Genoa Cricket and Football Club', a nod back to the days of its foundation as an exclusive club for British expats.

## The English doctor

The Via James Richardson Spensley in Genoa's Marassi district is a fairly modest marker for one of the founding fathers of Italian football. The street is a driveway that leads from the main road up to one of the entrances of the brown-brick edifice of the Stadio Luigi Ferraris, home to both Genoa and its city rival, Sampdoria. Spensley was a doctor from Stoke Newington in East London. He was 30 years old when he landed in Genoa in 1896. His job was to tend to British sailors transporting coal, rather like William Alexander Mackay had done when he arrived in Huelva, Spain, as a doctor to British miners. Spensley joined the Genoa Cricket and Athletics Club. The society had been formed in a small room on the Via Palestro on 7 September 1893 by members of the British Consulate. The ledger of the club's foundation in the club's museum contains the names of its English founders. The London draughtsman and designer Charles de Grave Sells is cited as president; Yorkshireman Charles Alfred Payton – an adventurer and diplomat – is cited as patron, along with eight other founder members. The Genoa Cricket and Athletics Club was very much a club founded *by* Brits *for* Brits. Spensley was something of a polymath. He wrote for the *Daily Mail*, was a keen boxer and also a cultured linguist, mastering both Greek and Sanskrit. On 10 April 1897, Spensley set up the football arm of Genoa Cricket and Athletics Club and persuaded the board to admit Italians. The football branch went on to eclipse the athletics arm, so the organisation switched its name to Genoa Cricket and Football Club.

## Calcio Italiano and the Nottingham connection

Now that Spensley had established his footballing arm, the question was whom to play against. This is where the other two founding fathers of Italian football come into play. A full decade before Spensley had set up his footballing branch of the Genoa Cricket and Athletics Club, Edoardo Bosio had already established Italy's very first soccer club, Torino Football and Cricket Club in Turin, aged just 23. Bosio, the son of a prominent Swiss brewer based in Turin, had first encountered football while working as an accountant for lace manufacturer Thomas Adams of Nottingham. At this time, Nottingham was a hotbed for English football, with two established teams in Notts County FC (founded 1862) and Nottingham Forest FC (founded 1865) based on either side of the River Trent. Bosio was hooked. His main sport was rowing; he was a champion team rower. At

1.81m tall, he would have stood out in 19th-century Italy. Even in the 21st century, the average height for an Italian male is 1.76m. Like Sheffield FC's co-founders, Crestwick and Prest, Bosio was looking for a winter sport to keep him active. Torino Football and Cricket Club practised cricket and rowing in the summer, and football in the winter, along with mountaineering. When he returned to Italy, he took footballs with him. On one of his business trips between Nottingham and Turin in 1891, he took his colleague at Thomas Adams, Herbert Kilpin, with him.

Kilpin is remembered in Italy as the founder of AC Milan. *Milanisti* ultras wave flags prematch featuring a moustachioed Kilpin looking rather like a Victorian drill ground major. In 2017, Kilpin's story was turned into both a novel and a film called *The Lord of Milan* by Nottingham-based writer Robert Nieri and a production company called LeftLion. 'I came across the story when I read the front page of the *Nottingham Evening Post*, and it said that a local lad had founded the world-famous football club,' Nieri told me. 'Herbert was a textile worker from Nottingham, he was an amateur footballer, and he left Nottingham to go to Italy for work purposes. He initially went to Turin, where he played for a club called Internazionale. In 1899, he founded the Milan Football and Cricket Club, and he led the side to its first three championship titles.' Kilpin, the son of a butcher and one of 16 children – some of whom died in infancy – was 21 when he headed to Italy. He had lived just a mile from Nottingham's Lace Market, and – while not good enough to play for either of Nottingham's established professional clubs, Forest and County – he had played for Notts Olympic and a church side, St Andrew's. 'The English father of Italian football is probably Kilpin,' Nieri states.

In 1891, the same year Bosio took Kilpin to Turin, Bosio's Torino Cricket and Football Club merged with another new team from the city, Nobili Torino – the 'Turin Nobles' – so named because the team contained the Duke of Abruzzi and the Marquis Ferrero of Ventimiglia. The newly merged team – Internazionale di Torino, for whom Kilpin turned out – retained Nobili's black and yellow stripes. 'That was two years before Genoa was founded,' Nieri points out. Other football clubs were to emerge before Genoa's soccer arm was launched by Spensley in 1897. Football Club Torinese was founded in 1894 and also wore black and yellow stripes, and later absorbed Internazionale di Torino in a merger in 1900. Bosio stayed on with the new set-up. The club should not be confused with the existing Torino FC, founded in 1906, the same year FC Torinese closed down, with many players jumping across to the newly formed *Toro*.

Kilpin also knew another Nottingham man, John Savage, who is credited with shipping black and white stripes from the Notts County team to Turin for the Juventus side that he played for in 1903. Juventus had been founded on 1 November 1897 by students of the Liceo D'Azeglio school. The story goes that the students – the eldest of which was just 17 – founded the club on a bench on the Corse Re Umberto in central Turin. Three names were put to a vote: 'Società Via Fort', 'Società Sportiva Massimo D'Azeglio' – after the players' school – and 'Sport Club Juventus' after the Latin word for 'youth'. These young men were students of the classics, after all. Now nicknamed 'La Vecchia Signora' ('The Old Lady'), due to its longevity, Juventus had originally worn pink at its outset before Savage brought over the famous *bianconeri* striped shirts. When Juventus inaugurated its new stadium in 2011, the club invited Notts County, then of the English third tier, to play an exhibition match. The game ended 1-1. Another Turin football club to emerge in 1897 was the soccer arm of the *Reale Società Ginnastica Torino* (Royal Gymnastic Society of Turin). In the nearby town of Vercelli, midway between Turin and Milan, Pro Vercelli was formed in 1903 from a gymnasium, while on 3 December 1906, Juventus dissidents led by the Swiss financier Alfred Dick met in the Voigt Brewery to form Torino Football Club. Its colours would be maroon, like those of Dick's favourite Swiss club, Servette FC.

## The first formal football match in Italy

Bosio may have introduced the game into Italy, but his matches will have been informal kickabouts. It was Spensley who gave Italian football structure and competition. Spensley looked at Turin's nascent football scene and decided to arrange a match. On 6 January 1898, Spensley's Genoa CFC took on Football Club Torinese in Genoa with the Turin side running out 1-0 winners. Some records survive from the match. For example, we know the name of the referee was Reverend Richard Douglas. More than 150 tickets were sold, and the event made a profit of more than 100 lire.[2] The Italian Football Federation – the *Federazione Italiana Football* – later Italianised in 1909 to the *Federazione Italiana Giuoco Calcio* (FIGC) – was formed after that first match. Engineer Mario Vicary was elected as its president.

On 8 May 1898, a four-club, one-day tournament was arranged at Turin's Velodromo Umberto I. Those four pioneer clubs were Spensley's Genoa CFC, Bosio and Kilpin's Internazionale di Torino, FC Torinese and Ginnastica Torino. It was a basic tournament with two semi-finals and a final. Internazionale beat FC Torinese 1-0 in the first match, which kicked off at 9am. In the second semi-final, Genoa – with Spensley in goal and fielding three other British players in the side – defeated Ginnastica 2-1. The teams took a lunch break before the final match at 3pm. Genoa needed extra time to beat Internazionale by another 2-1 scoreline, with Norman Victor Leaver notching the winner. The Duke of Abruzzi – you may remember him from the Nobili team – presented the trophy to Genoa. Genoa's Ponte Carrega ground hosted the finals tournament the following year, with Spensley's *Genovese* side once again lifting the trophy. Genoa won four more titles under Spensley as player-manager before he hung up his boots aged 40, but he hadn't finished contributing just yet to his adopted homeland – Spensley went on to found the Italian scouting movement.

One English observer of the nascent Italian game in 1901 wrote in the *Lancashire Evening Post* that the game was in 'very crude condition' but was on the up. He noted the role that keen Englishmen were playing in keeping the game alive in Milan, Genoa and Turin, but that the game needed more organisation if Italy were ever to 'become a power to be reckoned with on the Continent'.[3] Nieri says Spensley's role is important in the development of the game in the peninsula because he pushed for Italians to be involved in the traditionally expat-only Genoa Cricket and Football Club. At that time, a quota system was used by the club to guarantee British players a game. Kilpin also knew Spensley, Nieri says, and even played against him and – on occasions – with him. 'They played one or two finals against one another, and at times they even played together for representative sides against visiting foreign teams from Switzerland and from France,' Nieri adds. When they did play against each other, it was with a great spirit of camaraderie, Nieri tells me. Both Spensley and Kilpin were true gentlemen amateurs, so egos didn't come into it; they just played for the love of the game, and there was no competition between these two Englishmen over who was the more prominent in the Italian game.

## The Lord of Milan

Herbert Kilpin had set up his first club at the age of 13, called Nottingham Garibaldi, inspired by the great Italian hero of the Risorgimento – the unification of Italy. Nottingham Forest had donned 'Garibaldi red', so we can see his point of reference.

Milan was not a happy place when Adams sent Kilpin there in 1897. The wheat harvest failed that year and, coupled with the Spanish-American War adding to the cost of importing American wheat, prices soared. By May 1898, a series of food riots broke out across the city. These culminated in the 'Bava Beccaris massacre', named after the general who ordered his troops to fire on protestors. The death toll is unknown, but estimates put it up to 400. King Umberto I, who gave his name to the Turin velodrome, praised General Bava Beccaris for his actions and awarded him with the Great Cross of the Order of Savoy. On 29 July 1900, the anarchist Gaetano Bresci took revenge by assassinating the king in Monza.

It was into this tumultuous backdrop that Kilpin and his English friends founded the Milan Cricket and Football Club at the Fiaschetteria Toscana bar on 16 December 1899. As *The Lord of Milan* film recounts, Kilpin stated to those present: 'Our colours will be red, because we will be the devils, and black because of the fear we will strike into the hearts of our opponents.' The club president was Alfred Edwards from Shropshire – he was the British consul general – with Edward Berra Nathan as his vice-president. The secretary was the Mancunian Samuel Richard Davies, and there were three other directors, Messrs Barnet, Saint

John and Pirelli. Kilpin was coach, leaving the captaincy to the older David Allison. The *Gazzetta dello Sport* recorded the event in its Monday, 18 December 1899 edition[4] in a single paragraph. 'Finally, after many unsuccessful attempts, Milan will have a football club,' it proclaimed, citing that the Milanese team had been established to compete in the Italian Championship that spring and providing instructions on where new members could go to join. Members came from Italy, England, Wales and Switzerland, and played on a field where Mussolini's grand Centrale Station now stands. At 3pm on 15 April 1900, Milan Football and Cricket Club made its debut in the Italian Football Championship against Kilpin's former team-mate Edoardo Bosio's FC Torinese. The black and yellow side from Turin won 3-0, with Bosio himself scoring the first recorded hat-trick in competitive domestic Italian football. Milan dusted themselves down to win the *Medaglia del Re* (King's Medal) with a 2-0 win over Juventus the following month.

By 1901, Milan were Italian champions, breaking Spensley's grip on the trophy that Genoa had enjoyed since its inception in 1898. With Kilpin – nicknamed 'Il Lord' – as a utility player at its heart, Milan Football and Cricket Club won back-to-back titles in 1906 and 1907 before Kilpin's retirement. After Kilpin's departure, a schism emerged in the club. The Italian Football Federation was keen to promote local participation in soccer, and disagreements arose over the admission of foreign players to the Milan Football and Cricket Club. As a result, a group broke away to set up a new club on 8 March 1908. Its name was Football Club Internazionale and its founders described themselves as *fratelli del mondo* (brothers of the world). Within two years, this heavily Swiss-influenced team won its first championship. Inter Milan is the only club never to have been relegated from Italy's top division, Serie A.

Meanwhile, the cricketing arm of the Milan Football and Cricket Club had pretty much disappeared as the English drifted away, with the club dropping 'and Cricket' from its name in 1919. It was Mussolini's fascist regime that forced the club to Italianise to Associazione Calcio (AC) Milano in 1939, but after the Second World War the club reverted to the English spelling of the city and has been AC Milan ever since.

But what of Kilpin? We know he had married an Italian, Maria Capua from Lodi, in 1905 – under the condition that she didn't prevent him from playing football – and the two never had children. Kilpin died aged 46 on 22 October 1916, apparently the victim of his own love of a drink – he is alleged to have kept a flask by the goalposts during matches. *Gazzetta dello Sport* mentioned his passing, and then Herbert slipped into obscurity for eight decades – including AC Milan's most successful years in the 80s and 90s. In 1998, Milan-based football historian Luigi La Rocca uncovered Herbert Kilpin's final resting place. La Rocca discovered a mislabelled 'Alberto' Kilpin in the archive, listed in a humble Protestant graveyard. Since La Rocca's discovery, Kilpin has enjoyed something of a renaissance. In the most famous image of Kilpin, he is stood decked in a thin black and red striped shirt and cap, with white trousers tucked into long socks. His right hand is on his hip, and he sports a determined look and a strong moustache. This image has made its way on to the banners of AC Milan *ultrà* groups that are waved in the stands of the San Siro.

Kilpin now rests alongside the great and the good *Milanese* in the huge Cimitero Maggiore, thanks to the club he founded. What this lace maker from Mansfield Road,

Nottingham, would make of his fame in his adopted city we'll never know, but his place in the red and black half of Milan's hearts is secure, and maybe the blue and black half owes him a little too. One place where Kilpin's legacy is finally recognised is his hometown. Robert Nieri and LeftLion's work on *The Lord of Milan* book and film has certainly helped. Kilpin's story inspired the naming of a pub in Bridlesmith Walk, Nottingham, complete with his own pale ale.

## Italy pioneers early football tournaments

More tournaments began to appear in Italy's industrial north in the early 1900s. In 1908, Turin was the host of one of the first international club competitions, the *Torneo Internazionale Stampa Sportiva*, which was organised by Italian sports magazine *La Stampa Sportiva*. Host-city clubs Torino and Juventus were joined by fellow northern Italians Piemonte Calcio and FC Ausonia Milano, French club US Parisienne, Germans Freiburger FC and eventual winners, Servette FC from Switzerland. A year later, tea magnate Sir Thomas Lipton, who had already sponsored football tournaments in South America, held his own tournament in Turin. Amateur side West Auckland from the Northern League travelled to Turin as Britain's representative to take on invited clubs from Italy, Germany and Switzerland. West Auckland's team was made up of miners paying out of their own pocket to make the tournament. The team dispatched Germany's Stuttgarter Sportfreunde 2-0 on 11 April 1909 and beat the Swiss FC Winterthur by the same margin in the final the following day to win the trophy. In 1911, the Sir Thomas Lipton Trophy was held again in Turin and – again – the West Aucklanders triumphed to win the 'hundred guineas Challenge Cup', beating Swiss side Zürich in the semi-finals and thrashing Juventus 6-1 in the final. Juventus was just over a decade old at this point and nowhere near the power it is now. One English paper even spelled its name 'Juventers' in its report.[5]

Road signs into the County Durham town welcome visitors to the 'Home of the First World Cup'. The story of West Auckland FC's Sir Thomas Lipton Trophy adventures was brought to the screen by British actor Dennis Waterman in his 1982 biopic *A Captain's Tale*. The club launched its own documentary film, *Our Cup of Tea*, in 2019. West Auckland Town FC, as the club is now known, returned to Turin in 2009 for the centenary of the first competition, losing 7-1 to Juventus's Under-20s. Lipton's generosity was not limited to the north of Italy. Between 1909 until Italy joined the First World War in 1915, the Lipton Challenge Cup – or *Coppa Lipton* – was held in the south of Italy, featuring clubs formed in the first half of that decade, Naples Football Club (a forerunner of SSC Napoli), Palermo Football Club and other southern clubs.

While the first Italian clubs and tournaments had been formed in the northern regions of Piemonte and Liguria, the south was not far behind. Palermo Football Club had started life as the Anglo-Palermitan Athletic and Football Club, and was founded by Ignazio Majo Pagano on 1 November 1900. Pagano had been sent to London at the age of 22 by his parents, and he brought back a love of football. The Palermitans were also an Anglo-Italian outfit, playing in red and blue against groups of British sailors and administrators. Its honorary president was a member of the Whitaker family, which sponsored an annual challenge cup as early as 1905 for Palermo to contest against fellow Sicilian football pioneers, Messina. Three years after Palermo's foundation, William Poths, an Englishman in the employ of the Cunard shipping company, moved to Naples. He found a small football culture in his adopted home, with at least three clubs in existence already. Poths teamed up with local Neapolitan Ernesto Bruschini, and by early 1905 the Naples Football Club was formed,[6] marking its first match against the crew of the English ship *Arabik*. In 1909, a writer for *The Sketch* in Britain noted on his travels that, in the dozen or so towns he had travelled through, Italian boys had 'got the football fever'.[7]

## Italian football unites the peninsula

In 1910, the FIGC put together a national team which, playing in white, beat France 6-2 at the Arena di Milano. Against Hungary the following year, the Italian team wore blue for the first time, and the legend of the *Azzurri* (The Blues) was born. If Italy had followed the trend of many other major footballing countries and applied the colours of its national flag to its football kit, then the Italian outfit would probably be akin to the red, white and green combination of Mexico or Hungary. Rather, blue was chosen in honour of the House of Savoy. The country entered a team for the 1912 Olympic Games in Stockholm. Of the 18-man squad, only six were capped previously and all were drawn from clubs in the north. Italy lost its first-round match 3-2 after extra time to the Finns. Entering a consolation tournament, Italy beat the hosts Sweden 1-0 at Råsunda but were thrashed 5-1 by Austria four days later.

Domestically, the league system was in flux. The FIGC wanted to promote the development of Italian-born players and in 1907 divided the championship into the main Italian Championship for teams for Italian-only clubs, who competed for *La Coppa Buni*, and the Federal Championship for those with foreign players, for which the winners were awarded *La Coppa Spensley*. Genoa, Milan and Torino withdrew in protest. The matter was eventually resolved, but the championship was, by now, a league format, with Pro Vercelli dominating with five titles in six years between 1908 and 1913. Pro Vercelli's 1913 championship win marked the first time that a nationwide tournament had been held, with the league divided into a northern and a central-southern group. Genoa won its seventh title in 1915, before Italy's late entry into the First World War on the side of the Allies meant a postponement of most football until 1919. The war would claim more than half a million Italian lives, including Genoa's Luigi Ferraris, after whom the club's stadium is named. Dr James Richardson Spensley was also killed in no man's land in 1915 by a German sniper, while he was tending to a wounded German soldier. Internazionale lost 26 players and staff, but, despite this huge setback, Inter won the first championship that ran after the war.[8]

The 1920s would see major developments in the Italian game, including the introduction of a national knockout competition, the *Coppa Italia* in 1922, which got off to something of a false start. The tournament did not attract the best clubs to start with, and the first edition was won by third division Vado, a small town in Liguria. It then went into hiatus until 1926/27 and was cancelled mid-tournament. It would not start again in earnest until the 1935/36 season. It was in the 1920s that Italian football finally took shape into a structure that we recognise today.

### What's in a name? 'Calcio' or 'football'?

You'll have noticed that the Italian word for football – *calcio* – is nothing like other non-English naturalisations, such as the *fútbol* of Spanish, *futebol* of Portuguese, or *fußball* of German. Italian clubs founded in the 19th century often had an English name or connection, yet from the early 20th century, all this changed. The use of the word *calcio* – literally, 'kick' – is very deliberate. As in many parts of the world, a kicking game existed in Italy centuries before Association football arrived with its distinct regulations. In Italy, this game was *Calcio Fiorentino* or *Calcio Storico* (Florentine football or Historic football), which has undergone something of a recent revival. The Florentine game dates from at least the 16th century and is played by teams of 27 dressed in historical garb. These are brutal encounters: players can use their hands and their feet, with punches, headbutts, elbowing and even choking permitted, which would probably get Ebenezer Cobb Morley and his FA co-founders' moustaches twitching. The 50-minute final in Florence's Piazza Santa Croce is started by cannon fire. Oh, and there are no substitutes.

Italy was still politically weak after the devastation of the First World War. This instability gave rise to Italian fascism and in late October 1922, Benito Mussolini marched on Rome, taking the capital. Mussolini immediately saw the value of sport as a way to create *l'italiano nuovo* – the new Italian – whose physical prowess would drive forward his new empire. Italian dictator Benito Mussolini did much to reinvigorate the Florentine game, identifying it as the forerunner of Association football.[9] While the Florentine ball game shared some traits with Association football, the two are unconnected, yet the name stuck. Italy had been united less than six decades, and Mussolini was very much in the business of 'making Italians', and that included reinterpreting their history. Journalist Gianni Brera said that the English had only reinvented the game.[10]

For Mussolini, sport was a key part of the new Italian strength and a key unifying factor. After a fraught 1925/26 season during which refereeing disputes led to a crisis at the FIGC, three lawyers came together to create the *Carta di Viareggio*, a charter that would dictate the future of Italian football at a national level. Named after the town in which the lawyers met, the charter laid provision of a national league, set the boundaries for professionalism and player transfers, and – significantly – banned foreign players and managers. In his drive to italianise football, Mussolini forced clubs to change their English names to Italian ones. Internazionale, that dissident club founded by Swiss breakaways, was rebranded as Ambrosiana; the English-sounding Genoa became Genova 1893 Circolo del Calcio; Milan Football Club would become Milan Association Sportiva in 1936 and later Associazione Calcio Milan in 1939. In Florence, the fascist noble Luigi Ridolfi merged two clubs – Club Sportivo Firenze and Palestra Ginnastica Libertas to form Fiorentina in 1926. Mussolini, while not much of a football fan himself, saw the value of the sport for propaganda and as a way to unite the country. At his behest, Serie A was created in 1929 as the first championship to include teams from the entire peninsula. The 18-team season kicked off in the 1929/30 season, with Ambrosiana (Internazionale) winning by two points from Genova 1893 (Genoa). Another result of the nationalisation of the sport under the fascists was the consolidation of three Roman clubs in 1927 – Alba-Audace, Fortitudo-ProRoma and Football Club di Roma – to create a single club in the capital to compete at a national level.[11] AS Roma was the result, adopting the red and yellow colours of the city and its She-Wolf emblem. AS Roma immediately became a key rival of fellow Romans, SS Lazio, at the time one of the stronger sides in the centre and south of Italy.

Now he had sorted out the domestic situation, Mussolini set his sights on international football glory. Italy had fallen at the quarter-final stage at the Olympics in 1920 and 1924, and were only narrowly beaten in the semi-finals of the 1928 tournament by eventual winners, Uruguay. The Italians then thrashed Egypt 11-3 to take the bronze medal. Italy had its first international title. Two years later, Italy won the inaugural edition of the Central European International Cup, a competition created by Austrian football pioneer, Hugo Meisl. After seeing the success of the first World Cup in 1930 in Uruguay, Mussolini backed an Italian bid to host the tournament in 1934. It was essential for Mussolini that Italy won the trophy, so to strengthen an already impressive side, the *Azzurri* drew on *oriundi* – naturalised players of Italian descent who had been born outside the country. These *oriundi* included Raimundo Orsi, Enrique Guaita and Luis Monti from Argentina. Mussolini is alleged to have influenced referees in 1934, and several controversial decisions went Italy's way as the side won the second edition of the FIFA World Cup. The country would retain the trophy away in France four years later with an Olympic gold win sandwiched in between in 1936, proving that Italy could probably boast the world's best football team without the need of political influence.

## Modern Genoa Cricket and Football Club

What of Genoa today, the pioneer football club? After starting out wearing white shirts, the club adopted blue and white stripes at the turn of the 20th century. This kit only lasted one season before the club finally settled on its famous *rossoblu* red and blue halves. Genoa won six out of the first seven Italian championships between 1898 and 1904, missing out only in 1901 to Kilpin's Milan. From then the power shifted northwards, to Milan, Juventus and Pro Vercelli.

Spensley had led *Il Grifone* (The Griffin) to the club's first six Italian championships. Another Englishman would later bring further silverware to Genoa's trophy cabinet. William Garbutt, the former Arsenal and Blackburn Rovers winger, switched to coaching after a knee injury brought his playing career to an abrupt end. He became Italian football's first professional manager when he joined Genoa in 1912 and is credited with being the original *mister*, a term still used today in Italy for the manager. He also coached Roma and Napoli. Garbutt brought a new emphasis on tactics and physicality, and was the first coach in Italy to manage paid player transfers. Vittorio Pozzo, who coached Italy to its two World Cup triumphs and Olympic gold in the 1930s, said that Garbutt was the most important man in the history of Italian football. The *Scudetto*, the Italian flag champions wear on their shirts for the following term, was first awarded to Garbutt's Genoa after its last-ever title win in the 1923/24 season. Clubs that win a tenth *Scudetto* are awarded a gold star to place above their crest. Genoa CFC has been stuck on nine titles now for nearly a century, and a tenth looks a far-off prospect.

The English connection endures. After the fall of *Il Duce*, the club reverted to its original name of Genoa Cricket and Football Club, despite the lack of cricket. The team emerges on to the pitch at the Luigi Ferraris to the sound of 'You'll Never Walk Alone'. Genoa shares the Luigi Ferraris with cross-town rivals Sampdoria, formed in 1946 as a merger between Sampierdarenese and Andrea Doria, who had been a nearly team in the early days of the Italian Championship. Sampdoria fans have traditionally baited Genoa as it is their club which has fielded the British players in recent decades, from Graeme Souness and Trevor Francis in the 1980s, to David Platt and Des Walker in the

1990s. Lee Sharpe also had a stint at *Il Samp*. The Stadio Luigi Ferraris actually has the feel of a British ground. It's a tight, tiered rectangle with fans close to the action, unlike in many Italian grounds where an athletics track often separates spectators from the action. This closeness makes for an unforgettable atmosphere, helping make the Genoa-Sampdoria *Derby della Lanterna* (the Lighthouse Derby) so intense and captivating.

## Spensley's legacy

While Genoa CFC's long wait for a tenth *Scudetto* looks set to continue for some time yet, Spensley's name lives on in street names, supporters' groups and, of course, he founded the scouting movement. And the Genoese influence on football extends way outside the Italian peninsula. The massive influx of Italians to the River Plate was so strong it left its mark on the local language, providing much of the new slang of Buenos Aires and Montevideo, called *lunfardo*. Also, in 1905, a group of players from the docklands of Buenos Aires formed a football team and named it after their district, La Boca. The club they founded – Boca Juniors – is now one of South America's most successful sides and its fans are known as *Los Xeneizes* – the Genoese. In 1923, Genoa CFC toured the River Plate, winning one match versus a *Combinado Sud* (Southern Combination) team and losing to the Northern Combination, drawing with Argentina, and losing 2-1 in Montevideo to Uruguay.

1 Foot, John, *Calcio: A History of Italian Football* (London: Harper Perennial, 2007, p1)
2 Foot, John, *Calcio: A History of Italian Football* (London: Harper Perennial, 2007, pp4–5)
3 *Lancashire Evening Post*, 1 November 1901 (p5)
4 http://www.magliarossonera.it/189900_storia.html

5  *Hartlepool Northern Daily Mail*, Wednesday, 19 April 1911 (p4)

6  https://www.sscnapoli.it/static/content/History-81.aspx

7  *The Sketch*, 1 December 1909 (p8)

8  Foot, John, *Calcio* (London: Harper Perennial, 2007, p16)

9  Foot, John, *Calcio* (London: Harper Perennial, 2007, p2)

10  https://gentlemanultra.com/2016/04/01/mussolini-and-calcio-fascisms-legacy-in-italian-football/

11  https://www.asroma.com/en/club/history

# 21.

# Middle East and Africa

AFRICAN FOOTBALL reached its zenith on 3 August 1996. Emmanuel Amunike runs joyfully to the touchline, arms aloft. He has just put Nigeria 3-2 ahead in the last minute of the Olympic football final against Argentina, while the stunned South Americans appeal in vain for offside. While no African country came close to fulfilling Pelé's prediction of an African team winning the World Cup before the year 2000, Nigeria had just bagged a major global title. Nowadays, hundreds of African players ply their trade in Europe's top leagues. The leading three goalscorers in England's Premier League 2018/19 season were African – Mohamed Salah, Pierre-Emerick Aubameyang and Sadio Mané. Many other African players have played influential roles for adopted European countries, such as Mozambique-born Eusébio for Portugal, or Ghana-born Marcel Desailly and Senegal-born Patrick Vieira for France's World Cup-winning side of 1998. The Middle East is now a significant financial power behind many European clubs, with Qatar the host nation for World Cup 2022. Turkey attained the region's highest achievement in world football by reaching the semi-finals of the 2002 World Cup. In the Middle East and Africa, the craze for the round-ball game has its roots in colonialism and has – as in other occupied parts of the world – acted as a leveller for the local population against European occupiers.

## Football arrives in Africa

Twenty-first century Africa is football crazy, but it has been a long journey for the Association game in the region. The continent finally hosted its first World Cup in South Africa in 2010, in the country where the round-ball game most likely first arrived in Africa. For centuries, major European powers had exploited African resources: for human labour, agriculture and minerals. In the second half of the 19th century, colonisers set about carving the continent up for themselves, working their way inland from the coast. Where they went, football followed. Port Elizabeth, in the British-controlled Cape Colony, was the place where a football was probably first kicked in Africa. Situated on the southern tip of the African continent, by the 1860s, Port Elizabeth was a major harbour and well-connected into the interior by rail for access to mines and agricultural land. A match was recorded as taking place in Port Elizabeth in May 1862 between a team of white men born in the colony and a side made up of recent arrivals.[1] The game took place a full 17 months before the Football Association was founded and laid out its rule book. What form of 'football' took place at Port Elizabeth – like the scoreline – is lost to history.

But the Association game faced a fight in Southern Africa from its Rugby rival. Down in Cape Town, students of the Diocesan College were introduced to Winchester College rules football, which involved handling of the ball. The Rugby rules game, played by military garrisons and heartily adopted by the Dutch-speaking population, soon gained popularity, and several clubs were formed during the 1880s. The Association game had some advocates, with the foundation of the whites-only Pietermaritzburg County Football Club in 1879. Africa's oldest existing Association football club was founded in the Natal city of Pietermaritzburg in 1882 – Savage Football Club, now called Savages Football Club. South African society was to be defined by race from the moment that white settlers arrived in the 17th century. While whites-only establishments emerged, such as the Natal Football Association in 1882, the decade also saw the emergence of African and Indian-founded clubs in Durban and Johannesburg. Natal was key to the Association game's establishment in South Africa, with a healthy scene in the 1880s with strong competition and an established Challenge Cup. However, some clubs were forced to fold as they lost players to gold rushes upcountry. Eighteen ninety-two saw the foundation of the all-white South African Football Association (SAFA), and within three years it was affiliated with the Football Association in London. Scottish shipping magnate Donald Currie donated a trophy for an inter-provincial football competition, first held in 1892 for both Association football and rugby. The Currie Cup is still the premier competition in South African rugby.

In 1897, Corinthian FC arrived on its first overseas tour to bolster the growth of the game. The SAFA's honorary president, mining magnate Cecil Rhodes, guaranteed funding for the tour. The two-month trip started with a 4-0 win in Cape Town on 17 July and included 23 matches up until 13 September. Corinthians won 21 – including a 10-1 win over Griqualand and a 9-0 trouncing of Pretoria – and drew just two, both against Natal teams. The club's expenses totalled £2,100, but this amount was recovered in gate receipts, with takings in Johannesburg alone totalling

£970. As a sign of thanks, Corinthians presented G.A. Parker, honourable secretary of the South African FA, with a *kaross* (cloak) made from the skins of nine silver jackals.[2]

Significantly, in September 1899, a black South African team arrived in Southampton for an extensive four-month tour of England, Scotland, Wales, Ireland and France. The 16-man squad was made up of Orange Free Staters and played 49 fixtures. The Orange Free State FA and W.M. Williams of the Welsh FA arranged the tour. Sporting amber shirts and black shorts, the African team would have been the first black side the Europeans would have faced. The South African team was captained by 28-year-old Joseph Twayi, a powerful forward from Bloemfontein who by 1915 was treasurer of the organisation that would later become the African National Congress (ANC). The British press reports could not resist remarking on the appearance of the African players with terminology that would shock modern readers. At the time, in 1899, a game between black and white players would not have been possible back within South Africa due to racial segregation. The South Africans drew large crowds wherever they played, which included games in as varied locations as Sheppey in Kent to Greenock near Glasgow. Tottenham Hotspur, Aston Villa, Newcastle United and Portsmouth also hosted the tourists. Unfortunately, the tour was more of an entertainment spectacle put on for a curious British audience rather than a meeting of sporting equals. The 1899 tour drew criticism from many white South Africans, who were angry that a black South African team had toured Britain before a white team.[3]

Weeks after the team arrived, the South African War broke out between the British Empire and the Boer Republics, which included the Orange Free State. Twayi expressed his loyalty to the Queen to the British press, and the team even wore red, white and blue ribbons in a match against Aston Villa. The only match the South Africans won on their long tour was their only game in France, versus Sporting Club Tourcoing in Roubaix. Chris Bolsmann is a professor at California State University, Northridge, and a leading historian of African football. Bolsmann has studied the 1899 tour at length. 'The 1899 team were South African pioneers that were ridiculed in Britain and ignored in their homeland because they were black,' he explains. 'They rightfully deserve their place and acknowledgement in football history.'

Elsewhere across the South African racial divide, an Indian lawyer was putting his organisational skills to good effect. In 1903, Mohandas Gandhi helped found the South African Association of Hindu football. While Gandhi's first sporting loves were cricket and cycling, he certainly saw the appeal and potential power of football and helped establish it among the Indian community in South Africa. Also in 1903, the Corinthians returned to the Cape after the South African War and played 25 matches, winning all but three, drawing two and going down to a solitary 1-0 defeat to Durban. The English amateurs returned in 1907 to find that South African soccer was continuing to develop fast. This time, the Corinthians suffered five losses – including a 4-0 reverse against Western Province – and seven draws in a 24-match series. It was the last time Corinthian FC visited the Cape. Between the Corinthians' last two visits, a white South African team toured South America in 1906, funded by the Argentine FA. Of the 15-man squad, eight team members were born in Britain. The South Africans decided to tour South America rather than England as the South Americans and South Africans felt they were relatively equal in their footballing development. As it happened, the

South African side proved to be significantly better than their hosts on the 1906 tour. They won 11 of 12 matches, including a 14-0 opening-match win over a Buenos Aires university side. In their more significant matches, the South Africans enjoyed a 4-1 win over an Argentinian select XI, a 6-1 win against a combined Montevideo side, and a 6-0 win against a São Paulo XI with Charles Miller in its ranks. The only team to defeat the South Africans was the strong Alumni side in Buenos Aires.

In 1910, the South African FA became the first association from outside Europe to join FIFA. That year, an English FA side sailed on a ship named *Kinfauns Castle* from Southampton to Cape Town to play 23 matches against whites-only sides. The professionals would receive little opposition, returning having scored 143 goals to 16 against. A proposed tour from the Scottish FA in 1912 never happened. An English FA side toured again in 1920, and once more only played white clubs. They won all 14 matches, scoring 64 goals to ten against. The team's organiser, John Lewis of Blackburn, compared the South African players' standard to the English Second Division. He blamed the vast distance between clubs for the reason the game did not develop. He also described rugby as the 'national sport' but believed the prospects were bright for the Association game in South Africa.[4] A whites-only South African FA team toured Ireland and Britain in the second half of 1924 and were even inspected by King George V in the churchyard at Sandringham. By the time the South Africans wrapped up their four-month, 22-match tour with a 3-2 win over Everton, they had won 13 and lost nine, scoring 73 goals and conceding 44. The team was more than able to hold its own against amateur teams and even weakened professional sides from Britain and Ireland.

An English FA amateur side followed in 1929 to continue the 'education' of South African players – again the FA side only played against white teams. Scottish club Motherwell, who had toured South America in the 1920s, visited in 1931 and won 14 of their 15 matches. Motherwell's sole defeat was a 3-1 reverse to Natal, and the Scots were feted everywhere they went. Star striker Willie MacFadyen scored 30 goals. The Fir Park outfit returned three years later – a period during which it had won the Scottish League championship – after the South African FA had failed to attract FA Cup winners Everton or West Bromwich Albion to tour. On the 1934 tour, Motherwell went undefeated for all 16 games, and MacFadyen improved on his earlier outing by scoring 35 goals. Motherwell had endured a torrid tour of South America the year before, perhaps emphasising how far the South American game had developed, while the South African game had not advanced at such a rate. Still, from the 1930s to the 1950s, South Africa provided the highest level of overseas players to the English leagues of any country.

The early 1930s saw the game develop significantly across South Africa, and the first official interracial tournament, the Suzman Cup, was launched in 1935. This tournament enabled African, mixed-heritage and Indian teams from Transvaal to compete against each other, regardless of their background. Together with the Bakers Cup, established in 1932, and the Godfrey South African Challenge Cup, set up in 1936, competitive matches in South Africa were attracting crowds of 10,000-plus. While the private schools and richer whites had the elite sports of cricket and rugby, soccer was more democratic. Anyone could play. In this backdrop, the Orlando Boys Club was formed in Johannesburg in 1937 by boxing instructor Andries 'Pele Pele' Mkhwanazi. The boys played barefoot and without an official kit in a minor division of the Johannesburg Bantu Football Association, before gaining the name 'Pirates' a few years later.[5] Orlando Pirates is now one of Africa's most famous football clubs.

FIFA originally recognised the white Football Association of South Africa (FASA) only to suspend it in the early 1960s due to the country's – and the sport's – discriminatory racial divisions. It was not until post-Apartheid 1991 that a united South African Football Association (SAFA) was formed and welcomed into the African and global football family.

## Football spreads across North Africa

In the same year that the Natal Football Association and the Savage Football Club were founded in South Africa – 1882 – in the north of the continent, the British were busy extending their influence in Egypt. Victory in the Anglo-Egyptian War gave the British greater control over the Suez Canal. In this backdrop, Europeans brought their sports to North Africa, founding the Khedivial Sporting Club (now Gezira Sporting Club) on the Cairo island of Zamalek that year. Reports appear of matches played throughout the 1890s. These include the clash between the Military School of Cairo and the Ghelzeh Agricultural College in 1892, or the Cairo Football Challenge Shield and Regimental Challenge Shield, which were contested by British Army divisions. It was not until 1903 that British and Italian railway engineers in Cairo founded Egypt's first football team, El Sekka El Hadid SC. During its heyday in the 1920s the club won the Cairo League twice and the Sultan Hussein Cup once. The club has spent some seasons in the top flight but at the time of writing is in Egypt's second tier.

In 1907, the club that would go on to be labelled Africa's 'Club of the Century' was formed. Al-Ahly Sporting Club (The National Sporting Club) emerged as a multisports club for students on 24 April 1907. As its name suggests, Al-Ahly SC was very much an Egyptian club established in contrast to the occupying European sides. Its future nemesis, Zamalek Sporting Club, was founded in 1911 as the Kasr El-Nile Club by the Belgian lawyer George Marzbach. This club was inclusive, welcoming players of all backgrounds, but would not come under Egyptian directorship until 1917, by which time it was called Nady El Mokhtalat – Cairo International Sports Club. Marzbach was well connected in Cairo circles and was even close to Sultan Hussein Kamel, the country's head under the British protectorate. The club chose white – the colour of peace – as a base colour for its kit with two red horizontal stripes.[6]

In the same year that Zamalek SC was founded, a 20-year-old Egyptian made his way to England to study engineering at University College London. His name was Hussein Hegazi from the town of Kremlah. One of the ways he practised his aim was rather unpleasant. He would look out for people carrying goods in jars balanced on their heads and aim his shots at the jars. Hegazi's parents often had to pay compensation to the people whose jars and goods were damaged.[7] Hegazi had learned to play at school on hard sand and played against British teams, typically army sides, before representing the mostly expat National Sporting Club. In 1909, he was part of an Egyptian team that won a five-a-side tournament in Cairo that included many British military sides. In London, Hegazi joined Dulwich Hamlet, becoming the first Egyptian to play in England. At Hamlet, the teetotaller quickly earned a reputation for his dribbling and also turned out for Fulham, a select London XI, the University of Cambridge and Corinthian FC. In 1913, the *Pall Mall Gazette* reported: 'H. Hegazi (of Dulwich Hamlet), an Egyptian, has already proved a great acquisition in the forward line. He should go far.'[8] But the following year, with war looming, Hegazi returned to Egypt. Here, he went on to play for both Cairo rivals Al-Ahly and Nady El Mokhtalat (Zamalek), and to appear for the national team at two Olympic tournaments.

Egypt was a vital strategic location during the First World War for the Allies, during which time the British put Egypt under martial law. Football continued during the war, with Al-Ahly playing its first match against Nady El Mokhtalat on 9 February 1917. Al-Ahly won 1-0. Popular discontent with British rule in both Egypt and neighbouring Sudan – particularly over the exile to Malta of nationalist leader and first honorary president of the Al-Ahly SC, Saad Zaghul Pasha – led to the 1919 revolution. The British had changed the status of the country at the outbreak of the First World War to a protectorate, imposing martial law and replacing the pro-Ottoman Khedive Abbas Hilmi with a relative. An increase in British, Australian and New Zealand troops had led to a breakout of fights between allied soldiers and locals, a rise in prostitution, and open alcohol consumption in this devoutly Muslim country. For its part, Egyptians did not feel they received any benefits for their contribution to the war effort.

It was in this backdrop of violence at home that Egypt sent an XI into the 1920 Olympic football tournament, the first African team to enter an international football competition. Hegazi chose the 16 uncapped players that headed to Belgium, including ten from Al-Ahly SC, four from Nady El Mokhtalat, and one each from El Sekka El Hadid SC and Tersana.

The campaign lasted just one match as the Egyptians fell at the first hurdle to Italy 2-1. Al-Ahly forward Zaki Osman became the first man to score an international goal for the 'Pharaohs' with an equaliser on the half-hour mark in front of 1,500 spectators in Ghent. The Olympics may have ended early for the Egyptians, but they stayed in Belgium to play friendlies, including a 5-3 victory over Antwerp. Following the tournament, Nady El Mokhtalat forward Tawfik Abdullah became the second Egyptian to play in England, signing for Derby County before moving on to Cowdenbeath in Scotland after just one year. In 1921, the Egyptian Football Association was founded, and the Egyptians returned an Olympic side to the 1924 games in Paris. Egypt entered the tournament in the second round at the Stade de Paris against much-fancied Hungary. Egypt won 3-0, with Nady El Mokhtalat players Ibrahim Yakan (scoring twice) and Hegazi on the scoresheet. British news reports indicate that the Egyptians had won due to their superior speed and combination play, while the defence was well marshalled to repel the Hungarian attacks.[9] The Egyptians then crashed out 5-0 to the Swedes three days later at the Stade Pershing.

Domestically, the game continued to develop, with the Sultan Hussein Cup. Founded in 1916 by the British, the plan was to include both Egyptian teams and allied military sides. Nady El Mokhtalat would have been the only Egyptian side but Al-Ahly – the club of the nationalist resistance – decided to join. The knockout tournament ran between 1916 and 1938, with Nady El Mokhtalat winning the first two editions. Soon after, in 1921, what is now the Egypt Cup was founded with Nady El Mokhtalat again winning the first final with a 5-0 thrashing of Ittihad Alexandria. A year later, the Cairo League was established, with Nady El Mokhtalat again taking home the trophy first. Increased competition strengthened the national team. The team that headed to Amsterdam for the 1928 Olympic tournament thrashed Turkey 7-1 in the first round. Al-Ahly's Mahmoud Mokhtar chipped in with a hat-trick. Mokhtar scored again in the quarter-finals against Portugal, with the Pharaohs going through 2-1 to face a tough Argentina side in the semi-finals. At the Olympic Stadium that day, the Egyptians succumbed 6-0 in front of nearly 8,000 people. This time, it was Boca Junior's Domingo Tarasconi's turn to bag a hat-trick. Two days later, Egypt played the bronze medal play-off against Italy, which featured three hat-tricks, with Schiavo, Banchero and Magnozzi netting in Italy's 11-3 win.

As FIFA's sole African member in 1930, Egypt was invited to enter the first World Cup in Uruguay but did not make the journey.[10] However, Egypt would go on to become Africa's first representative at a FIFA World Cup in Italy in 1934 under the guidance of former Clyde, West Ham and Manchester United player, Scotsman James McCrae. Of the 20-man squad, seven were drawn from Nady El Mokhtalat and five from Al-Ahly. It would be a short-lived campaign, with the Egyptians losing in the first round of the knockout format tournament 4-2 to the Hungarians in Naples. The teams had been level at half-time, with the North Africans having pegged back a two-goal deficit before fading in the second half.

Hegazi's legacy lives on in the name of a street in Cairo, and he was to be the oldest goalscorer at an Olympic football tournament from 1924 until Ryan Giggs scored for Team GB at London 2012. 'The sports journalists who saw him play regarded the charismatic genius as unmatched among his generation,' Hegazi's biographer Jack McInroy writes. 'His contribution to Egyptian football is immense.'[11] Nady El Mokhtalat changed its name to Nady Farouk El Awal in 1941, then back to Zamalek Sporting Club in 1952. And what of the Zamalek and Al-Ahly rivalry? James Montague is author of *When Friday Comes: Football, War and Revolution in the Middle East*. Montague tells me that the rivalry between Al-Ahly and Zamalek stems from the origin stories of both clubs, with Al-Ahly as the 'Egyptian' club and Zamalek the foreign-founded institution where Egyptians couldn't get a look in. 'Al-Ahly fans never let Zamalek fans forget their foreign roots to this day,' he adds. Ultras of both clubs played a key role in Egypt's Arab Spring of 2011, which saw the country's long-time dictator Hosni Mubarak removed from power. The Muslim Brotherhood-aligned Mohamed Morsi became Egypt's first democratic president shortly afterwards. But Morsi was toppled in a coup and the forces of opposition that led the Arab Spring have, one by one, been neutered. That included the ultras, who have now been banned, viewed by pro-government cheerleaders as 'terrorists'.

## The Francophone experience

In the summer of 2019, while France hosted the eighth FIFA Women's World Cup tournament, I went along to the *Foot et le Monde Arabe (*Football and the Arab World) exhibition held at the Institute du Monde Arabe (Institute of the Arab World) in Paris. The building stands by the banks of the Seine just around a watery bend from the recently burned carcass of Notre-Dame. The exhibition held a wealth of memorabilia from one of the often forgotten corners of football. Algeria and Morocco, under foreign occupation at the time of football's entry into the region at the end of the 19th century, have also been key actors in the African football story. Algeria is the ancestral homeland of the great Zinedine Zidane and also Rabah Madjer, scorer in FC Porto's 1987 European Cup Final upset against Bayern Munich. The country's first club, Le Club Athletique d'Oran, was founded in 1897 as the reserve of Europeans.

In Morocco, war dominated the early years of the 20th century. It was in this environment in 1914 that one of North Africa's first great players was born. Larbi Ben Barak was born in Casablanca, then under a French protectorate, and would be among the first African players to grace the French and Spanish football leagues. Ben Barak started his career at Idéal Club Casablanca as a 16-year-old before moving across town to US Marrocaine. He made his first big club move in 1938 to Olympique Marseille, where he would average a goal every three games. The Second World War curtailed his career before he resumed as an even more prolific striker with Stade Français, netting 43 goals in 87 games over three years. That's one goal every two matches! He retained that phenomenal strike rate at Atlético de Madrid between 1948 and 1953, when he was already deep into his 30s. Here, under Helenio Herrera, Ben Barek's dazzling skills helped the Madrid club to two La Liga titles. This feat is considerable considering the context. Spanish dictator General Francisco Franco had made his name in Morocco in Spain's Rif War against the local Berber. He later hired Morocco's most fearsome fighters to support his Civil War efforts (1936–39), and he was famously suspicious of outsiders. Ben Barak also played for France on 19 occasions, turning out first in 1938 and again, aged 40, in 1954 against Germany, where injury ended his match – and playing career.

Morocco's clubs had emerged in the first and second decades of the 20th century as Spanish and French colonials played on its sand. In the Spanish enclaves of Ceuta and Melilla, organised football matches began to emerge in 1912, with a league lasting in Melilla until 1921 when the Rif War brought it to a close.[12] In neighbouring Algeria, records show the game to be popular among both expats and locals in the 1890s, with games played on Sundays. The British community in Algeria had sent for a copy of the *Football Annual 1896/97* to keep up with developments in the mother country and were arranging match locations. These matches featured a truly cosmopolitan crowd, including local Algerian, French, Italian, Greek, Spanish and Maltese participants. One report notes that the 'Arabs' were noted for their speed and endurance, and were better at accepting defeat than their Southern European opponents.[13] British teams were touring North Africa as early as 1905, but in 1923 the English North Nottinghamshire League team visited to play three games against a select local XI. The team were presented with gold watches by their hosts on their departure from Oran. From 1930 to 1956, the *Coupe d'Afrique du Nord* (North African Cup) provided a platform for the cup winners from the Francophone countries of North Africa – Algeria, Morocco and Tunisia – to compete. It was run under the auspices of the French Football Federation (FFF).

## Football arrives on the Bosphorus

In the late 19th century, Turkey – the heart of the Ottoman Empire – was ruled by Sultan Abdul Hamid II. The sultan came to the throne in 1876, and his reign was marked by economic and political turmoil. The sultan appears to have become increasingly paranoid, including around the practice of football. Football matches involving Turks were broken up for fear the players could be plotting against the sultan, while the Ottoman authorities turned a blind eye to foreigners and non-Muslims' games.[14] It was in the modern Turkish capital of Izmir, then known to British expats as Smyrna, that the Association game was first played on Turkish soil, probably as early as the 1870s. Here in 1894 the Smyrna Football Club – sometimes recorded as the Bournabat Football and Rugby Club – was founded by Englishmen and managed by a bowler hat-wearing gentleman, Herbert Octavius Whittall.

Englishmen in Istanbul introduced the game to the Bosphorus and kickabouts began in the bay neighbourhoods of Kadiköy and Moda, which were at the time covered by meadows. The Kadiköy Football Club was founded by James Edward La Fontaine – recently moved from Izmir, where he had played – and Horace Armitage. The club was made up of English and Greek players. La Fontaine is regarded by some as the 'father of Turkish football', along with the British lawyer Harry Pears, for their role in introducing the game to Izmir and Istanbul.

All the while, Sultan Abdul Hamid II's spies were ever on the lookout for Turks breaking the rules. The first Turkish team to play the game was founded in 1899 and adopted the English name 'Black Stockings' – they wore black socks and red jerseys. The club was founded by Fuat Hüsnü, who played under the English name 'Bobby' to avoid detection and went on to play for Galatasaray and Fenerbahçe. Although the team wouldn't play its first game until 1901, the match was broken up by a police raid when the Turks were losing 5-1 to a team of Greeks. Officers chased the fleeing players around the pitch, and the club was forced to close. Black Stockings' co-founder Resat Danyal even had to go into exile in Tehran.[15] In March 1903, the first of Turkey's 'Big Three' was formed. The Bereket Gymnastics Club was given special permission to practise sports, and the sultan's own son attended training sessions. The club that would later become Besiktas Jimnastik Kulübü (BJK) was based on the European side of the Bosphorus, although it did not practise football until 1911 when Ahmed Serafettin Bey, the chairman and founder of the nearby Valideçesme Football Club, joined with his players.[16] Soon after, another local team – Basiret Club – also joined Besiktas, and it is interesting to note the professions of its players, which include doctors and poets.

While Besiktas was still solely a gymnastics club, Istanbul's first football league – The Constantinople Football League – was held in 1904/05 by the newly formed Istanbul Football Association. The first edition was contested between teams from Kadiköy, Moda FC, Elpis and HMS Imogene. The players would have been made up exclusively of Brits, Greeks and Armenians living in the city, and matches were played on Sundays. A year after the formation of the league, students of the Lycée de Galatasaray, led by Ali Sami Yen, listed as 'Member No.1' and its first president, formed the Galatasaray Spor Klubü (SK). The club's aims were to 'play collectively like the British, to have our colours and our name, and to beat non-Turkish teams'.[17] Galatasaray's Ali Sami Yen was pivotal in the early development of the sport, according to Turkish football historian, Mehmet Yuce. 'As well as founding Galatasaray, he arranged the first match for any Turkish side with another European club, in this case Kolojvar (now Cluj FC) of Romania, in 1911, plus the return match. In addition, Ali Sami Yen was the first president of the Sports Association of Turkey in 1922, so his role is crucial to the story of Turkish football,' Yuce tells me. 'Another Galatasaray influence was Yusuf Ziya Öniş, who was the first Turkish Football Federation president at a critical time in the country's development.'

Galatasaray's chance would come in time, but in 1906, Athens hosted The Intercalated Games, a special meeting held between the 1904 and 1908 Olympiads, which included an unofficial football tournament. The Ottoman Empire was represented by two of the four sides in the tournament – Smyrna FC and Thessaloniki, now part of modern-day

Greece. The Smyrna team was made up entirely of non-Turkish players, including five members of the Whittall family. Smyrna lost 5-1 to Denmark in their opening match before smashing Thessaloniki 12-0. In 1907, Turkish graduates from the Frerler Mektebi school formed their own football club and named it the 'Lighthouse Garden' – Fenerbahçe – because of its location, and eventually settled on yellow and blue shirts. Fenerbahçe's founders included members of Black Stockings FC, and would feature 'Bobby' Fuat Hüsnü Kayacan, reputed to have been the first Turkish footballer and goalscorer in Black Stockings' only game. He first played the sport as a soldier based in Izmir in 1898. Fenerbahçe would come to see itself as the most Turkish of the big three as it is based on the Asian side of the Bosphorus.

Towards the end of the first decade of the 20th century, the sultan's grip on power was waning and before he was deposed in 1909 after the Young Turk Revolution, the sultan was forced to make concessions, including liberalising the playing of sports for Muslims. This move opened the door wide for football in Turkey. Galatasaray, Fenerbahçe and other Turkish clubs and players joined the Sunday League. Galatasaray became an early force with Ali Sami Yen dictating play in the middle of the park, winning three championships in a row. By 1912, a new league had formed in Istanbul. The Friday League included Darülfünun SK, Istanbul Jimnastik, Anadolu SK, Sanayli FK, Sehremini SK and Fenerbahçe's second team. Fenerbahçe was instrumental in promoting the Turkish game abroad, featuring in a short series of matches in Odessa, Ukraine, in 1914. Here, the Istanbul side won one match, drew another and lost three. The games were filled to capacity with thousands more locked out.[18]

The First World War would pit Turkey against the British who had introduced the game to the country. Turkey's defeat led ultimately to the break-up of the Ottoman Empire at the Treaty of Sèvres in August 1920.

The power vacuum led to a Turkish nationalist uprising led by Mustafa Kemal Atatürk to defeat the remnant Ottoman forces who had signed the treaty. In 1923, the Treaty of Lausanne secured the establishment of the Republic of Turkey. The Turkish Football Federation was founded on 23 April 1923 and joined FIFA later that year. At its helm was Yusuf Ziya Öniş, the former Galatasaray player who had also turned out for Servette in Switzerland. Football continued during this period of upheaval, including football matches between occupying British and French forces and local teams. Football at this time became a proxy war, with local nationalist feelings of revenge on the football field whenever a Turkish side beat the occupying foreign army sides. Fenerbahçe were particularly successful against the foreign sides, winning 41 matches out of the 50 it played. On 29 June 1923, a send-off match was held between the best British Army players, assembled by its commander in Turkey, General Charles Harington, and Fenerbahçe, at Taksim Stadium. While Harington wanted to give the locals a final defeat to remember, it did not turn out that way. The occupying force took the lead on the half-hour mark with a goal from Scotsman William Ferguson, who played for both Chelsea and Queen of the South during his career. In the second half, Fenerbahçe's Zeki Riza Sporel scored twice to give the Turkish side a 2-1 victory. The Harington Cup resides in Fenerbahçe's club museum.[19]

The allied forces left and Turkish football was now fully in control of its own destiny. Sporel again netted twice in Turkey's first international match against Romania in

1923 in a game that finished 2-2. Overseeing the Turkish team was Ali Sami Yen, now a key administrator of the Turkish game. He would act as president of the Turkish delegation to the 1924 Olympics in Paris, where Turkey was eliminated in the first round 5-2 by Czechoslovakia. Nineteen twenty-four was a pivotal year for Turkish football. Local leagues existed in Istanbul and also in Adana, Ankara, Izmir, Trabzon and Eskisehir. The challenge was to create a national championship. The Turkish Football Championship (*Türkiye Futbol Şampiyonası*) was a knockout tournament contested by regional league champions. The team of the Turkish Military Academy (*Harbiye*) won the first edition, but only two editions were held before 1932 due to the cost of travel.[20] At the 1928 Olympic Games, Turkey repeated its failure of four years earlier, exiting in the first round to a 7-1 thumping from Egypt in Amsterdam. It would take decades to build club sides that were ready to compete at the top table, peaking at the turn of the 21st century when one of the nation's pioneer clubs, Galatasaray, won the UEFA Cup in 2000. This was swiftly followed by a World Cup semi-final place for the national side in 2002.

## Football in West Africa

We met the world's first black professional footballer, Arthur Wharton, back in the first chapter of football's global journey. Wharton was born in Accra, Ghana – known at the time of his birth in 1865 as the Jamestown on the Gold Coast – and moved to England as a missionary aged 19. He played in goal for a number of clubs in the north of England, including Sheffield United. As with many other countries, the school system was key to the introduction of football into West Africa. It is thought that games were being played as early as 1882 and that Ghanaian students followed English football scores at the end of the 19th century. In 1903, a group of students from the Cape Coast Government Boys School trained under cover of darkness at Victoria Park with footballs gifted to them from European sailors. The boys' headmaster had encouraged them to take up the sport. This group of 22 formed the core of Ghana's first football club, Excelsior. On Boxing Day 1903, the group formed two teams and performed an exhibition match at Victoria Park, which was attended by Sir Frederic Hodgson, governor of the Gold Coast.[21] Excelsior also played against ships' crews and European resident sides. The Excelsior players acted as evangelists for football within the Gold Coast, heading in-country over the coming months playing demonstration matches in nearby towns. In 1910, the Invincibles club was founded in Accra. The following year, Accra Hearts of Oak Sporting Club, Ghana's oldest surviving team, was founded by Christopher Brandford Nettey to provide the Invincibles with competition. By 1912, at least six new football clubs had been founded. The Gold Coast Football Association (now the Ghana Football Association) was established in 1920 and in 1922 the first league was launched by league founder, British governor Sir Gordon Guggisberg. Hearts of Oak won the inaugural Guggisberg Shield title.

In Nigeria, the first recorded match took place on 15 June 1904 in the port city of Calabar when local students played a team of visiting British sailors and won 3-2. This indicates that the students must have had some practice, so football in Calabar probably goes back further.[22]

It was not until the 1920s that football became organised in then capital Lagos, although it was not until 1933 that the Nigerian Football Association was founded. Ugandan winger Yuno Kalemba Dimmock became the first East African player to appear in English football, turning out for South

London side Nunhead in the Isthmian League between 1927 and 1930 while a university student in London.[23]

Despite Nigeria's 1996 Olympic triumph, only Cameroon (1990) and Ghana (2010) – denied when Uruguay's Luis Suárez handled a goal-bound header in the final minute – have come close to a World Cup semi-final. Both fell short in quarter-final extra time or penalties. Turkey's 2002 semi-final appearance remains the best run of any Middle Eastern team at a World Cup. When will Africa and the Middle East's day finally come?

1 Hawkey, Ian, *Feet of the Chameleon: The Story of African Football* (London, Portico, 2010)

2 *Sunderland Daily Echo and Shipping Gazette*, 15 January 1898 (p3)

3 *Lancashire Evening Post*, 16 September 1899 (p2)

4 *Lancashire Evening Post*, 12 August 1920 (p5)

5 https://www.orlandopiratesfc.com/club/history

6 http://el-zamalek.com/

7 https://www.southwarknews.co.uk/history/the-forgotten-story-of-hossein-hegazi%e2%80%88the-dulwich-hamlet-fc-striker-who-became-the-father-of-egyptian-football/

8 *Pall Mall Gazette*, 8 November 1913 (p17)

9 *Western Daily Press*, 30 May 1924 (p4)

10 https://www.egypttoday.com/Article/15/51955/The-Pharaohs-at-FIFA-World-Cup

11 McInroy, Jack, *Hussein Hegazi: Dulwich Hamlet's Egyptian King* (London: Hamlet Historian, 2019, p131)

12 https://thesefootballtimes.co/2017/10/01/melilla-and-ceuta-the-spanish-clubs-based-in-morocco/

13 *Isle of Wight County Press and South of England Reporter*, 3 October 1896 (p7)

14 McManus, John, *Welcome to Hell? In Search of the Real Turkish Football* (London: W&N, 2018, p40)

15 https://www.goal.com/tr/news/2556/editoryal/2012/10/17/3456310/goalcom-%C3%B6zel-gol-atan-ilk-t%C3%BCrk-futbolcusu-bahriyeli-fuat

16 https://bjk.com.tr/en/cms/tarihce/2/76/

17 https://www.galatasaray.org/s/galatasaray-nasil-kuruldu/13

18 Dougan, Andy, *Dynamo: Defending the Honour of Kiev* (London: Fourth Estate, 2013, p26)

19  https://www.fenerbahce.org/club/general-harington-cup

20  http://www.rsssf.com/tablest/turkhist.html

21  https://www.modernghana.com/sports/588673/today-in-history-ghanas-first-football-club-formed.html

22  https://www.premiumtimesng.com/entertainment/artsbooks/271594-new-book-reveals-football-in-nigeria-started-in-calabar.html

23  http://nunhead1888.co.uk/

# 22.

# Asia-Pacific

IN 2004, the then FIFA president, Sepp Blatter, visited China. On his visit, he announced that FIFA would recognise China as the birthplace of football. He probably had commercial interests at heart with the oncoming of the 'Chinese Century', and no doubt one day China will host the World Cup. But why credit China with inventing football? As Dr Kevin Moore explains to me, 'Fans around the world recognise that the English invented modern football, Association football. Yet many countries then claim to have invented football, in that they had an earlier version of the game, their own form of football. And it's true, there were many earlier football games around the world, going back thousands of years.'

According to Dr Kevin Moore, the Chinese have the best claim to have invented the first organised form of football. There were different versions of this ancient football game, called *cuju*, and the game evolved over time, beginning in military exercise in the third century BC. *Cuju* had a delineated pitch, a set number of players, clear laws, and at one point a league with professional players. It appears to have lasted until the 16th century. It has no connection with modern soccer but is an important part of wider football history.

*Cuju* or *Ts'u-chu* – literally 'kickball' – had been played since the Han Dynasty (206 BC–221 AD) as a martial training sport in the city of Linzi and peaked during the Song Dynastic (960–1279 AD). The game took different forms – such as the ceremonial *zhuqiu* – and involved the kicking of a leather ball filled with fur or feathers by teams of between 12 and 16 players. These teams sported different colours, and the 'goals' were made out of bamboo or coloured rope. The shape of these goals varied from crescent to round. Use of the hands was prohibited, but everything else was fair game as players contested to head or kick the ball through a goal that would be several metres above the ground. *Cuju* handbooks have been discovered, teams had distinguishable positions and captains, and successful players became feted celebrities. Even emperors played the game. Victors enjoyed the rewards of flowers, wine and silver while the captain of the losing side could, potentially, expect to be flogged.

Goals were celebrated with music and toasts of wine, and points were deducted for unfair play. The highest-scoring team won the match. *Cuju* also came with its own code of respect around gamesmanship and behaviour. We also know from both writing and illustrations that women were both fans and players.

The modern spelling of the ancient game – *zuqiu* – is still used in China for Association football, which has become huge in the country during the 21st century. The riches of the Chinese Super League have managed to attract some of the world's finest players – some in the middle of their careers, not at the tail end as is often the case with non-European leagues. The Chinese state has massive ambitions to develop players from a young age and improve the ranking of both the men's and women's teams. A kicking game existed in China hundreds – even thousands – of years ago, but then kicking games existed in other places that would not have had contact with China, such as Central America. The Greek kicking game of *episkyros* was even a contemporary of early *cuju*. Would the English have even encountered *cuju*?

Direct British involvement in modern China did not take root in earnest until English traders first sailed into Portuguese-run Macau in the 17th century. It was not until the early 19th century that British influence in Southern China led to the Opium Wars and the cession of Hong Kong to Britain in 1842. And it was here in the island colony that both Association and Rugby rules were played first in modern-day China. The Hong Kong Football Club (HKFC) was founded on 12 February 1886 by colonial official Sir James Stewart Lockhart. On 16 February that year its team made up of civilians played a British Army garrison team stationed on the island. The match took place on a pitch within the verdant gully of Happy Valley, near where the club is still based today. A month later, HKFC played its first Association rules match against Royal Engineers. Writing in 1895, the *Illustrated Sporting and Dramatic News* described Happy Valley as 'perhaps the most picturesque arena in the world where such [sporting] struggles for supremacy take place', while noting that the Association game enjoyed more supporters than rugby.[1]

In 1895, the Hong Kong Challenge Cup Shield was launched as a knockout competition. Kowloon won the first final 3-0 against a team from HMS *Centurion* at Happy Valley. The second edition a year later featured the same teams in the final, with HMS *Centurion* winning 2-1 in front of 3,000 spectators. Mrs Steward Lockhart presented the Shield and 11 gold medals to the winning team. Many of the early competitors were military regiments, including companies of the Royal Welsh Fusiliers, Royal Navy crews from various ships and even the Royal West Kent Regiment. HKFC won its first Shield in 1899. In 1908, a Hong Kong football league was established, making it among the first in Asia. While many of the participating teams were British, there were Chinese teams. That year, the sports club now known as South China Athletics Association was founded by Chinese college students in the territory. In 1910, when founder Mok Hing established its football division – South China Football Club – it had only 40 members.[2] The South China club was invited to represent China at the 1913 Far Eastern Championship Games in Manila, Philippines. This multisport event was the brainchild of American sports organiser Elwood Brown, and also included representatives from Japan, Malay, Siam (Thailand) and Hong Kong. One of the South China players, midfielder Tong Fuk Cheung, scored China's first international football goal in a 2-1 defeat to the Philippines.

The Hong Kong Football Association (HKFA) was founded in 1914 to administer the game although it would not join FIFA for another four decades. Football would continue in the British territory throughout the First World War, with military teams still dominating competitions. That was until South China won the league in 1923/24, the first Chinese team to do so. By the time the Hong Kong league was interrupted by the Japanese invasion in December 1941, South China had won the title eight times, more than any other club. Over in the mainland in 1924, the Chinese Football Association was founded and affiliated to FIFA in 1931. British and Irish newspaper reports from the early 20th century indicate that forms of folk football were being played across entire towns in China. The message was spread, even then, that the Chinese were the true inventors of the game.

In 1927, mainland China descended into civil war, but it did not deter the Chinese from their newfound love of the Association game. A British soldier writing to the *Sports Argus* in late 1928 wrote that football matches continued, even with the sound of gunfire in neighbouring fields. The paper reports that football is doing a lot in China to improve the relations between the British and Chinese.[3] *Cuju* was encouraging sportsmanship and fair play centuries before the arrival of the codified Association game but it is unlikely that the former influenced the latter. Hong Kong Football Club is a member of the Club of Pioneers.

## Kick it back: the birth of football in India

In India, the world's second-most populous country, cricket is a national religion. But that does not mean for a second that there is no room for other sports. The Kolkata (formerly Calcutta) derby between India's oldest existing football club, Mohun Bagan, and East Bengal is a century old, has regularly attracted crowds of more than 100,000 and has been played more than 350 times. The 'Boro Match' ('Big Match' in Bengali) holds the record for the highest-attended sports fixture in Indian history when 130,000 people witnessed a 4-1 Federation Cup semi-final win for East Bengal at Salt Lake Stadium in 1997.

As with many Commonwealth countries, the story of football in India begins with British regiments using the sport for training and recreation. Both Rugby and Association rules were used at the outset, which led to two 20-a-side teams of English and Scottish players contesting a Rugby rules game on Christmas Day 1872 in Calcutta. This match led to the foundation of the Calcutta Football

Club and – ultimately – the Calcutta Cup. The trophy – a silver tankard with three cobra handles and an elephant on the lid – was crafted by Indian silversmiths. The Calcutta Cup is still contested between the England and Scotland rugby union sides each year as part of the Six Nations tournament. Calcutta was the British capital in India at the time and as such the game gained a foothold in the Bengal area. While the game started out as the preserve of the British ruling classes, it would not stay that way for long. The legend goes that in 1877, the eight-year-old Nagendra Prasad Sarbadhikari was travelling with his mother in a horse-drawn carriage when he stopped to watch British soldiers playing in the Calcutta FC ground. The ball bounced towards him, and one of the soldiers asked him to kick it back.[4] Transfixed, Sarbadhikari and his friends obtained a ball from a shop and took it into the Hare School the next day. One of the English schoolmasters informed the boys that they had, in fact, bought a rugby ball, so he himself purchased a round ball and taught the students the Association rules.

By the late 1880s, a number of India's early clubs were formed, including the Aryan Club, the Jubilee Club (later named Mohammedan Sporting Club) and Sovabazar Club – captained by Kalicharan Mitra, a childhood friend of Sarbadhikari. In 1888, the Durand Cup was launched for both British and Indian Army teams, with the Royal Scots Fusiliers defeating fellow Scots regiment the Highland Light Infantry 2-1. Scottish regiments dominated the early years of the Durand Cup, winning all but one until 1900. The Durand Cup still runs, making it the fourth-longest-running knockout football cup competition in the world after the English, Scottish and Welsh FA Cups. Other tournaments, such as the Rovers Cup, Coochbehar Cup and Trades Cup, were also established to provide competition for footballing clubs in Bengal. Mohun Bagan Sporting Club (now Mohun Bagan Athletic Club) began life on 15 August 1889. It was founded by the prominent lawyer, Bhupendra Nath Basu, who assumed the presidency of the club. The club's foundation was attended by numerous distinguished Indian gentlemen, including two *maharaja* – Indian princes – and its grounds were within the Mohun Bagan Villa, a large tract of land in Calcutta.

In 1893, the Indian Football Association (IFA) was founded by British residents in India. In keeping with many other establishments of the Empire, no Indians were permitted to sit on the board, until the 1930s. The organisation launched the IFA Shield, which quickly became Indian football's most prestigious trophy. By the end of the decade, the Calcutta Football League was up and running. The Gloucester Regiment won the first edition in 1898. Mohammedan Sporting Club was the first Indian club to win the Calcutta Football League in 1934 and the Durand Cup in 1940, but it was Mohun Bagan that created the first key breakthrough for Indian football. In the first decade of the 20th century, Mohun Bagan improved markedly under the training of Subadar Major Sallen Basu. He brought his training from the military to improve the fitness of the players. By 1905, the club had defeated that year's IFA Shield winner, Dalhousie, 6-1, and in the following three years won and retained the Trades Cup. This was a time when the Indian independence movement was gaining momentum, so games between Indians and European teams could prove fractious. At a match between Dalhousie and Mohun Bagan in 1908, the Bengali crowd broke the rope in reaction to a refereeing decision and had to be quelled by baton charge.

What made Indian football teams unique is that they often played barefoot. 'In India, I have seen wonderful developments of football,' *The Clubman* columnist reported in *The Sketch* in 1909. He goes on to describe a 'regiment of Pathans [Pashtuns] with naked feet and hair flying' as they chased the ball.[5] In a famous photo, the Mohun Bagan team in their green and maroon shirts are pictured barefoot with the massive IFA Shield they won in 1911. This was a historic cup final victory. By beating the East Yorkshire Regiment 2-1, Mohun Bagan became the very first Indian side to win the IFA Shield. It had already defeated the Second Rifle Brigade and the Third Middlesex Regiment after a replay en route to the final. An estimated 80,000 Bengalis attended the final, many of whom could not even see the play, so were informed of the score by kites that were flown closer to the action. East Yorks took the lead direct from a free kick by its captain Jackson before Shibdas Bhaduri and Abhilas Ghosh wrote themselves into Indian sporting immortality, both scoring within minutes of each other in the second half. British media reported an absence of racial tensions; local Bengalis even cheered the losing team.[6] This match was a huge moment for the Indian resistance movement – proof that Indians could beat European teams. Mohun Bagan also won the Gladstone Cup, Nawab Asanullah Challenge Shield and Bengal Jimkhana Shield in what was something of an annus mirabilis for the club.

The 1911 IFA Shield win for Mohun Bagan proved a catalyst for Indian football among the Bengali youth but the British-run IFA rules of the time permitted only two Indian football clubs in the First Division of the league. The rest of the Indian sides were restricted to the cup competitions. In the years immediately after the First World War, teams made up entirely of Indian players acted as football ambassadors around Asia-Pacific, playing in Australia, the Dutch East Indies (Indonesia), Japan and Siam (Thailand). In August 1920, Mohun Bagan's future derby rival East Bengal FC was founded by former members of the Jorabagan Club, including Manmatha Nath Roy Chaudhuri, the Maharaja of Santosh. The club faced opposition from fellow Calcutta sides Mohun Bagan and Aryans as it joined the IFA but was admitted to the Second Division in 1922. East Bengal FC's co-founder Chaudhuri is remembered in the name of the Santosh Trophy, now the top domestic knockout tournament in India. He also served as president of the IFA in the 1930s, and his diplomatic skills were critical to promoting Indian teams and guiding the creation of a nationwide governing body. Football gradually nationalised with the Bengal-based IFA looking to create an India-wide federation. This led to the creation of the All-India Football Federation in June 1937 by six regional associations. A newly independent India appeared at the London Olympics in 1948, losing in the first round to France before turning down the chance to appear at the 1950 World Cup in Brazil. India is yet to appear in a World Cup finals tournament but, with a huge population and two major league competitions, it is surely only a matter of time.

## Football: big in Japan

When Japan co-hosted the 2002 FIFA World Cup with South Korea, it was the culmination of a long journey of football development. Like China, Japan had its own ancient kicking game – *kemari* – which had been inspired by China's *cuju*. The first references to *kemari* come from the seventh century, although a common code would not emerge until the 13th century. The game was played with hollow balls around 20cm in diameter made of deerskin and coated in egg white. The pitch was in a square with trees in each corner between six and seven metres apart, and two teams of eight players had to keep the ball in the air for as long as possible. *Kemari* took on major social and even religious significance, with evidence suggesting that *marikai* (game meetings) were held to assuage droughts and other misfortunes. The Association game arrived in Japan as early as 1871, where games are recorded as taking place in Kobe docks. Most notably, a game took place in September 1873 at the Imperial Japanese Navy Academy in Tsukiji, Tokyo, arranged by military instructor, Lieutenant Commander Archibald Douglas.[7]

In the late 19th century, Japan, a traditionally isolationist culture, was opening up to foreign ideas to keep pace economically and militarily. This influx of foreigners into Japan's major ports led to the establishment of small communities and − as elsewhere in the world − associated sports clubs. Into this environment, Scotsman James Pender Mollison founded Yokohama Country & Athletic Club in 1868. He had arrived a year earlier to find a city still recovering from the great fire of 1866.[8] It was not long before compatriot Alexander Cameron Sim, a pharmacist, founded the Kobe Regatta & Athletic Club in September 1870. Sim, a stern-looking man with piercing blue eyes and a rich moustache, was an all-round athlete and spent 30 years of his life in Kobe. He was the driving force behind the playing of western sports in Kobe and over time the club hosted meets for baseball, lawn bowls, basketball, cricket, rugby and tennis, and − on 18 February 1888 − held the first official Association football match in Japan. Kobe played its counterpart, the Yokohama Country & Athletic Club, with Sim's team winning.[9]

The game was played in schools, universities and local social societies, with reports reaching Britain by 1904 that

Japanese students were taking to football 'like babes to their bottles'.[10] Much of the credit goes to physical education teacher Gendou Tsuboi, who taught football in Tokyo schools for around four decades. Speaking English enabled Tsuboi to learn foreign football theories and practices, and in 1885, together with his student Morinari Tanaka, he published a book called *Kogai Yugi Ho* (Rules of Outdoor Games). It included a chapter on football – a first for Japan.[11] Tsuboi was sent to Europe in 1900 to investigate western sports further and returned two years later with a table tennis set from England. Many regard Tsuboi as the father of Japanese football, and he would go on to publish more books on the sport.

Ties between Japan and Britain were strengthened by the 1902 Anglo-Japanese Alliance designed to check the growing influence of Russia. Indeed, Japan was an important regional ally of the British during the First World War, taking over German-leased territories in Asia and even helping suppress a mutiny by Indian troops against Britain. By the end of the war, Japan still lacked an internal infrastructure for the promotion of the game. In 1918, a Kanto regional high school tournament, which pitted the best teams from Tokyo and Yokohama, was attended by the British ambassador Sir William Conyngham Greene and embassy secretary William Haigh. Wheels were put in motion for the promotion of the game as a diplomatic gesture. In January 1919, the Football Association sent a silver cup to Japan to establish a contest that 'shall be run on the same lines as govern such competitions in this country [Britain] so far as circumstances permit'.[12] The Silver Cup was designed around the English FA Cup and was donated with the aim to bring order to an informal footballing culture and arrived with a letter with instructions that the cup should be awarded to 'the winning team of the Japanese national championship'.[13] Tairei Uchino, who ran the football club at a Tokyo school that is now Tsukuba University, consulted Haigh at the British embassy for advice on how to proceed. Uchino lay the foundations for the creation of the Japan Football Association (JFA) in 1921, which led in turn to the All-Japan Association Football Championship for teams to compete for the Silver Cup.

The first winner of the Silver Cup in 1921 – since rebranded as the Emperor's Cup – was Tokyo Shukyu-Dan (Tokyo Football Club). This club was founded in 1917 by Tairei Uchino and is the oldest existing entity in Japan that was founded specifically as a football club. The inaugural tournament held at Tokyo's Hibiya Park had just four entrants. The list of participants in the tournament's first decade demonstrates how far Association football had spread across Japan, with entrants from Tokyo, Kobe, Hiroshima, Kyoto and Nagoya. On 23 May that year, what is recognised as Japan's first international took place in the Far Eastern Games in Osaka, with Japan losing 2-1 to the Philippines and 5-1 to China, represented again by South China Athletic Association of Hong Kong, the following day. Japan would not secure a first international win for another four years. On 1 September 1923, disaster struck. Aged just 32, one of the pioneers of football in Japan, William Haigh, died in the Great Kanto earthquake that destroyed much of Tokyo and Yokohama. Haigh was one of an estimated 140,000 casualties from the 7.9 magnitude quake and resulting firestorm.

By the end of the decade, the JFA was fully affiliated within FIFA although it would be expelled during the Second World War and not readmitted until 1950. In 1930, the national side picked up its first silverware in the three-team football tournament at the Far Eastern Games held in Tokyo. Takei Wakabayashi of the Kobe Icchu Club bagged four in a 7-2 rout over the Philippines, which was followed by a 3-3 draw with China, Japan twice having to come from behind. The Japanese sent a team to the 1936 Olympics in Berlin, stunning Sweden 3-2 at the Hertha-BSC-Platz in what was the first time an Asian team had played at either a World Cup or Olympic football tournament. Following the 'Miracle of Berlin', Japan succumbed 8-0 to world champions and eventual gold medallists Italy in the second round, with Frossi scoring a hat-trick and Biagi netting four. Anglo-Japanese relations collapsed at the onset of the Second World War. In 1945, with Japan desperate for materials for the failing war effort, even the Emperor's Cup was melted down and used in armaments *against* the trophy's original donor country, Britain, and its allies. In 2011, on the 90th anniversary of the foundation of the JFA, the organisation sought to create a replica of the original Silver Cup. JFA president Junji Ogura met with his counterpart at the Football Association, David Bernstein, at Wembley Stadium to apologise formally for the melting down of the Silver Cup and asked permission to create a replica. Bernstein informed Mr Ogura that the FA would be happy to recreate it as an anniversary gift.

During the decades of national reconstruction following the Second World War, Japanese football clubs began to spring from company sides rather than academia and its unique and colourful football fan culture developed. However, the game itself is less popular than baseball domestically. Kobe Regatta & Athletic Club and Yokohama Country & Athletic Club still play their annual inter-port match. In recognition of the fixture's significance in the Japanese game, the clubs were invited to play their 2002 fixture ahead of the South Korea and Japan World Cup finals at the 70,000-seat Yokohama Stadium. Yokohama Country & Athletic Club is in the Club of Pioneers. Tairei Uchino, who was also the brains behind the JFA's three-legged crow crest, was admitted to the Japanese Football Hall of Fame in 2006, 53 years after his death. The Tokyo Shukyu-Dan club that he founded still plays in the Tokyo Regional League. As for Japan's 2002 World Cup co-host South Korea, the game probably arrived with British seamen onboard the HMS *Flying Fish* in June 1882. The ship was docked at Incheon while Vice Admiral Willis was signing a treaty between Britain and Korea. The crew were ordered to stay on board but decided to play football on the pier instead to enjoy more space. They apparently left two balls behind. The game was definitely being played at the Royal English School in Seoul in 1896.[14]

## Soccer down under

Despite the vast distance between Australia and New Zealand and Britain, in the Victorian era the cultural bonds were strong between the colonies and the 'Mother Country'. So much so that an entire state – Victoria – was named after the Queen. Historically, people in the area now known as western Victoria had their own kicking game – *Marn Grook*, which means 'ball game' – long before European settlers arrived in the 18th century. The game involved the kicking and catching of a possum-skin ball. Games of up to 50 men and boys took place over a wide-open space. As in England, codes of football emerged among the European settlers to keep cricketers occupied during the winter months. Codified football in the gold-rich state of Victoria – now known as Australian Rules football – predates the foundation of the Football Association by five years. Much of the credit goes to Tom Wills, the son of a wealthy landowner who had been sent to Rugby School in England and captained the football team there before returning to Melbourne in 1857. Wills may well have witnessed *Marn Grook* in his youth. Wills umpired the first football match on 7 August 1858 between the prestigious Scotch College and Melbourne Grammar Schools. Wills established the initial ten rules of Australian football the following year along with his cousin Henry Harrison, and journalists William Hammersley and James Thompson at the Parade Hotel in East Melbourne. The writers had drawn inspiration from both the Rugby and Eton rules, but the game was very much its own Victorian invention and, by 1866, a competition had been established. This was just three years after the Football Association rules had been written down in England and a year before Scotland's Queen's Park FC was founded.

By the time the Association game was ready to approach Australia, the colony already had its own favoured code – in Victoria, at least. By the late 1870s, 'inter-colonial' football matches were taking place at the Melbourne Cricket Ground involving teams from Victoria and New South Wales. One such occasion in 1878 involved the Carlton Football Club of Melbourne and the Waratah Club of Sydney. One match was played under Rugby rules and the other under Victorian rules. Carlton won both games. A year later, the first matches took place between state sides, with Victoria beating South Australia at the East Melbourne Cricket Ground in front of 5,000 spectators.

It was to the Melbourne rules that New Zealand's first football club in Nelson turned. Its first match in 1868 involved a hybrid mix of Melbourne and Association rules played with a round ball, until Charles John Monro returned from three years in the English schooling system, bringing with him back to Nelson a Rugby rule book and four oval balls. Monro convinced Nelson Football Club to try the Rugby rules, and on 14 May 1870 organised and played in the country's first rugby match in Nelson. New Zealand caught the rugby bug and never looked back. Association rules games probably took root around dockland areas of New Zealand throughout the 19th century but it is known that the Canterbury Association Football Club in the South Island played the round-ball game as early as 1882. In the North Island, in Auckland, North Shore United Football Club – New Zealand's oldest Association rules club and a member of the Club of Pioneers – was founded in 1886. Within a year, there were 13 clubs in Auckland. In the South Island, the Northern Association Football Club of Dunedin was founded in April 1888. The Canterbury Football Association was not founded until 1903.[16] In 1891, the New Zealand Football Association (now New Zealand Football) was formed but would not affiliate to FIFA until 1948.

Back across the Tasman Sea in Sydney, New South Wales, English émigré John Walter Fletcher established the Wanderers Football Club in 1880. It is considered by many to be Australia's first soccer club. A schoolmaster, Fletcher had been living in the colony for five years. In the western suburb of Parramatta on 3 August 1880 at Aarons Hotel he and a friend, J.A. Todd, formed Wanderers FC. Its kit was all white with blue socks, and its crest was a simple Southern Cross badge. The club's first match using Association rules took place just 11 days later against members of the King's School rugby team on Parramatta Common, which attracted an impressive crowd of 1,000 spectators. Pockets of soccer cultures emerged in the coal mining areas of New South Wales, including Newcastle and Illawarra, but the lack of a railway restricted any state-wide development of the sport.

The Newcastle and District League was dominated in its early years by the Scots-founded Minmi Rangers.[17] The first effort at a cup competition in New South Wales was the Gardiner Cup in 1885, which ran until 1928. Balgownie Rangers Football Club was founded in 1883 in the coastal town of Wollongong, 70km south of Sydney. One of the co-founders was Scots miner Peter Hunter, who had played junior football in Scotland. The club joined the New South Wales Football Association – recently established by John Walter Fletcher – in 1890, two years after a new railway joined the two towns.[18] As a mining town club, Balgownie's players wore pit boots with leather bars on their soles, which appears to have drawn comments from their Sydney-based opponents. Balgownie Rangers FC is believed to be the oldest soccer club still running in Australia and dominated the local Illawarra District League in the mid-1890s. Meanwhile, up in Brisbane, the Anglo-Queensland Football Association was founded in 1884 to promote the game. In the same year, the Anglo-Australian Football Association was founded in Victoria.

By 1904, trans-Tasman matches were played between Australian and New Zealand sides. The NZFA invited an Australian team to tour, and a party of 15 New South Welshmen led by manager and captain Fred Robinson sailed from Sydney to Auckland, where on 29 June the tourists and their North Island hosts shared a 1-1 draw. Reports indicate that the New South Wales side had dominated the game. NSW then beat Auckland 3-2 before losing to a Wellington side 2-1 in terrible weather. The team then went on the rampage in South Island, winning three matches against Canterbury, Otago and Southland by an aggregate of 20-3. To cap off the tour, a New Zealand national side was put together for the very first time. But even with a combined effort the Kiwis couldn't overcome New South Wales, who won 1-0. A second match took place in Wellington the following week, which ended in a 3-3 draw.

The Australian states all had their own Football Associations until 1911, ten years after independence from Britain, when the Commonwealth Football Association was founded to govern the game throughout the country. In 1911, Australian soccer pioneered something that would go on to become the norm in the sport across the world. In a match between Sydney Leichardt and HMS *Powerful*, the teams became the first to wear squad numbers on their backs. A year later, squad numbers became mandatory throughout NSW soccer. The practice would not catch on in Europe until 1928 when the first shirt numbers were worn in a match between Sheffield Wednesday and Arsenal. In 1921, the Commonwealth Football Association became the Australian Soccer Association. A year later, the first official soccer international took place between an Australian national side and New Zealand at Carisbrooke Park, Dunedin. A crowd of around 10,000 saw the home side run out 3-1 winners. At the second match in Wellington, 12,000 witnessed a 1-1 draw while the third 'Test' in Auckland attracted 15,000 and resulted in a 3-1 win for the hosts. New Zealander Ted Cook has the distinction of scoring in all three Tests. In December of the same year, Captain C.B. Prickett of the Royal Navy cruiser HMS *Chatham* presented a silver replica of the English FA Cup to the New Zealand FA to thank the country for the hospitality his crew had enjoyed during their tour of duty.[19] The first winner of the Chatham Cup – which is New Zealand's longest-running football competition – was Seacliff from the South Island area of Otago in October 1923, defeating the Wellington YMCA 4-0 at Athletic Park, Wellington. By the mid-20s, there were around 460 soccer clubs in New Zealand with 6,000 active players, not far behind the number of rugby clubs (670).[20]

Back in Australia, the first English touring party arrived in May 1925, presenting the Australians with a chance to test their skills against the originators of the code. The English side played 25 matches and won them all, scoring 139 goals with just 13 conceded, attracting crowds of up to 45,000. In 1927, Czech side AFK Vršovice toured Australia, rebranding as Bohemians to make it easier for the Australian public to pronounce the team name. The Australians gifted their Czech visitors with two kangaroos to take back with them. The marsupials ended up in Prague zoo, while Bohemians incorporated a kangaroo into their crest.

## Modern soccer down under

Soccer itself was a peripheral sport in Australia until the last quarter of the 20th century. It had existed largely in the margins among Italians, Greeks, Croatians, and other communities from countries with a soccer culture that did not have a tradition of Australian Rules, cricket and either format of rugby. When I played non-league soccer in Melbourne in the early 2000s, I played for a multicultural team with players drawn from all over the world. But we would typically find ourselves somewhere in Melbourne's seemingly endless suburbs playing a team from one or other Mediterranean communities. In my view, the Croatians were always the toughest opponents!

It would take decades of post-war immigration and new communities to help build a foundation to make Australian soccer challenge more established codes of football. A 'golden generation' built largely but not exclusively by the sons of Croatian and Italian migrants in the 1990s and early

2000s, supported by the general globalisation of the game, has led to a successful and popular A-League set-up hosted in large, modern arenas. So why didn't soccer take off as well as Australian Rules in Victoria, or the Rugby codes in New South Wales, Queensland and New Zealand? It may just be a case that the Association arrived too late to establish itself when other codes had already put down solid roots in the late Victorian era when the code war was being fought. A century later, soccer began to finally take a hold in sports-mad Australia in the men's game with the successful A-League. In 1979, a women's national soccer team, the Matildas, took to the field for the first time. In 2023, Australia will co-host the FIFA Women's World Cup alongside New Zealand. And what of the pioneer men's clubs? Balgownie Rangers still plays in local Illawarra soccer leagues in an area that has always been one of Australia's soccer heartlands. North Shore United has joined the Club of Pioneers. It plays in the NRFL Premier league for Auckland area clubs and has six Chatham Cups in its trophy cabinet.

1  *Illustrated Sporting and Dramatic News*, 1 June 1895 (p13)

2  https://www.scaa.org.hk/index.php/About/about_history.html

3  *Sports Argus*, 22 December 1928 (p1)

4  http://www.thehardtackle.com/2012/legends-of-indian-football-the-pioneers/

5  *The Sketch*, 1 Dec 1909 (p8)

6  *Dundee Courier*, 31 July 1911 (p7)

7  https://www.soccerphile.com/soccerphile/archives/wc2002/fo/co/jf.html

8  https://ycac.jp/wp/history/

9  http://www.krac.org/about.php

10  *Globe*, 26 September 1904 (p1)

11  https://www.jfa.or.jp/eng/history/index.html

12  *Lancashire Evening Post*, 3 January 1919 (p5)

13  https://www.jfa.or.jp/eng/history/index.html

14  http://theaccidentalgroundhopper.blogspot.com/2013/11/a-british-history-of-south-korean.html

15  https://www.sydneyswans.com.au/news/59357/the-story-of-marn-grook
16  https://teara.govt.nz/en/1966/association-football
17  https://scottishfootballmuseum.org.uk/scottish-influence-implementing-football-in-australia-and-france/
18  http://www.balgownierangers.com.au/?page_id=5
19  https://nzhistory.govt.nz/page/first-chatham-cup-football-final
20  https://teara.govt.nz/en/football/page-1

# 23.

# Epilogue

ASSOCIATION RULES football continues to expand and evolve, causing controversy and dividing opinion much as it has since its very earliest days. The game's very simplicity is one reason it has achieved and maintained global appeal and the fact it arrived in many places before other codes gave it a distinct edge. The first codifications of the sport may have taken place in the Victorian drawing rooms and public houses in England, but the development of Association rules football into the world's favourite spectator sport has been a global team effort.

There are some major footballing countries that I didn't cover in this book. For example, Mexico, where the Aztecs had practised a ball game called *ulamaliztli* in an I-shaped court known as a *tlachtli* for millennia prior to the arrival of the Spanish *conquistadores* in the 16th century. Association football in Mexico dates back to as early as 1892, with the English-founded Pachuca Football Club, which is still active in the Mexican top division as Club de Fútbol Pachuca. In Europe, Yugoslavia was a significant participant in tournaments from its creation after the First World War to its dissolution in the 1990s. As with many other countries, it was

British industrialists who first brought Association football to Croatia in the coastal city of Rijeka at the end of the 19th century. The rules were first printed in Croatian in Zagreb in 1896. It was also in the capital that the first Croatian-formed club, First Football and Sports Club Zagreb, was founded in 1903. In Poland, the first exhibition match took place in 1894 during a jamboree for a popular team gymnastics practice, known as *sokol*. The game between representatives of Lwów and Kraków lasted just six minutes when, after the first goal was scored, organisers brought the showcase to a close and continued with the *sokol*. In Russia, Scotsman Arthur MacPherson created the All-Russian Football Union in 1912 but fell victim to the Russian Revolution five years later. He was arrested by Communists opposed to what they perceived as a 'bourgeois' import and he was found dead in a Moscow prison in 1919.

We owe a great deal to the visionaries who nurtured the seeds of the game into solid roots. The game needed its mavericks to survive. Charles W. Alcock, creator of the FA Cup and international football, and key protagonist in the fight for professionalism, deserves special credit. As do William Prest and Nathaniel Creswick for galvanising the Sheffield scene; Ebenezer Cobb Morley for getting early clubs together to found the Football Association and standardise the rule book; Pa Jackson for founding the global evangelists, Corinthian FC; William Sudell at Preston North End for pressing the professionalism debate; and Billy Meredith for driving the protection of players. And where would the women's game be without Nettie Honeyball and the Dick, Kerr Ladies? In the 21st century the women's game is now making great advances.

The Association game owes a great deal to Scotland, where Queen's Park FC gave us the combination game.

Scotsmen planted the seed of football in Spain, Sweden, Argentina, Ukraine, Japan and elsewhere, and often stayed to see it grow and bear solid fruit. We must salute the evangelists who undertook long journeys to play exhibition games to encourage the uptake of the game. The Corinthians and the Casuals teams, in particular, but also Clapton FC, Tunbridge Wells FC and other pioneers travelling abroad in the last decade of the 19th century. Where would the game be without the publishers? John Lillywhite was the first to publish the FA rules and create the *Football Annual* alongside Charles W. Alcock. What about Bensemann's *kicker* in Germany, still going strong into the 21st century?

Gymnasiums played a key role in Association football's emergence, especially in Berlin, Bilbao and Budapest. The health benefits of physical education were promoted by British doctors, such as James Richardson Spensley in Genoa and William Alexander Mackay, while the role of the clergy as neutral arbiters and promoters of muscular Christianity is interesting, as we saw in Le Havre, Dresden and Genoa.

Here's to the pioneering coaches who nurtured the first generations of talent across the world to surpass the Home Nations at their own game: Messrs Hogan, Garbutt, Madden, Robertson, Pentland et al. Let's also remember Archibald Leitch, who recovered from tragedy to drive forward stadium design that would stand the test of time. We also owe a debt to the organisers and enthusiasts who drove international competition. Herr Meisl, Monsieurs Rimet, Delaunay, de Coubertin and Guérin, Sir Thomas Lipton, and more. Some countries relied on royal approval for the game to flourish, as in King Carol's Romania or Alfonso XIII's Spain, while even an autocratic regime in Italy succeeded in unifying a country under soccer.

Often, football has been the leveller. Whether it was Blackburn Olympic's first FA Cup win upsetting the public-school order in England, Mohun Bagan's IFA Shield triumph in India, or Brazil's victory over Exeter City, every country has its breakthrough moment.

Without these people, these moments, football would not be where it is today. We would not have more than a century and a half of drama, controversy, might-have-beens and legends.

Football is the world game. But we owe the pioneers who laid the foundations and gave us our origin stories.

# Credits and Thanks

I COULDN'T have created *Origin Stories: The Pioneers Who Took Football to the World* without the time and insight of some extremely knowledgeable people.

In the UK, I owe a huge thanks to Dr Kevin Moore, Richard Tims at Sheffield FC, Andy Mitchell, Belinda Scarlett, Paul Brown and Clint Jones for their input. Also, to John Forrest and Llew Walker at Corinthian-Casuals, a remarkable club that keeps appearing in the early story of the game across the world. Thanks also to Gerard Farrell and Alan McLean for helping me tell the complex Irish football story, and to David Berg and Claus Bermann in Sweden and Denmark respectively. Also, to Stéphane Louwens, Jurryt van de Vooren and Bert Vermeer for their knowledge of the scene in Belgium and the Netherlands.

In Spain, Alejandro López, Colin Millar, Charlotte Mackay and Andrew Gillan; Ricardo Serrado, Filipe d'Avillez, Arquivo Histórico Municipal de Cascais, Casa Pia Atlético Clube and Vintage Football City Tours (Lisbon) in Portugal; on the Uruguayan game, Juan Carlos Luzuriaga and Vadim Furmanov; in Argentina, Esteban Bekerman; in the United States, Brian D. Bunk and Jim Brown, Stephen C. Brandt, Ryan Moniz and André Ruette. I found the North American chapter particularly interesting, purely because I had no idea of its rich soccer history.

I couldn't have told the story of the Central European experience without the expertise of Christoph Wagner (Germany), Alexander Juraske (Austria), Péter Szegedi and Dominic Bliss (Hungary), and Mojmir Staško (Slovakia). To bring the Italian story to life, it was brilliant to speak to Robert Nieri, the team at *The Gentleman Ultra*, and also Aidan Williams, whose knowledge of Mussolini-era Italy is incredible. In the Middle East, John McManus and Mehmet Yuce in Turkey were extremely helpful, as was James Montague. In Africa, Peter Alegi and Chris Bolsmann's insights were invaluable, and a big thanks to Dulwich Hamlet historian Jack McInroy. In Asia, Chris Hough in Japan set me on the right path.

Finally, thanks to Jane and the team at Pitch Publishing for bringing the story to life, Pete Gentry, Duncan Olner, Graham Hales and Dean Rockett, and all my friends who volunteered to read chapters and feed back.

# Bibliography

**Books**

Ball, Phil, *Morbo: The Story of Spanish Football* (London: WSC Books Ltd., 2002)

Bellos, Alex, *Futebol: The Brazilian Way of Life* (London: Bloomsbury, 2014)

Bliss, Dominic, *Erbstein: The Triumph and Tragedy of Football's Forgotten Pioneer* (London, Blizzard Media, 2014)

Bolchover, David, *The Greatest Comeback: From Genocide to Football Glory: The Story of Béla Guttmann* (Hull, Biteback Publishing, 2017)

Brown, Paul, *Savage Enthusiasm: A History of Football Fans* (County Durham, Goal-Post, 2017)

Brown, Paul, *The Victorian Football Miscellany* (County Durham: Goal-Post, 2013)

Campomar, Andreas, *¡Golazo! A History of Latin American Football* (London: Quercus, 2014)

Collins, Tony, *How Football Began: A Global History of How the World's Football Codes Were Born* (London: Routledge, 2019)

Dougan, Andy, *Dynamo: Defending the Honour of Kiev* (London: Fourth Estate, 2013)

Finch, M.H.J, *The Political Economy of Uruguay since 1870* (London: Palgrave Macmillan, 1981)

Foot, John, *Calcio: A History of Italian Football* (London: Harper Perennial, 2007)

Galeano, Eduardo, *Soccer in Sun and Shadow* (New York: Nation Books, 2013)

Glanville, Brian, *The Story of the World Cup* (London, Faber & Faber, 2018)

Goldblatt, David, *The Ball is Round: A Global History of Football* (London: Penguin, 2007)

Hawkey, Ian, *Feet of the Chameleon: The Story of African Football* (London, Portico, 2010)

Hesse, Ulrich, *Tor! The Story of German Football* (London: WSC Books, 2003)

Hubbard, Ryan, *From Partition to Solidarity, The First Hundred Years of Polish Football* (Leicester: RAH, 2019)

Johnes, Martin, *A History of Sport in Wales* (Swansea: University of Wales Press, 2005)

Lacey, Josh, *God is Brazilian: Charles Miller, The Man Who Brought Football to Brazil* (Stroud: Tempus Publishing, 2005)

McInroy, Jack, *Hussein Hegazi: Dulwich Hamlet's Egyptian King* (London: Hamlet Historian, 2019)

McManus, John, *Welcome to Hell? In Search of the Real Turkish Football* (London: W&N, 2018)

Mitchell, Andy, *First Elevens: The Birth of International Football* (Dunblane, Andy Mitchell Media, 2012)

Moore, Dr Kevin, *What You Think You Know About Football is Wrong: The Global Game's Greatest Myths and Untruths* (London, Bloomsbury, 2019)

Morris, Terry, *Vain Games of No Value? A Social History of Association Football in Britain During its First Long Century* (Bloomington: AuthorHouse, 2016)

Roberts, Benjamin, *Gunshots & Goalposts: The Story of Northern Irish Football* (Eastbourne: Avenue Books, 2017)

Sanders, Richard, *Beastly Fury: The Strange Birth of British Football* (London: Bantam, 2010)

Serrado, Ricardo, *História do Futebol Português – Volume I* (Estoril: Prime Books, 2010)

Smith, Rory, *Mister: The Men Who Taught the World to Beat England at Their Own Game* (London: Simon & Schuster, 2016)

Szegedi, Péter, *Az első aranykor* (Budapest: Akadémiai Kiadó, 2016)

Westby, Martin, *England's Oldest Football Clubs 1815–1889* (Self-published, 2019)

Wilson, Jonathan, *Angels with Dirty Faces: The Footballing History of Argentina* (London: W&N, 2017, p6)

Wilson, Jonathan, *Inverting the Pyramid: The History of Football Tactics* (London, Orion, 2014)

**Online resources**

BBC.co.uk
BleacherReport.com
British Newspaper Archive
CanadianSoccerHistory.com
Corinthian-casuals.com
Fifa.com
FootballPink.net
History.com
LevantineHeritage.com
National Archives
NationalFootballMuseum.com
Marca.com
RSSSF.org
Rugby Reloaded Podcast
SAHistory.org.za
ScottishFootballMuseum.org.uk
ScottishSportHistory.com
SoccerHistoryUSA.org and Soccer History USA Podcast
Teledoce.com/programa/el-origen/
TheseFootballTimes.co and These Football Times Podcast
Official websites of football clubs and national football associations cited
Official websites of schools and colleges cited
Local government and tourism websites

*Newspapers and other websites cited in text*